American Police Systems

PATTERSON SMITH REPRINT SERIES IN
CRIMINOLOGY, LAW ENFORCEMENT, AND SOCIAL PROBLEMS

A listing of publications in the SERIES *will be found at rear of volume*

PUBLICATION NO. 53: PATTERSON SMITH REPRINT SERIES IN
CRIMINOLOGY, LAW ENFORCEMENT, AND SOCIAL PROBLEMS

American Police Systems

BY

RAYMOND B. FOSDICK

Author of "EUROPEAN POLICE SYSTEMS"

With a New Introduction by
DONAL E. J. MACNAMARA

Montclair, New Jersey

PATTERSON SMITH

1969

SBN 87585-053-7

Library of Congress Catalog Card Number: 69-14925

INTRODUCTION TO THE REPRINT EDITION

One cannot but be amazed at Raymond Fosdick's depiction of American police organization, operations, and problems a half-century ago — for with little up-dating, both his facts and his strictures, his analyses and his recommendations, would duplicate the most recent, informed writing in the field. Visiting some seventy of America's larger municipal police departments in the years 1915 to 1917 and drawing on the research that went into his earlier work (*European Police Systems*, 1916), Fosdick noted political interference, public apathy (and in fact sympathy with the criminal), judicial irresponsibility, too short tenure for police administrators, lack of proper selection criteria and inadequate training for recruits, corruption, unenforceable sumptuary laws, a high crime rate, the impact of the narcotics traffic, uncoordinated police operations, and a host of other problems later to be elucidated in greater detail by August Vollmer, Bruce Smith, O. W. Wilson and more recent authorities.

Some of Fosdick's recommendations might well have been taken from the federal government's report, *The Challenge of Crime in a Free Society* (1967) and *Task Force Report: Police* (1967), *e.g.*, lateral entry at higher than police recruit rank for administrative and specialist personnel, more attention to crime prevention (a principle of Sir Robert Peel's as early as the 1820's), greater organization and operational flexibility, and a central crime intelligence bureau to serve all of America's 40,000 police agencies (realized in part only in the late 1960's). One of Fosdick's most important contributions was his early emphasis on the wastefulness and ineffectiveness of the uniformed foot patrol — a traditional operational technique which still characterizes America's police forces and wastes hundreds of thousands of police man-hours per annum.

The resistance of the police to the introduction of new techniques (such as fingerprinting in the World War I era) has changed little in half a century, and the readiness to "pass the buck" to others for deficiencies in crime control, particularly to the criminal court judges, finds its counterpart in the speeches and testimony of many police officials of our time. For example, Boston Police Commissioner Stephen O'Meara's criticism of the leniency of his city's magistrates presages by more than fifty years today's sharp attacks on the Warren Court.

The author takes to task the police of the early twentieth century for anti-labor union attitudes and operations but is himself guilty of anti-Negro, anti-alien bias — the latter somewhat surprising since he is so outspoken an admirer of the German, French and English police. His comparisons of European and American crime rates, despite the sorry state of crime statistics then and now, stand up quite well — as do his somewhat superficial analyses of the reasons for the differences they show.

In his chapter on the prevention of crime, the author quotes one statistic that will astound many students of the narcotics problem today, namely that there were 300,000 narcotics addicts in New York City alone in 1919. This unsupported estimate and a number of similar statements may have been exaggerated to engage public interest and support for a well-taken stand on the importance of eliminating crime-breeding conditions. Neither in this chapter nor elsewhere does Fosdick mention organized crime (despite the then recent lynching of the reputed Mafia murderers of a New Orleans police chief), but attention is given to assaults and extortions by ethnic and neighborhood gangs in New York, Boston, and other cities.

Until Bruce Smith's *Police Systems in the United States* became available twenty years after Fosdick's pioneering efforts, *American Police Systems* was preeminently the basic reference work for serious students of American police administration. It remains today a resource of unquestioned value.

—DONAL E. J. MACNAMARA

John Jay College of Criminal Justice
City University of New York
January, 1969

FOREWORD

This study, which I undertook at the invitation of the Bureau of Social Hygiene, as a companion volume to *European Police Systems,* was practically completed when the United States entered the war in 1917. Thereafter for over two years and a half my time was so occupied that there was no opportunity to get the manuscript ready for the press. Only recently have I had leisure to finish it, and its publication now is due largely to my associate, Mr. Leonard V. Harrison, whose research and investigation in the last six months have brought my material up to date.

The book is based upon personal study of the police in practically every city in the United States with a population exceeding 100,000, and in many communities of lesser size. In all, seventy-two cities were visited, and Mr. Harrison has recently duplicated my itinerary of several years ago to discover any alterations or new developments in the police situation occurring in the interval. During the last year, too, I have had an opportunity to follow up certain lines of research in London and Paris, so that the comparisons between European and American conditions occurring in the book are based upon the latest information available.

I am very glad to have the opportunity of making grateful acknowledgment of the aid and assistance which I received from police officers and other municipal officials

Foreword

throughout the country. It is impossible to mention by name all those to whom my thanks are due, but I may perhaps be permitted to testify in this general way to the patience and courtesy with which I was everywhere treated. I am under peculiar obligations to Professor William Bennett Munro of Harvard University, Dr. Walter Laidlaw of the New York City 1920 Census Committee, Professor Felix Frankfurter of the Harvard Law School, and Colonel Arthur Woods of New York, for their thoughtful and discriminating criticism of portions of the manuscript which they were kind enough to read. In justice to these gentlemen, however, I hasten to acquit them of any responsibility for the statements made and the opinions expressed in this book, or for any errors of omission or commission. The book is mine, and I am solely responsible for it.

Finally, it is my privilege to acknowledge the generous assistance and counsel of Mr. Harrison, who has been associated with the investigation from the beginning, and the long-tried patience and faithfulness of my secretaries, Mrs. Jasper J. Mayer, and Miss Helen T. Wisherd.

RAYMOND B. FOSDICK.

233 Broadway,
New York City,
August 5, 1920.

CONTENTS

CHAPTER I

THE AMERICAN PROBLEM

CHAPTER II

THE DEVELOPMENT OF AMERICAN POLICE CONTROL

CHAPTER III

THE PRESENT STATE OF POLICE CONTROL

Contents

CHAPTER IV

SPECIAL PROBLEMS OF POLICE CONTROL

CHAPTER V

THE ORGANIZATION OF THE DEPARTMENT

CHAPTER VI

THE COMMISSIONER OR DIRECTOR

Contents

CHAPTER VII

THE CHIEF OF POLICE

CHAPTER VIII

THE RANK AND FILE

CHAPTER IX

THE DETECTIVE FORCE

Contents

CHAPTER X

THE PREVENTION OF CRIME

CHAPTER XI

CONCLUSION

CHARTS

AMERICAN POLICE SYSTEMS

AMERICAN POLICE SYSTEMS

CHAPTER I

THE AMERICAN PROBLEM

Contrast between European and American police.— American police problem far more difficult.— Heterogeneity of America's population.— Preponderance of crime in America.— Comparative statistics: murder, burglary, robbery.— Relation of heterogeneity to crime.— The relation of court procedure to the police problem.— The law's delays.— The technicalities of procedure.— Faulty personnel on the bench.— The sentimental attitude of the public.— Relation of unenforceable laws to American police problem.— Sumptuary laws.— Borderland between live and dead law.— Embarrassment of the police.

To the American student of European municipal police bodies the contrast with similar institutions in the United States furnishes slight basis for pride. The efficiency of the Metropolitan Police Force of London, the operation of the detective bureau of Paris, the work of the Carabinieri in Rome and of the Politi in Copenhagen have little comparable to them in America; while even as regards the police of smaller cities like Zurich, Edinburgh or The Hague, an American looks almost in vain for equal effectiveness at home. This is so well recognized, indeed, and we have become so accustomed to think of our police work as perhaps the most pronounced failure in all our unhappy municipal history, that we are inclined to accept the phenomenon without analysis and charge it up generally to " politics." That politics lies at the root of much of it cannot of course be denied. No one can trace the development of police organization in the United States, as we shall follow it in Chapter II, without realizing how true the generalization is; but to believe that the unfavorable comparison between European and American police systems is chargeable solely to politics or to the personnel of our forces is to overlook certain fundamental divergencies in national conditions, customs and psychology which pile up obstacles in the way of efficient police work in America almost beyond the conception of the average European official.

In a word, the police of an American city are faced with a task such as European police organizations have no knowledge of. The Metropolitan Police Force of London with all its splendid efficiency would be overwhelmed in New York, and the *Brigade de sûreté* of Paris, with its ingenuity and mechanical equipment, would fall far below the level of its present achievement if it were confronted with the situation in Chicago. It is to the discussion of some of these external factors which complicate police function in America that the present chapter is devoted.

I. HETEROGENEITY OF POPULATION

With rare exceptions, the populations of European cities are homogeneous. The population of American cities is heterogeneous to an extent almost without parallel. Only 3% of London's population is foreign-born.[1]

[1] Census of 1911, Vol. 9. Wherever in this book London is

The American Problem

Paris has 6%,[1] Berlin 2.9%,[2] Vienna approximately one per cent.[3] In America — to use only a few illustrations at random — New York's foreign-born population is 41%, Chicago and Boston 36% each, Cleveland and Providence 34% each, Detroit 33%. Where London has 211,000 foreign-born, Paris 170,000, and Berlin 60,000, New York has 1,944,357, of which 1,563,964 are of non-English speaking peoples, while Chicago has 783,428, of which 653,377 are from non-English speaking countries.[4]

This contrast can be emphasized in another way. London has 14,000 Italians among her foreign-born; Paris has 26,000. New York has 340,000; Chicago has 45,000. London has 45,000 foreign-born Russians; Paris 18,000. New York has 485,000; Chicago 121,000. Where Paris has 7,000 Austro-Hungarians, New York has 267,000. Where London has 27,000 Poles, Chicago has 126,000. London's 42,000 foreign-born Germans must be contrasted with New York's 280,000 and with Chicago's 185,000. New York's Italian-born population is greater than the combined populations of Bologne and Venice. She has more German-born residents than has Bremen, Konigsberg, Aix la Chapelle, Posen, Kiel or Danzig. Only three cities of old Austria-Hungary — Vienna, Budapest and Prague — have a larger Austro-Hungarian population than New York, while in Chicago

mentioned, the reference is to the Metropolitan Police District which covers an area of 699 square miles and includes a population of 7,231,701.
[1] *Annuaire statistique de la Ville de Paris,* 1912.
[2] *Statistische Jahrbuch der Stadt Berlin,* 1913, pp. 40–41.
[3] That is, born outside the limits of the old Austro-Hungarian Empire. Meyer's *Konversationslexikon,* Vol. 20, annual supplement 1910–11.
[4] Federal Census of 1910.

the foreign-born Austro-Hungarians outnumber the population of Brunn, Cracow or Gratz. In only five Russian cities — Petrograd, Moscow, Odessa, Warsaw and Kiev — can a Russian population be found greater than that of New York.

But this is not the whole contrast. The forebears of London's present population for generations back were Englishmen, bred to English customs and traditions, just as the forefathers of modern Parisians were Frenchmen, born to French institutions and ideals. In New York, Chicago and other large cities of the United States there are hundreds of thousands of residents whose mothers or fathers or both were born abroad. If we add this class to the foreign-born population, of which we have been speaking, to form what may be called the foreign-stock element, we find that it comprises 80% of New York's population, and that of the total number, amounting to 3,769,803, nearly three-fourths came of non-English speaking people.[1] Similarly, this foreign-stock element constitutes the majority of the population in the nineteen largest cities of the United States. In other words, the native white population of native parentage amounts to less than one-fifth the total population of New York and less than one-fourth of the populations of Chicago, Boston, Cleveland, Detroit and Milwaukee; while in cities like Fall River, Massachusetts, it constitutes little more than 10%. In only fourteen of the fifty largest cities of America does the native parentage population equal fifty per cent of the total.

[1] *Ibid.* Congestion adds to the difficulties of heterogeneity. London in 1911 had only 180,000 people housed 219 to the acre; New York in 1910 had 1,171,000 people so housed.

The American Problem

Again, the contrast can be emphasized in terms not only of race but of color. In London and other cities of Great Britain the negro population is so negligible that the census statistics make no mention of it. Only rarely does one see negroes on the streets and a " color problem " does not exist. In America, in consequence of the great numbers of negro inhabitants, this problem has assumed startling proportions. Its extent can be judged from the following figures: [1]

City	Negro population	Percentage of negroes to total population
Atlanta	51,902	33.5
Baltimore	84,749	15.2
Birmingham	52,305	39.4
Charleston (S. C.)	31,056	52.8
Indianapolis	21,816	9.3
Kansas City	23,566	9.5
Louisville	40,522	18.1
Memphis	52,441	40.0
Nashville	36,523	33.1
New Orleans	89,262	26.3
Richmond	46,733	36.6
Savannah	33,246	51.1
Washington	94,446	28.5

The consequences of this mixture of race and color are far reaching, particularly in their effect on such functions as policing. Homogeneity simplifies the task of government. Long-established traditions of order and standards of public conduct, well-understood customs and prac-

[1] Census of 1910.

tices which smooth the rough edges of personal contact, a definite racial temperament and a fixed set of group-habits by which conflicting interests are more readily comprehended and adjusted — in short, the social solidarity and cohesiveness which come only from a common language and a common heritage — all these factors, so interwoven in French and English community life, and so essential in facilitating the maintenance of law, are utterly unknown in many of the towns and cities of the United States. Our larger cities, indeed, are often divided by more or less well defined lines into nationalistic sections: Italians, Chinese, Poles, Russians, Czechs, Slavs, each with their own districts, where they settle in colony fashion. Here, frequently in comparative isolation, they speak their own language, read their own newspapers, maintain their own churches and their peculiar social life. Occasionally the so-called foreign-section of a city comprises within a narrow area a heterogeneous mixture of races. In a single ward in St. Louis — to use an illustration that could be duplicated many times — are 900 Austro-Hungarians, 830 Irish, 2301 Germans, 2527 Italians, 7534 Russians and 493 Roumanians — all of them foreign-born — in addition to 14,067 native residents of foreign parentage and 1602 negroes.[1] The official census proclamation of 1920 in New York City was printed in 22 languages.

It is this complex problem of nationality that the police are called upon to grapple with. They must enforce the same laws among a score of races and maintain a standard of conduct in a population coming from radically dif-

[1] Personally communicated.

ferent environments. They must be prepared to understand the criminal propensities of Sicilians and Poles, of
Chinese and Russians. They must become expert in de-
tecting crime characteristics as shown by twenty races.
They must deal with people who have no knowledge of
public health regulations or safety ordinances or of those
sanitary laws which distinguish the modern city from the
medieval town. They must have a ready knowledge of
national customs and habits so as to be forearmed against
an Italian festival, a Polish wedding or a Russian holiday. They must constantly realize that the juxtaposition
of separate racial groups is a factor of potential disorder.

To see the London " Bobby " at work, dealing with
people of his own race who understand him and whom he
understands, is to learn a larger sympathy for his brother
officer who walks the beat in New York, Chicago or San
Francisco.

II. PREPONDERANCE OF CRIME IN AMERICA

The task of the police is further handicapped in the
United States, as compared generally with Europe, by the
greater volume of crime committed here. Police statistics show that crime is far more prevalent in American
cities than in the cities of England, France or Germany.[1]
The point will undoubtedly be made that inasmuch as the
prime duty of the police is the prevention of crime, this
unhappy condition is the *result* of our police ineffectiveness rather than one of the *causes* of it. In part this

---

[1] German criminal statistics after 1914 are not available, and
French statistics since that date are unsatisfactory for the use of the
careful student. The English statistics maintain their standard of
excellence and completeness in spite of the war.

9

point is well taken, and it must be admitted that in assessing responsibility for the condition which we shall shortly describe, we are in a borderland where exact analysis is impossible. At the same time the large preponderance in America of certain types of crime which are, generally speaking, unaffected by police activity — such as premeditated murder and many kinds of commercial frauds — affords a basis for the belief that our greater comparative propensity to crime is to a certain degree due to the make-up of our population, quite apart from the inefficiency of our police forces. To that extent, therefore, this condition may be placed in the list of those external factors which complicate our police problem.

Comparative Statistics — Murder.

As to the fact of our excessive criminality, the statistics furnish startling evidence. London in 1916, with a population of seven millions and a quarter, had nine premeditated murders. Chicago, one-third the size of London, in the same period had 105, nearly twelve times London's total.[1] In the year 1916, indeed — and it was not an exceptional year — Chicago with its 2,500,000 people had twenty more murders than the whole of England and Wales put together with their 38,000,000 people.[2] The Chicago murders during this year total one

[1] These figures, in both instances, do not include abortion cases. I am indebted for my Chicago figures to the Bureau of Records of the Chicago police department which prepares perhaps the best analysis of homicidal deaths to be found anywhere in the United States. The London figures are from the annual reports of the Commissioner of the Metropolitan Police. It must be emphasized that these statistics in both instances are based not on judicial determinations, but on a police analysis of crime complaints.

[2] Figures obtained from the *Judicial Statistics of England and*

The American Problem

more than London had during the five year period from 1910 to 1914 inclusive. In 1917 Chicago had ten more murders than the whole of England and Wales and four more murders than all England, Wales and Scotland.[1] In 1918 Chicago had fourteen more murders than England and Wales. In 1919 the number of murders in Chicago was almost exactly six times the number committed in London. A tabulation of some of these statistics follows:[2]

	Murders				
	1914	*1915*	*1916*	*1917*	*1918*
England and Wales	92	81	85	81	81
Scotland	8	12	9	6	*
London	16	21	9	16	26
Liverpool	5	4	4	4	5
Chicago	87	77	105	91	95

* Figures not available.

But Chicago is not exceptional. Other American cities suffer equally from comparison with crime conditions abroad. New York City in 1916 had exactly six

Wales — Criminal Section (Table on police returns). These statistics are published annually by the Home Office. The figures quoted above — indeed the crime figures quoted in this entire section of the chapter — do not represent judicial findings — that is, they are not based on the results of trials. They are *complaints of crime,* or, as they are called in England, *crimes known to the police,* regardless of arrests, convictions, or the particular degrees of crime for which prisoners are sentenced. Thus the police in a given community might know that 100 burglaries had been committed in the course of a year. Perhaps 50 arrests are made and 40 convictions secured in varying degrees of burglary and housebreaking. The index of crime in that community is not found in the arrests or the convictions, but in the 100 burglaries known to the police to have been committed.

[1] Figures obtained from the *Judicial Statistics of Scotland,* published annually by the Scottish Office.

[2] Exclusive of abortion cases and infanticides.

times the number of homicides (murder and manslaughter) that London had for the same year, and only ten less homicides than all of England and Wales. In 1917 New York had six times more homicides than London, and exceeded the total homicides of England and Wales by 56. In 1918 New York again had six times more homicides than London, and exceeded the total homicides of England and Wales by 67.[1] This contrast cannot be attributed to the peculiar conditions in London induced by the war. In each of the years from 1914 to 1918 inclusive New York had more homicides than occurred in London during any three year period previous to the outbreak of the war in 1914.[2] A tabulation of homicide statistics follows:

[1] The New York figures are taken from the annual reports of the New York police department. The homicide figures in all instances are exclusive of abortion cases and vehicular accident and other criminal negligence cases. Every effort has been made to verify the accuracy of these statistics and careful studies have been undertaken in New York, Chicago and London (at Scotland Yard) to test their comparability.

[2] At the same time it cannot be denied that the war had some effect upon criminal statistics in England, although the reduction in homicides is not as marked as might be expected. The following table shows murders and manslaughters in London during the ten years preceding the war:

Year	Murder	Munslaughter	Total homicides (murder and manslaughter)
1904	19	30	49
1905	20	24	44
1906	16	20	36
1907	12	35	47
1908	18	35	53
1909	18	24	42
1910	21	22	43
1911	21	31	52
1912	24	40	64
1913	22	38	60

These figures, compiled from the reports of the London police, are

The American Problem

Homicide (*murder and manslaughter*)[1]

	1914	1915	1916	1917	1918
England and Wales	220	226	196	180	154
Scotland	39	57	53	29	*
London	46	45	31	39	37
Liverpool	8	8	8	9	5
Glasgow	11	23	18	11	9
New York	244	234	186	236	221
Chicago	216	198	255	253	222
Detroit	*	*	62	94	42
Washington, D. C.	26	25	24	24	27

* Figures not available.

Statistics of this kind could be multiplied at length. In the three year period 1916–1918 inclusive, Glasgow had 38 homicides; Philadelphia, which is only a trifle larger, had during this same period 281.[2] Liverpool and St. Louis are approximately the same size; in 1915 St. Louis had eleven times the number of homicides that Liverpool had, and in 1916 eight times the number.[3] Los Angeles, one-twentieth the size of London, had two more homicides in 1916 than London had for the same period; in 1917 she had ten more than London had. Cleveland, Ohio, one-tenth the size of London, had more than three

exclusive of abortions, infanticides, justifiable homicides and all vehicular accident and criminal negligence cases.

[1] Exclusive of abortions, infanticides and vehicular accident and other criminal negligence cases. New York and Chicago figures are based upon police reports, except the 1915 New York figure, which is based on a personal examination of the records. This examination showed twelve more homicides than were indicated in the annual report.

[2] Philadelphia statistics from annual reports, Bureau of Police.

[3] The St. Louis statistics were obtained from the police department records.

13

times the number of homicides in 1917 and approximately twice the number in 1918.[1]

The chief constable for Edinburgh in his annual report for 1915 wrote as follows: " I regret to state that while crimes against the person have considerably decreased, a number of serious crimes under the heading of homicide were reported during the year — namely, one murder, one attempted murder, and five cases of culpable homicide." [2] The one murder was an abortion case; two of the culpable homicides were cases in which infants had died from neglect; a third was a vehicular accident case; and two others, " after full investigation by the Crown Authorities were not proceeded with." [3] Edinburgh is a city in excess of 300,000 population. Surely a chief of police in an American city of equal size would have reasons for pride rather than regret if he could point to such a record.

We have already noted that as a result of the war reliable crime statistics are not available in Continental Europe. It is pertinent to note, however, that for a long time before the war Berlin had an average of 25 murders a year, and Vienna an average of nineteen.[4]

[1] Statistics obtained from police records.
[2] *Report on Crime and the Police Establishment, 1915,* p. 6.
[3] *Ibid.* In his report for 1918 the chief constable of Edinburgh says: "The only crime of a serious nature recorded during the year was that of a young unmarried woman charged with culpable homicide." This was an infanticide case (p. 8). In his report for 1919 this same official said: " I regret to state that while crime has slightly decreased during the year, crimes against the person have considerably increased. . . . Two cases of murder and one case of culpable homicide were reported to the police during the year." These cases included one abortion and one vehicular accident case. (p. 8.)
[4] These figures I verified in 1914 at police headquarters in *Alexanderplatz,* Berlin, and at the *Agentenreferat* in Vienna.

The American Problem

Comparative Statistics — Burglary.

Equally significant is the comparison of burglary statistics between Great Britain and the United States. In 1915, for example, New York City had approximately eight times as many burglaries as London had in the same period, and nearly twice the number of burglaries reported in all England and Wales.[1] In 1917 New York had four times as many burglaries as London, and approximately the same number as occurred in England and Wales. In 1918 the burglaries which the police reported in New York were approximately two and a half times those in London.[2] While war conditions undoubtedly served to heighten this contrast, they were by no means entirely responsible for it; in 1915 New York City had more burglaries than occurred in all England and Wales in 1911, 1912, or 1913.[3] Chicago in 1916 had 532 more burglaries than London, in 1917, 3459 more, in 1918, 866 more, and in 1919, 2146 more. Detroit and Cleveland generally report several hundred

[1] In New York there were 11,652 burglaries in 1915; in London 1,459; in England and Wales 6,737. In order to establish a comparison I have grouped within the classification "burglary" several crimes which in England are listed under such titles as housebreaking, shop-breaking, sacrilege, etc. The crime burglary as used in the above comparison includes housebreaking by day or night.

[2] It seems probable that these New York figures for 1918 represent an under-statement of the actual number of burglaries.

[3] The burglaries occurring in London and in England and Wales from 1910–1915 inclusive are as follows:

Year	London	England and Wales
1910	3,057	12,215
1911	3,048	11,045
1912	2,974	11,112
1913	2,911	11,166
1914	2,352	9,844
1915	1,459	6,737

more burglaries per annum than London, although London is seven or eight times larger. In each of these two cities in 1917 and 1918 the number of burglaries averaged one-fourth the number committed in all England and Wales. The annual burglaries in St. Louis always exceed those in London.

A table of burglaries follows:

Burglary, including housebreaking by day or night, shop-breaking, sacrilege, etc.[1]

	1916	1917	1918
England and Wales....	7,809	9,453	10,331
Scotland	3,977	5,073	*
London	1,581	2,164	2,777
Liverpool	1,135	1,361	1,136
New York	*	9,450	7,412
Chicago	2,113	5,623	3,643
Detroit	2,736	3,080	2,047
Cleveland	*	2,752	2,608
St. Louis	3,212	2,483	2,989

* Figures not available.

The disproportionate number of burglaries occurring in American cities as compared with English cities is reflected in the prevailing burglary insurance rates of the two countries. Due to differences in insurance practices

[1] The American figures in this table are taken from police department records. Their accuracy cannot be vouched for, because in many of our departments, complaints of crime are deliberately and systematically concealed. It can safely be assumed, however, that these figures represent an under-statement rather than an over-statement. The English statistics, on the other hand, are kept with meticulous care, and after a careful study of the records and methods at Scotland Yard and elsewhere in Great Britain, I do not believe that complaints of crime are ever concealed to avoid unfavorable appearances.

and methods, exact comparisons are impossible, but enough has been gathered from careful investigation to warrant the general conclusion that burglary rates in American municipalities are from fifteen to twenty times higher than in the principal cities of England.[1]

Comparative Statistics — Robbery.

Even more startling are the statistics of robbery.[2] New York City in 1915 reported 838 robberies and assaults with intent to rob where London had 20, and England, Wales and Scotland together had 102. In 1916 New York had 886 such crimes to London's nineteen, and England, Wales and Scotland's 227. In 1917 New York reported 864 to London's 38, while England, Wales and Scotland reported 233. In 1918 New York had 849, while London had 63 and England and Wales had 100. This contrast is by no means ascribable to war conditions, although such conditions undoubtedly heightened it. In each of the four years from 1915 to 1918 inclusive, New York City had from four to five times more robberies than occurred in all England and Wales in any one of the five years preceding the war.

[1] This statement is based on quite a detailed study of burglary insurance in London and New York and I am indebted to various insurance company representatives in both cities for their courtesy and assistance. An interesting comparison in burglary insurance rates for private residences is possible between different American cities. The rates prevailing in June, 1920, for seven municipalities are as follows: Chicago and San Francisco, $19.80 per thousand; New York, St. Louis and Detroit, $16.50 per thousand; Atlanta, $13.75 per thousand; Boston, $11.00 per thousand.

[2] The astonishing discrepancy in these statistics led to a careful investigation. The legal definitions of robbery are practically identical on both sides of the Atlantic. The fact remains that highway robberies or "hold-ups" do not occur in Great Britain with anything like the frequency they do in America.

Practically the same proportion exists between Chicago's robberies and those in Great Britain. In 1918, for example, Chicago had 22 robberies for every one robbery in London and 14 robberies for every one robbery in England and Wales. Washington, D. C., in 1916 had four times the number of robberies that London reported; in 1917 three times the number; and in 1918 one and one-half times the number. Los Angeles in 1916 had 64 more robberies than all of England, Wales and Scotland put together; in 1917 she had 126 more than these three countries. Cities like St. Louis and Detroit, in their statistics of robbery and assault with intent to rob, frequently show annual totals varying from three times to five times greater than the number of such crimes reported for the whole of Great Britain. Liverpool is about one and a third times larger than Cleveland, and yet in 1919 Cleveland reported 31 robberies for every one reported in Liverpool.

Comparative Statistics — Miscellaneous.

Differences in definition and classification of crime between England and America make it difficult to push the comparison much further. One or two illustrations, however, may be noted to emphasize the contrast developed in the foregoing statistics. Automobile thefts are much more prevalent in America than in Great Britain, as is shown by the following table:

Thefts of automobiles reported in 1919 [1]

New York 5527
Chicago 4316

[1] Figures in all cases obtained from the police records. I am

The American Problem

Detroit 3482
St. Louis 1244
Cleveland 2327
Buffalo 986
London 290
Liverpool 10

Comparative statistics as to the number of automobiles in American and English cities are impossible to obtain, but it is probably a fair assumption that the proportionate excess of thefts in the United States far exceeds the admittedly larger supply of machines in our communities as compared with the communities of Great Britain.

Similarly in comparing the total number of arrests for all crimes and offenses in the United States and Great Britain, one is struck by the high figures in American cities.[1] The number of arrests in Boston for the year 1917 exceeded the number of arrests in London for the same year by 32,520. Philadelphia's arrests for 1917 exceeded London's by 20,005. Chicago's arrests for 1917 exceeded London's by 61,874. New York's arrests for this same period exceeded London's by 111,-877. Indeed New York had almost two and a half times

especially indebted to the Honorable Trevor Bigham, assistant commissioner at Scotland Yard, for his courtesy in aiding me to obtain the London figures.

[1] Figures of arrests must always be taken with some qualification, as they are subject to various interpretations. They may denote crime conditions, or excessive zeal on the part of the police, or too many laws and regulations to be observed, or any one of half a dozen other situations. Because in this case the American arrests exceed the English arrests by such large figures, I have felt free to use the comparison as at least throwing some further light on criminality in the United States.

19

as many arrests in 1917 as were made in London. Glasgow with an estimated population of a third of a million larger than either St. Louis or Boston, recorded in 1918 22,290 arrests and summonses, while St. Louis in the same period showed 54,400 and Boston 90,293. This same disproportion is to be found in cities of lesser size.

Relation of Heterogeneity to Crime.

To what extent the excessive volume of crime in America is attributable to the heterogeneity of our population cannot be precisely determined. Even where they exist at all, our criminal statistics are so crude and incomplete that deductions are difficult to make and when made are little better than rough estimates. The number of arrests in the course of a year is practically the only classification available for our purposes, and the fact that this basis of measurement makes no allowance for unsolved crimes or for cases subsequently discharged in court, shows its unsatisfactory character. However as an indication of the causal connection between the presence in America of large numbers of foreign races, uprooted and often adrift, and our overwhelming preponderance of crime, the figures of arrest may profitably be studied. They show, for example, that Irish-born inhabitants of Boston, constituting 9.8% of the population, are charged with 15% of the total arrests.[1] In New York City the Russian-born inhabitants, constituting 10.15% of the population, are credited with 20% of the total arraignments before the magistrates' courts, while the Italian-

[1] Calculation based on U. S. Census report and Annual Report of the Police Department for 1918.

The American Problem

born, who equal 7.15% of the population, have 11.8% of the arraignments.[1] The total figure of arraignments before the magistrates' courts in New York for 1917 can be calculated as follows:

Nativity	Percentage of total population	Percentage of total arraignments
Foreign born	40.8%	52.9%
Native born	59.2	47.1
(of native, foreign or mixed parentage)		

These figures, however, are largely made up of misdemeanors, including violations of sanitary regulations, health ordinances, etc., which as far as the foreigner is concerned may be often the result of ignorance. Certainly they do not necessarily imply criminality. A fairer judgment can be based on cases of felony as distinguished from misdemeanor. Arrests for felony in 1918 in Chicago, for example, can be illustrated as follows:[2]

Country of Origin	Percentage of total population	Percentage of total felony arrests
U. S. white	62.1%	55.1%
U. S. colored	2.0	13.2
Poles	5.8	6.4
Russia	5.6	5.9
Italy	2.06	4.3
Germany	8.3	2.4
Lithuania (including Letts)	.9	2.3
Other nationalities	12.+	10.+

[1] Calculations based on Annual Report of City Magistrates for 1917.
[2] Compiled from annual police report of Chicago for 1918.

American Police Systems

This can further be illustrated by figures showing the respective percentages of felony arrests and misdemeanor arrests in the total arrests of each of the above nationalities: [1]

Nationality	Percentage of felony arrests	Percentage of misdemeanor arrests
U. S. white	9.97%	90.03%
U. S. colored	15.8	84.2
Poles	11.3	88.7
Russia	15.97	84.03
Italy	15.3	84.7
Germany	11.5	88.5
Lithuania	14.6	88.4
Other nationalities	8.5	91.5

The problem presented by the colored race is shown in the following statistics of arrest from Washington, D. C., for the year 1919: [2]

	Percentage of total population	Percentage of total arrests
White	71.5%	57.57%
Colored	28.5	42.43

Another calculation follows showing the number of arrests for serious offenses in the same city for the same year: [3]

[1] *Ibid.*
[2] Compiled from annual report of the Metropolitan Police of the District of Columbia for 1919.
[3] *Ibid.* Similar statistics are obtainable in other cities which have large colored populations.

22

The American Problem

Nature of Offense	Number of Arrests	
	White	Colored
	(constituting 71.5% of population)	(constituting 28.5% of population)
Murder	15	34
Manslaughter	6	8
Assault with dangerous weapon	33	249
Assault with intent to kill	6	10
Housebreaking	139	323
Robbery	40	283

An intensive study of homicide records furnishes similarly interesting results. For example, the general homicide return for New York City in 1915, exclusive of abortions, vehicular accidents and justifiable homicides, shows that 240 cases were known to the police in which a total of 251 persons were killed.[1] Of this number, six were infants below the age of one year, and one was an adult who was never identified. Distributing the remaining 244 decedents according to nativity we find that 93 were born in the United States of native parents, 26 were natives of the United States with foreign-born parents, and 125 were foreign-born. Of the 240 cases, arrests were made in 161, and 222 persons were charged with homicide. Of the 222, 60 were natives of native parentage, 65 were born in Italy, while twelve others were native-born of Italian parentage. The Russian-born numbered 21, and the native-born of Irish parentage were next in order with a total of nineteen.[2]

[1] These statistics are the result of personal research at Police Headquarters in New York.
[2] The complete list of the nativities of the 222 persons apprehended

American Police Systems

The Chicago Police Department reported 77 cases of premeditated murder for the year 1915, accounting for the death of 77 people. Of the 59 persons arrested on the charges of murder and accessory to murder, 25 were native whites, nineteen were Italians, ten were native negroes, two were Poles, and three were of other nationalities.[1]

was as follows: Italy, 65; United States, 60; Russia, 21; United States (parents Ireland), 19; United States (parents Italy), 12; Austria, 11; United States (parents Germany), 8; Ireland, 7; Germany, 4; United States (parents Austria), 3; England, 1; England (parents Russia), 1; Finland, 1; Greece, 1; Hawaiian Islands, 1; Hungary, 1; Scotland, 1; Turkey, 1; United States (parents Canada), 1; United States (parents Russia), 1; United States (parents Sweden), 1; West Indies, 1.

It is possible to push this analysis a little further. We have seen that arrests were made in 161 of the 240 cases of homicide known to the police. In 27 cases the perpetrators committed suicide, in one case the perpetrator was killed, so that there remained 51 cases which were not solved by the police and in which no arrests were made. Considerable importance attaches to these cases, as unsolved crimes are more likely to be planned by the wary and seasoned criminal. In homicides, the very fact that no clue is left may indicate greater caution and more carefully laid plans. To include in the calculation, therefore, only those cases in which arrests have been made, is to eliminate the most dangerous and vicious crimes and criminals. For these reasons a careful examination was made of the Detective Bureau records pertaining to the 51 unsolved murder cases, and personal interviews were had with the detectives having the cases in charge. In many of them, while the perpetrator was known with reasonable certainty, the evidence was not sufficient to warrant an arrest. On the basis of this calculation, of the 51 unsolved cases, 31 can with reasonable accuracy be charged to natives of Italy; 4 perpetrators are believed to be natives of the United States, one a native of Irish parentage, and one an Austrian. In 14 cases no clue whatever was established.

[1] A study similar to that carried on in New York was made of Chicago's 1915 cases. As in New York, it consisted of close examination of the Detective Bureau records and consultation with the detectives. The unsolved cases amount to 30 cases of murder and 10 cases of manslaughter, and the perpetrators can with reasonable certainty be distributed among the following nationalities: United States (white), 6; United States (colored), 6; United States (parents Polish), 1; United States (parents Irish), 1; Italian, 13; Poland, 2; Russia, 2; Serbian, 1; Turk, 1; Chinese, 1; no clue, 6.

The American Problem

In St. Louis during 1915 there were 71 cases of murder and manslaughter [1] in which there were 71 decedents and 72 perpetrators. The nativity of the perpetrators in these cases almost coincided with the nativity of the decedents. Of native whites there were 34 decedents and 35 perpetrators; of the native colored there were twenty decedents and 24 perpetrators; seven decedents were of Italian parentage as were six perpetrators; there were three Albanian decedents and two Albanian perpetrators; seven decedents of other nationalities, with five perpetrators of other nationalities. [2]

In Memphis in 1915 there were 76 cases of murder and manslaughter in which 78 people were killed. Of the persons killed, nineteen were white and 59 were colored. Of the 77 alleged perpetrators, the whites numbered seventeen, the colored 53, unknown four, patrolmen in the performance of duty, three. [3]

In Washington, D. C., in the five years between 1915 and 1919, 143 homicides were committed. In all but five of these cases the police succeeded in apprehending the persons charged with the crime. Of the 138 cases thus

[1] This figure does not include abortions, justifiable homicides or criminal carelessness cases. Arrests were made in 56 cases, in two the perpetrators committed suicide and thirteen remained unsolved by the police.

[2] These statistics were gathered by personal research. It is worthy of note that in St. Louis in this period (1915) one negro was charged with murder or manslaughter for every 1,832 of the colored population, and one white was charged with the same offense for every 13,385 of the population.

[3] Arrests were made in 37 cases, 15 of the perpetrators being white and 22 being colored. Of the remaining 36 unsolved cases, two white perpetrators were known but not apprehended, 29 colored perpetrators were unapprehended, four cases remained without clue, and one perpetrator committed suicide. (Statistics gathered by personal research.)

American Police Systems

cleared up, 45 were committed by white persons and 93 by negroes.[1] Of the 45 white persons, five were foreigners.

Calculations such as these furnish indisputable evidence that America's crime rate is greatly augmented by the presence of unassimilated or poorly assimilated races. It must not be supposed, however, that our foreign and colored population is the sole cause of our excessive crime rate. If the offenses of our foreign and colored races were stricken from the calculation, our crime record would still greatly exceed the record of Western Europe. With

[1] The complete tabulation of these homicides is as follows:

	1915	1916	1917	1918	1919	Total
Total number of homicides....	25	24	24	26	44	143
Cleared up	25	23	24	26	40	138
Not cleared up	0	1	0	0	4	5
Committed by whites	13	5	9	4	14	45
Committed by negroes	12	18	15	22	26	93

The details of the above totals are as follows:

	1915	1916	1917	1918	1919	Total
White men killed by negroes..	0	2	3	5	4	14
Negroes killed by white men..	2	1	1	0	3	7
White men killed by white women	0	1	0	0	1	2
White women killed by white men	4	2	3	3	3	15
Negro women killed by negro men	6	7	4	4	4	25
Negro men killed by negro women	0	0	2	0	3	5
Negro men killed by negro men	7	9	6	13	15	50
White men killed by white men	6	1	5	1	7	20

The above figures, which were furnished through the courtesy of the late Major Pullman of the Washington force, are exclusive of abortions, infanticides, and justifiable homicides. The record made by the police of Washington, D. C., in clearing up all but five cases out of 143 is most unusual and compares favorably with the best records of European police departments. As will be noted by the above table, the Washington police department in three different twelve-month periods scored a hundred per cent record in their work. In some cities the record of homicide cases cleared up is only thirty and forty per cent of the total.

all its kindliness and good nature, the temper of our communities contains a strong strain of violence. We condone violence and shirk its punishment. We lack a high instinct for order. We lack a sense of the dignity of obedience to restraint which is demanded for the common good. We lack a certain respect for our own security and the terms upon which civilized communities keep the peace.

"There is probably more undisciplined, egotistic, mischievous force in the United States than in any country of first rank in the world." [1] This indictment, framed by an indignant newspaper, is scarcely exaggerated. There is hardly a community where its accuracy is not vindicated. It is little wonder, therefore, that the task which we have set before our police has all but proved impossible.

III. THE LAW'S DELAYS, THE COURTS, AND THE PUBLIC

The police are but one part of the machinery of justice. Their function is to maintain order and if necessary apprehend offenders. With the prosecution, trial and punishment of these offenders, however, they have little to do. They start the process but they do not finish it. The prosecuting attorneys' offices, the courts and the prisons take up the thread of their work where the police leave it. The operation of justice is a single operation working through a number of agencies.

It follows, therefore, that the effectiveness of the police cannot be judged apart from the effectiveness of

[1] Chicago *Tribune* (Paris edition), January 31, 1919.

other agencies with which they are associated in working for a common end.   If the district attorney's office is lax in its prosecutions, if legal procedure makes for delay and uncertainty, if the court is slothful or open to unworthy influence in its decisions, the ends of justice for which the police are working are apt to be defeated.   The failure of a single agency impairs the work of all.

This is a point which cannot be too strongly emphasized.   In the popular mind the police are often held responsible for results over which they have no control. They share the ignominy which belongs to other parts of the machine, as well as the discouragement of association with an enterprise which so often fails.   Efficient work on their part in the detection of a criminal, for example, or in the prevention of an abuse, stands an excellent chance of being mangled and destroyed in the subsequent processes.   Indeed, without the support of an administration of justice that is prompt and certain, consistently effective police work is out of the question.

It is, of course, a notorious fact that such support is not given our police forces.   There is no part of its work in which American law fails so absolutely and so ludicrously as in the conviction and punishment of criminals. " It is not too much to say," said President Taft in 1909, " that the administration of criminal law in this country is a disgrace to our civilization, and that the prevalence of crime and fraud, which here is greatly in excess of that in European countries, is due largely to the failure of the law and its administration to bring criminals to justice." [1]

[1] Chicago Speech, September, 1909.   Quoted in *The Reform of Legal Procedure* by Moorfield Storey, Yale University Press, 1911, p. 3.

The American Problem

The Technicalities of Procedure.

Space is not available for more than a hasty discussion of this important factor. In the first place, our legal procedure with its red tape and technicalities is fantastically employed to aid the criminal. When a verdict of murder is set aside because the word " aforethought " is omitted after the word " malice ";[1] when a man convicted of assault with intent to kill is freed because the copying clerk left out the letter *l* in the word *malice;*[2] when an indictment for rape is held defective because it concluded " against the peace and dignity of State " instead of " against the peace and dignity of *the* State ";[3] when another murderer is discharged because the prosecution neglected to prove that the real name of the victim and his alias represented one and the same person;[4] when a horse-thief is released because the indictment ended in the words " against the peace and dignity of the state of *W*. Virginia," instead of " against the peace and dignity of the state of *West* Virginia "[5]— briefly, when in a manner utterly unknown in Europe, such absurdities can be spun to defeat the ends of justice, it is not surprising that the police are slack and careless.[6] The morale of the best

[1] Etheridge *vs*. State, 141 Ala. 29.
[2] Wood *vs*. State, 50 Ala. 144.
[3] State *vs*. Campbell, 210 Mo., 202.
[4] Goodlove *vs*. State, 82 O. S. 365.
[5] Lemons *vs*. State, 4 W. Va. 755.
[6] Although there are a few recent cases, I believe that the courts as a whole are less inclined than formerly to upset convictions because of faulty indictments. See *Garland vs. Washington*, 232 U. S. 642 (1914), overruling *Crain vs. U. S.*, 162 U. S. 625 (1896). See also *Valdez vs. U. S.*, 244 U. S. 432. It is noteworthy too that Congress in 1919 passed the following amendment to the Judicial Code:

" Sec. 269. All of the said courts shall have power to grant new trials, in cases where there has been a trial by jury, for reasons

police organization in the world would soon be broken down in such an environment. "It's small satisfaction to catch the crooks," a chief of detectives told me, "when you know all the time that some sharp legal trick will be used to turn them free."

A member of the Alabama Bar, addressing the Bar Association of that State, said: "I have examined about 75 murder cases that found their way into the reports of Alabama. More than half of those cases were reversed and not a single one of them on any matter that went to the merits of the case; and very few of them upon any matter that could have influenced the jury in reaching a verdict." [1] This same story comes from all over the country.

Again, the special defenses which the common law throws about the defendant have been so interpreted and developed as to afford the accused a degree of protection out of all relation to modern conditions. The principle that no person shall be compelled to give evidence against

for which new trials have usually been granted in the courts of law. On the hearing of any appeal, *certiorari,* writ of error, or motion for a new trial, in any case, civil or criminal, the court shall give judgment after an examination of the entire record before the court without regard to technical errors or defects or to exceptions which do not affect the substantial rights of the parties."

This reform has in substance been adopted in the following 25 states: Alabama, Arizona, California, Florida, Illinois, Indiana, Iowa, Kansas, Kentucky, Michigan, Minnesota, Missouri, Montana, Nebraska, Nevada, New Hampshire, New Jersey, New Mexico, New York, Ohio, Oklahoma, Pennsylvania, Texas, Wisconsin and Wyoming. (A summary of the statutes and decisions in these states is to be found in 66 U. of P. L. Rev. 12. For further discussion see Third Annual Report of the Standing Committee of the American Bar Association to Suggest Remedies and Propose Laws Relating to Procedure, dated June 10, 1919.)

[1] Storey, *loc. cit.,* p. 231.

himself, or shall be placed twice in jeopardy for the same offense, furnishes the basis for constantly recurring perversions of justice upon which foreign jurists look with amazement. The accused has wide privileges of challenge in the choice of a jury which are denied the prosecution; he cannot be made to take the stand in his own defense and his failure to do so cannot be used against him; he has the right of appeal to higher courts while the state has none. As many prosecuting officers have pointed out, the criminal law in America is a game in which the defendant is given every chance to escape, fair and unfair, while every possible obstacle is placed in the way of the prosecution. To such an extent has this situation developed that under present conditions it would seem to be the community that stands in need of protection rather than the criminal.[1] "The wonder now is not that so many guilty men escape," said a prominent member of the Philadelphia Bar, "but that under our present system any guilty men are ever convicted. Where they have money enough to employ the most able counsel and to take advantage of every delay and technicality available, they practically never are convicted." [2]

In a single year in Oregon — to use an illustration that could be duplicated everywhere — there occurred 56 homicides. Forty-six of the offenders were arrested.

[1] "The fact is that our administration of criminal law has as nearly reached perfection in guarding the innocent (and guilty) from conviction as is possible for any human institution; but in securing the safety and order of the community by the conviction of the guilty, it is woefully inadequate." Judge Carl Nott in *Coddling the Criminal, Atlantic Monthly,* February, 1911.
[2] Samuel Scoville, Jr., in *The Evolution of Our Criminal Procedure,* Annals of the American Academy of Political and Social Science, March, 1914.

Of these, ten committed suicide and 36 were held for trial. Of the 36, only three were convicted at all, and of these only one for murder in the first degree.[1] In 1913 in the City of New York there were 323 homicides, 185 arrests and only 80 convictions. Of the 80 convictions, ten received death sentences. In 1914 in the same city there were 292 homicides, 185 arrests and 66 convictions. Of the 66 convictions, six received death sentences.[2] In 1917 in New York there were 236 homicides, 280 arrests and 67 convictions, of which nine received death sentences. In 1918 in the same city there were 221 homicides, 256 arrests, and 77 convictions, of which six received death sentences.[3] In Detroit during the fiscal year 1917 there were 89 murders, 104 arrests, and fourteen convictions; in the fiscal year 1918, there were 71 murders, 147 arrests and 22 convictions.[4] The annual homicide calculations of the Chicago *Tribune,* which, after careful checking, seem to be as accurate as any criminal statistics can be under our present system, indicate the following facts regarding culpable homicide in the United States:[5]

[1] Reports of the American Bar Association, 1908, p. 495.
[2] See *Report of a Study of the Homicide Records, New York Police Department,* 1913–14, prepared by the Bureau of Municipal Research, March, 1915.
[3] See annual Report, New York Police Department, 1918.
[4] In the same city in 1917 there were 843 robberies, 494 arrests and 115 convictions, while in 1918 there were 688 robberies, 458 arrests, and 101 convictions. (See Annual Report of Detroit Police, 1918.)
[5] These figures are exclusive of infanticide, justifiable and excusable homicide, and all vehicular and other accident cases. I use these figures because from all facts which I can secure they seem to represent an understatement rather than an overstatement. They are substantially supported by the annual homicide analyses of Mr. Frederick L. Hoffman, published in the *Spectator* (see, for example,

The American Problem

Year	Total number of culpable homicides	Total number of legal executions
1916	8,372	115
1917	7,803	85
1918	7,667	85

In England the situation is far different. Any volume of judicial statistics or any report of the Police Commissioner of London bears out the contrast. In 1904, for example, in London — to pick up a random report — there were twenty cases of premeditated murder. In six the perpetrators committed suicide; one man was sent immediately to an asylum, and one escaped to Italy. Of the twelve persons arrested and brought to trial, one was acquitted, five were adjudged insane and confined in an asylum, and six were sentenced to death. In 1917 in the same city, there were 19 premeditated murders. Three cases remained unsolved; five perpetrators committed suicide, and eleven were arrested. Of the eleven arrests, there were eight convictions. In the whole of England and Wales for 1916, 85 murders were committed and 59 people arrested in connection therewith were committed for trial. Fifty-three trials resulted during the year. Twelve of the accused were found insane on arraignment and were confined; sixteen were found guilty but were adjudged insane and confined; ten were acquitted, and fifteen were sentenced to death.[1]

It was from England that we borrowed the foundations

Vol. XCV, No. 26). No more emphatic commentary could be made upon the lamentable condition of criminal statistics in the United States than the bare statement that calculations such as these are not based upon exact information.

[1] Judicial Statistics for England and Wales, 1916.

of our criminal system. The special position of the accused, the assumption of innocence until guilt is proved, our jury system, in fact our whole attitude and point of view in regard to the man on trial, are of English origin, and were handed down from generation to generation before they were carried to America. It is an inescapable conclusion, however, that the English machine works smoothly and effectively while ours does not. A parasitic growth of technicality and intricacy has thwarted and choked our whole criminal process.

The Delays of Justice.

The delays of the courts furnish another reason for the failure of our administration of justice. A random examination of almost any volume of appellate court decisions will fully substantiate this charge. For example, in Illinois one Sam Siracusa was tried for murder in October, 1913, and pleaded guilty. On a writ of error the case was carried to the Supreme Court of Illinois where judgment was affirmed exactly three years from the date of conviction. The case was not finally disposed of until three months later when a rehearing was denied.[1] Dominick Delfino was convicted of murder in Pennsylvania in October, 1916. One year and three months later the judgment was affirmed.[2] In New York Charles Sprague was convicted of murder on February 8, 1912. Judgment was affirmed by the Court of Appeals four years and one month later.[3] Oresto Shilitano in the same state was convicted of murder on March 6, 1914.

[1] 275 Ill. 457.
[2] 259 Pa. State 272.
[3] 217 N. Y. 373.

Judgment was affirmed two years and two months later.[1]
Similarly, Leo Urban was found guilty in New York of
robbery in the first degree on December 14, 1915. Judgment was affirmed by the Court of Appeals July 3, 1917.[2]
These are not unusual cases. They are picked at random
from miscellaneous law reports.

A study of criminal court dockets brings similar results. For example — to cite a single case out of many
at hand — one Ben Kuzios was indicted in Chicago on
May 16, 1917, for assault with intent to rob. He was
found guilty on July 25, 1917, a motion for a new trial
was over-ruled, and he was sentenced to the penitentiary.
A week later his attorney entered another motion for a
new trial and the prisoner was released on bail. The
transcript from the docket tells the rest of the story:

Aug. 24, 1917 — motion for new trial continued to October term.

Nov. 3, 1917 — motion for new trial continued to Nov. 7,
1917.

Nov. 7, 1917 — motion for new trial continued to Nov. 14,
1917.

Nov. 14, 1917 — motion for new trial continued to Nov.
28, 1917.

Nov. 28, 1917 — bail forfeiture and *capias* issued.

Oct. 22, 1918 — motion for new trial continued to Nov.
12, 1918.

Nov. 26, 1918 — order of court, cause off call.

Jan. 29, 1919 — order of court, cause set for Feb. 1, 1919.

Feb. 1, 1919 — motion new trial granted. Prisoner released on $500.00 bail.

[1] 218 N. Y. 161.   [2] 36 N. Y. Crim. 70.

Feb. 18, 1919 — judgment in bond forfeiture, heretofore entered, set aside by order of county commissioners; costs paid.

Sept. 22, 1919 — on motion of defendant, cause continued to October 21, 1919.

Oct. 22, 1919 — by agreement cause continued to Oct. 30, 1919.

Nov. 6, 1919 — former verdict of guilty set aside.[1]

Records of this kind are not exceptional. They are commonplace occurrences with which every prosecuting attorney is familiar.

Radically different is the situation in Great Britain. Under the English law appeals to the Court of Criminal Appeal must be taken within ten days after conviction. Ordinarily the court renders its decision in from seventeen to twenty-one days, although in murder cases involving the death penalty this period is often shortened. An appeal never postpones execution in a capital case by more than three weeks. Thus, William Wright was convicted of murder at the London Assizes on February 2, 1920; his appeal was filed on February 10, was denied on February 23, and he was hanged on March 10. George Lucas was convicted of murder on January 15, 1920; his appeal was filed on January 17 and was dismissed on February 2. Andrew Fraser was convicted of murder on February 19, 1920; his appeal was filed on February 27 and was denied on March 8.[2]

---

[1] Records of the clerk of the Criminal Court, Docket 11,413. This transcript and many others of similar nature have been published in the bulletins of the *Chicago Crime Commission* during 1919 and 1920.

[2] The Court of Criminal Appeal, which was established in 1907, sits in London with jurisdiction over England and Wales. (7 Edw.

The American Problem

In this fashion it would be possible to quote case after case from the records which the Registrar of the Court of Criminal Appeal kindly placed at the writer's disposal. One gets the impression of a swiftly moving, silent machine — the embodiment of the certainty of justice in England.

The same impression is gained by one who watches the conduct of English criminal trials. The business of choosing a jury is a matter of minutes only.[1] The judge

7. ch. 23). It is composed of the Lord Chief Justice of England and eight judges of the King's Bench Division of the High Court. The following table shows convictions quashed and sentences reduced by the Court of Criminal Appeal from its inauguration to date. The figures for 1915 and 1916 are not available.

Year	Appellants	Convictions quashed	Sentences reduced
1909	627	27	39
1910	706	39	42
1911	679	25	31
1912	664	30	17
1913	655	31	47
1914	554	25	35
1917	299	16	16
1918	285	10	21
1919	355	17	17

The word "appellants" includes all persons who have appealed either against their conviction on a point of law or against their sentence as of right, or who have applied to the court for leave to appeal against conviction or against sentence, or against both conviction and sentence. There have been a very few cases where the sentence has been increased by order of the Court of Criminal Appeal, although in most cases where an unsuccessful application for leave to appeal is made to the court, the time from the signing of the notice of appeal to the final refusal of leave to appeal does not count as part of the sentence of the appellant, and so his term of imprisonment is automatically increased to that extent.

[1] In New York when Thaw was tried, and in Tennessee when the murderers of Senator Carmack were at the bar, weeks elapsed in choosing a jury. In the selection of a jury to try Calhoun in San Francisco, 91 days were consumed. To obtain a jury to try Cornelius Shea in Chicago, 9,425 jurymen were summoned, of whom 4,821 were examined, the cost of jury fees alone being more than $13,000. See Storey, *loc. cit.*, p. 210.

37

takes an astonishingly prominent part in the proceedings in a manner that an American judge would scarcely dare do, examining witnesses, instructing counsel and openly exerting his influence to guide the jury. He does not hesitate to comment upon the failure of a defendant to take the stand in his own behalf, and his general conduct of the case is such that in almost any state in the Union there would be no difficulty in securing a reversal by an appellate court on any one of a dozen technical points. The unrestricted flow of objections to questions by opposing counsel on the grounds of irrelevancy, incompetency and immateriality which forms so conspicuous a part of an American trial, is surprisingly absent. The proceedings are direct, simple and even colloquial. They would be intelligible to a layman. There are no hypothetical questions, no haggling over the admission of evidence. Counsel on both sides give the appearance of striving to arrive at the truth by the quickest and most direct route. On direct examination the questions of the attorneys are often " leading " questions and are put without objection. Thus they do not hesitate to ask their witnesses such questions as this: " Did you look through the door and see the defendant speaking with Williams, and after a few seconds did you see him fire a shot? " In an American trial it would take a dozen questions and answers to elicit this information, and each of them would likely involve objection and argument.

Briefly, our criminal procedure not only makes delay possible but encourages it. Our methods are formal, diffuse, and inflexible; we are enmeshed in technicalities which we revere as the attributes of justice, confusing

The American Problem

them with the essentials of a criminal system. We do
not seem to realize that simplicity, directness and a moderate degree of speed are consistent with fair, impartial
trials.

Faulty Personnel.

Another contributing factor in the failure of our administration of justice lies in the poor quality of some
of our magistrates and prosecuting officers. On no point
are policemen throughout the country so unanimous as
in their emphatically expressed opinion that they are not
fairly or properly supported by the prosecuting attorneys
and the courts. And it must be admitted that the charge
is not without considerable substantiation. From Massachusetts comes the authenticated story of the county attorney who on the last day of his term quashed 200 cases
without consulting the complainant officers. From the
police in many other states there are allegations, often
with specifications, of prosecuting attorneys conniving at
the acquittal or inadequate punishment of criminals. Indictments remain untried and accumulate on the calendars
of the courts, often dating back as far as three and four
years, with the result that witnesses leave the jurisdiction
and evidence disappears. The abuse and misuse of the
bail system are notorious.[1] Cases are often postponed to

[1] As illustrative of the abuse of the bail system, the Grand Jury of
Cook County, Ill., in May, 1919, handed down a presentment in part
as follows: "One of the most aggravated cases we have handled was
the case of three notorious criminals who were indicted by this
grand jury for robbery and hold-ups committed while out on bail.
We fixed the bail at $25,000.00 in each case. When we handed
these indictments to the judge we also requested him to prevent
any reduction in the amount of the bail. In addition to the above,
we asked the state attorney's office to fight any reduction of the bail

39

wear out the patience of the police. "There are instances on record," said former Police Commissioner Woods of New York, "where a case has been postponed and re-postponed until the patrolman has been obliged to come to court twenty-six times before it actually was called to trial." [1]

Illustrations of this laxity and neglect are legion. For example, on February 10, 1911, Thomas Chap, a bartender in Chicago, shot and killed a seventeen year old boy. Chap admitted the shooting and justified his act by accusing his victim of striking matches on the bar-top and of kicking a dog. He was indicted for murder on March 4, 1911. On April 7, 1911, he was released on $10,000 bail. No further record of his case appears until 1916, when the docket shows the following:

March 20, 1916 — case continued to April 17, 1916.
April 17, 1916 — continued to May term.
(Another gap in the record.)
Jan. 23, 1918 — continued to March 4, 1918.
March 28, 1918 — continued to April 22, 1918.
April 22, 1918 — continued to May 13, 1918.
May 13, 1918 — cause off call, order of court.
Sept. 23, 1919 — on motion of State's Attorney, cause reinstated.
Sept. 23, 1919 — *capias* order issued.

of these notorious criminals. Two members of the state's attorney's office fought this reduction to the limit. Notwithstanding our recommendations and their efforts, within a day or two we learned that the amount of the bond had been reduced from $25,000.00 to $10,000.00 in each of the three cases, and that these men were again at large in the community and able to continue their depredations on the public. We believe that bail for persons having a record of crime should be made extremely difficult."

[1] In a public address delivered in 1916. Manuscript unpublished.

Nov. 12, 1919 — on. motion of State's Attorney continued to Nov. 17, 1919.

Nov. 13, 1919 — by agreement bond reduced to $7,500.

Nov. 17, 1919 — on motion of State's Attorney set for December 1, 1919.

Dec. 1, 1919 — plea of not guilty entered, jury trial. Jury sworn; testimony heard in part.

Dec. 2, 1919 — further testimony heard; jury returns verdict of " not guilty." [1]

In some jurisdictions, moreover, it is not unusual for committing magistrates to throw cases out of court for frivolous and sometimes capricious reasons — because the officer is late, or because his hand-writing on the complaint is poor, or because his coat is unbuttoned. Often, too, the sentences imposed are absurdly inadequate. Dangerous criminals with long records are returned to civil life after undergoing minimum punishment. Sometimes they escape punishment altogether. Occasionally this is the work of politics; [2] more often it is due to haste and carelessness or to a failure on the part of the magistrates to realize the true significance of the struggle of society against crime. "One of the most discouraging things about police work," former Commissioner O'Meara of Boston told me, " is to work for weeks and months getting evidence on a particular case only to have

[1] Grand Jury No. 137; P. G. D. No. 95,897; Term No. 2,459; and General No. 84. This and other similar cases taken from the records of the Criminal Court Clerk in Chicago are published in the Bulletin of the *Chicago Crime Commission* of Dec. 20, 1919.

[2] Anyone who would see the American judicial system at its worst and lowest should read the report of the Congressional investigation of the negro riots in East St. Louis. (65th Congress, 2nd Session, Document 1,231, July 5, 1918.)

the court let the defendant off with a $25 fine. Then
we have to begin our work all over again." The annual
report of the General Superintendent of Police of Chicago
for 1910 carries a paragraph equally significant:

> " An honest effort has been made to reduce all gam-
> bling to a minimum, and many arrests and raids have
> been made, and the best results have been obtained that
> were possible under existing conditions. *The average
> fine for gambling was $4.20.*" [1]

Moreover the decisions of the courts are often based
on ignorance. In New York in 1915 a man well known
to the police was arrested for having concealed on his
person a burglar's " jimmy " and a flashlight. He was
immediately discharged by the magistrate on the ground
that intent to use these tools was not established. Another suspicious person, arrested with skeleton keys in his
possession, was similarly discharged.[2] Cases of this kind
can be duplicated in other cities. In 1911 in New York,
a judge of the Court of General Sessions frequently directed juries to acquit defendants because of the alleged
misconduct of the prosecuting attorney or of witnesses.
For example, in one such case, in which two men were
on trial for burglary, the district attorney wanted to
show that when arrested the men had dropped a " jimmy "
which was later found exactly to fit the marks on the
door of the premises in question. The following col-
loquy ensued:

[1] P. 8. The italics are mine.
[2] Cases of Proctor and Rentz in the Magistrate's Court in January, 1915.

The American Problem

The District Attorney: Q. (To Detective Murray) Did you ever take this jimmy upstairs into the building?

The Court: How is that material? I will sustain an objection.

The District Attorney: I want to show that the jimmy marks fitted into the door.

The Court: In view of the statement made by you I will direct the jury to render a verdict of not guilty.

The District Attorney: I stated it in my opening. I could n't prove it in any other way. The officer went back and fitted it.

The Court: The officer did not go back in time. You have no right to repeat that now so I sustain the objection. Sit down. I direct a verdict of acquittal for improper conduct of the district attorney in the trial of the case.[1]

Comment in cases such as these is superfluous. They are cited only because they illustrate some of the difficulties under which our police are laboring in their unequal fight with crime.

Attitude of the Public.

The weak sentimentality of the community in relation to crime and the criminal is a final factor in the failure of our administration of justice which cannot be overlooked. Offenders go unpunished and the laws are used as a shield for crime because such laxity is after all in substantial accord with public opinion, or at least with that element of public opinion which follows the daily news-

[1] People vs. Ristino, p. 18. For a discussion of this and other cases, see report dated May 23, 1912, submitted to the Mayor of New York by the present writer when serving as Commissioner of Accounts of New York.

paper stories of our criminal courts. Our hereditary sympathies are for the under-dog, for the man who is down and out, and the criminal is too frequently pictured as being only the victim of hard luck or a bad environment, fighting for his life or freedom against the powerfully organized, impersonal forces of the commonwealth. Sometimes this sentiment is little short of maudlin, and the man whose crime has been picturesque or unusual becomes in public imagination, if not a hero, at least a very interesting character, in the discussion of whose case the rights of society and the claims of justice are lost sight of. Sensational publicity whets the popular interest; the sordid details of the crime and its motive are blazoned in hysterical headlines. The attorneys issue or inspire statements in the press, presenting their proofs of innocence or innuendoes of guilt, and long before the case is tried, public sympathy is vociferously arrayed on one side or the other. In three different parts of the country I was told by prosecuting attorneys that it was impossible to secure the conviction of a woman for murder, no matter how conclusive the evidence. " It is not considered a fair sporting proposition," one such official said. " Every important case in which a conviction is obtained brings me a flood of letters urging clemency," a western judge told me. And he added: " Often the letters precede the conviction."

This false perspective — this irrational public attitude which first shrieks for the punishment of the perpetrator and then seeks to find excuses for his act and reasons for his pardon — has done much to vitiate the restraints of

The American Problem

the law and weaken its administration. "The evidence shows that Anton Jindra's treatment of her was most tantalizing, annoying and brutal; and because of this we believe the said Pauline Plotka should be given the benefit of the doubt, and we, the jury, recommend that she be released from custody." [1] This verdict, handed down by a coroner's jury in Chicago in the case of the murder of a man by his sweetheart, is typical of the atmosphere of false public sentiment in which criminal justice is administered in the United States. In Indianapolis in 1919 a negro shot and killed another following a quarrel over a girl. Upon apprehension the perpetrator admitted the act, but was freed by the Grand Jury presumably upon the ground of justification in shooting a trespassing rival. Upon release from custody he called at the coroner's office to get his pistol which he had left beside the body of his victim and which had been held as evidence. [2]

These are not isolated instances. While more prevalent in some parts of the country than in others, they can be duplicated in almost every jurisdiction. They are typical of the maladjustment of our attitude toward crime. "We have three classes of homicide," I was told by the chief of detectives in a large southern city. "If a nigger kills a white man, that's murder. If a white man kills a nigger, that's justifiable homicide. If a nigger kills another nigger, that's one less nigger." While of course brutally exaggerated, the statement is none the less

[1] New York *Times*, February 28, 1918.
[2] Personally communicated by the coroner of Marion County, Indiana. The investigator happened to be in the coroner's office at the moment when the negro called for his pistol.

too nearly a correct portrayal of the actual condition of public opinion in many parts of the country to be altogether or even largely discounted.

Crime is an offense not only against the individual victim but against the whole structure of society. Until public opinion adjusts its own point of view on these matters we cannot expect our courts to reflect anything better.

In discussing these four phases of the administration of justice in America — our technical criminal procedure, the long delays and the uncertainty of punishment, the badly chosen personnel on the bench and in the department of the prosecuting attorney, and finally the unhealthy state of public opinion toward crime and the criminal — the aim has been to emphasize the point, too often overlooked, that our police suffer from connection with a system that has all but broken down. From time to time, in our indignation at the obvious growth of crime, we rise up and cry out at the police. Why are they not at their business? Why do they not succeed? The answer is obvious. The task before us is far greater than the regeneration of our police. It is the regeneration of our whole system of administering justice and the creation of a sound public attitude toward crime.

IV. UNENFORCEABLE LAWS

A final disadvantage under which American police departments are laboring is to be found in the presence on our statute books of laws which, because they interfere with customs widely practised and widely regarded as

innocent, are fundamentally unenforceable. The willingness with which we undertake to regulate by law the personal habits of private citizens is a source of perpetual
astonishment to Europeans. In no country in Europe,
with the exception of Germany, is an attempt ever made
to enforce standards of conduct which do not meet with
general public approval, or, at the behest of what may
be a minority, to bring a particular code of behavior
within the scope of criminal legislation. With us, however, every year adds its accretion to our sumptuary laws.
It suits the judgment of some and the temper of others
to convert into crimes practices which they deem mischievous or unethical. They resort to law to supply the deficiencies of other agencies of social control. They attempt to govern by means of law things which in their
nature do not admit of objective treatment and external
coercion. " Nothing is more attractive to the benevolent
vanity of men," said James Coolidge Carter, " than the
notion that they can effect great improvement in society
by the simple process of forbidding all wrong conduct,
or conduct which they think is wrong, by law, and of
enjoining all good conduct by the same means." [1]

It is to this temptation and to this fallacy that our legislatures habitually succumb. The views of particular
groups of people on questions of private conduct are
made the legal requirements of the State. We are surrounded by penal laws whose only purpose is to enforce

[1] *Law: Its Origin, Growth and Function.* New York, 1900, p. 221.
See, too, *The Limits of Effective Legal Action,* an address by Roscoe
Pound before the Pennsylvania Bar Association, June 27, 1916 (a
pamphlet) ; and *The End of Law as Developed in Legal Rules and
Doctrines,* by the same author, in 27 Harvard L. Rev. 195.

by threat certain standards of morality. We are hedged about by arbitrary regulations, which, while they may have at one time perhaps satisfied the consciences of those responsible for them, no longer represent community public opinion, or at best represent only a portion of it. These regulations have not grown as we have grown and they do not ease up as we push the whole social weight against them. Indeed this presents one of the strange anomalies in American life: with an intolerance for authority and an emphasis upon individual rights, more pronounced, perhaps, than in any other nation, we are, of all people, not even excepting the Germans, pre-eminently addicted to the habit of standardizing by law the lives and morals of our citizens. Nowhere in the world is there so great an anxiety to place the moral regulation of social affairs in the hands of the police, and nowhere are the police so incapable of carrying out such regulation. Our concern, moreover, is for externals, for results that are formal and apparent rather than essential. We are less anxious about preventing a man from doing wrong to others than in preventing him from doing what we consider harm to himself. We like to pass laws to compel the individual to do as we think he ought to do for his own good. We attack symptoms rather than causes and in doing so we create a species of moralistic despotism which overrides the private conscience and destroys liberty where liberty is most precious.

From this condition arises one of the most embarrassing phases of the whole question of law enforcement. Mayors, administrations and police forces are more often and more successfully attacked from this point than from any other, and the consequences are corrupted policemen and shuffling executives who give the best excuse they can think of at the moment for failing to do the impossible, but are able to add nothing to the situation but a sense of their own perplexity. Of all the cities visited by the writer, there was scarcely one that did not bear evidence of demoralization arising from attempts to enforce laws which instead of representing the will of the community, represented hardly anybody's will. " I am always between two fires," the chief of police in New Orleans told me. " If I should enforce the law against selling tobacco on Sunday, I would be run out of office in twenty-four hours. But I am in constant danger of being run out of office because I don't enforce it." At the time of my visit to New Orleans the enforcement of this particular law was in a state of compromise by which green curtains were hung to conceal the tobacco stands on Sunday. The curtains served the double purpose of advertising the location of the stands and of protecting the virtue of the citizens from visions of evil!

It is this sort of hypocrisy that one encounters everywhere, and the number of such statutes is legion, most of them honored in the breach or perhaps in some compromise that brings the law and its administration into public contempt. " There has never been serious attempt to modify our strict Sunday laws," I was told by the prosecuting attorney in a large southern city. " In the first place it is n't necessary because the laws are n't enforced, and in the second place any attempt to modify them would meet with determined opposition from our good people." This happy philosophy fails to take account of the spasmodic efforts on the part of the good people to enforce the laws. One constantly comes across such situations as the following newspaper item portrays:

" ABERDEEN, Miss., April 15.— The W. C. T. U. is seeking to have all soda fountains closed on Sunday in the future. This was done once before but it did not last. The W. C. T. U. officials say they are going to hold this time and that they intend to see that the law is carried out to the letter and that every violator is prosecuted to full extent." [1]

Most chiefs of police confess frankly that in these cases they do not act except upon specific complaint. " And then we have to act," said one chief, " but of course nothing ever comes of it because judges and juries will not convict." Said a criminal court judge in Kentucky: " On ample evidence furnished by a Church Federation I placed several cases of Sunday violations before the Grand Juries of March, April, May, June, September, October and November, 1915. Not a single indictment was returned. It is my experience that prosecutors, judges and juries will not convict people of crime for doing things that are the community habit and practice." [2]

A county solicitor from Alabama writes me as follows: " While we have a statute making it unlawful to play tennis and golf on Sunday there is no effort made to enforce it. A great deal of effort has been made in the past to convict negroes for playing cards on Sunday, but this has

[1] Birmingham *Age-Herald*, April 16, 1915.
[2] Personally communicated.

been due to the fee system, and has been looked upon with disfavor by both courts and juries." [1]

Clearly it is a bungling arrangement which leaves a borderland between the live and the dead law to be explored at the discretion of individual officers. Our police departments are torn apart by constant controversies as to the existence and location of this shadowy area. Recently in Baltimore, the police suddenly descended in a series of raids to arrest all violators of the Sunday law. One hundred and thirteen people were taken into custody in one day and 223 summonses were served. Those arrested included druggists, drivers of ice-cream trucks, barbers, and bakery-shop keepers. Two men were arrested for balancing their books in their own homes. Selling a child a stick of candy constituted a heinous offense and the buying of a piece of chewing gum or a loaf of bread caused the arrest of the store-keeper. One man was arrested for painting the gate in his back yard. Policemen did not hesitate to approach a man who happened to be smoking a cigar and question him as to how he came in its possession. If satisfactory answers were not forthcoming the man was arrested. Efforts were made to persuade the police to allow a few men to continue working in a garage on the ground that a hundred motor trucks stored there would freeze if not attended to. The police, however, refused, and two arrests were made of men who attempted to preserve their property.[2] "This satire upon religious observance," said the Baltimore *American,* "bore no fruit of holiness, but on the

[1] Letter dated May 8, 1915.
[2] See Baltimore newspapers for December 1, 1919.

contrary fermented bitter feeling and vindictiveness. The public was strained almost to the verge of physical violence. The arrests were a disgrace to the city, and even the policemen who under orders made them, and the magistrates who held the preliminary hearings, shrank with disgust from the tasks that were laid upon them." [1]

Equally ludicrous results follow everywhere from legislative incursions into the sphere of morals. In Massachusetts where golf-playing on Sunday is illegal, a certain golf course lies partly in one township and partly in another. The authorities in one jurisdiction enforce the law; the authorities in the other do not. Consequently on Sunday the members are limited in their play to the holes in the " liberal " township. In Tennessee the law against the sale of cigarettes is enforced in Nashville and disregarded in Memphis. In Alabama the law against Sunday golf and tennis is nowhere enforced, while the law against Sunday baseball is enforced only in Birmingham. In New Orleans at the time of my visit a policeman was stationed every evening in each of fourteen cabarets where liquor was sold. These officers were on duty from 8 P. M. to 4 A. M. except on Saturday nights, when they were withdrawn at midnight for the reason, as stated to me by the commissioner, that their presence in the cabarets after midnight "might seem to countenance the violation of the Sunday liquor law "!

Often the laws are such as to defy enforcement even if they had behind them a substantial body of public opinion. Thus there are laws against kissing, laws against face powder and rouge, laws against ear-rings, laws regulating

[1] December 1, 1919.

the length of women's skirts, laws fixing the size of hat-
pins. In Massachusetts one may not play cards for
stakes even with friends in the privacy of one's home.
In Texas, card-playing on trains is illegal. One would
have to scan the ordinances published by the Police President of Berlin to find any parallel to the arbitrary regulations in regard to private conduct with which American
citizens are surrounded.[1]

The argument of those who hold the police responsible
for our lax observance of these sumptuary laws marches
with a stately tread. " The police," they say, " are sworn
to enforce all laws. It is not for them to use discretion
in determining what laws shall be enforced and what shall
not be." This argument fails to take account of the
practical situation in which the police find themselves.
It is estimated that there are on the average something
like 16,000 statutes, federal, state and local, applicable to
a given city.[2] To enforce all of them, absolutely, all the
time, is of course to any mind but that of the theorist

[1] Statutes such as these are frequently enacted apparently on the
theory that the function of law is to register the protest of society
against wrong. Dean Roscoe Pound of the Harvard Law School,
makes the following comment on this theory: "It is said that
Hunt, the agitator, appeared on one occasion before Lord Ellenborough at circuit, *apropos* of nothing upon the calendar, to make
one of his harangues. After the Chief Justice had explained to
him that he was not in a tribunal of general jurisdiction to inquire
into every species of wrong throughout the kingdom but only in a
court of assize and jail delivery to deliver the jail of that particular
county, Hunt exclaimed, ' But, my Lord, I desire to protest.' ' Oh,
certainly,' said Lord Ellenborough. ' By all means. Usher! Take
Mr. Hunt into the corridor and allow him to protest as much as
he pleases.' Our statute books are full of protests of society against
wrong which are as efficacious for practical purposes as the decla-
mations of Mr. Hunt in the corridor of Lord Ellenborough's court."
(Address before Pennsylvania Bar Association, June 27, 1916.)
[2] See Brand Whitlock: *Enforcement of Laws in Cities,* Indianapolis, 1910, p. 79.

and doctrinaire utterly impossible. With ten times the number of policemen it could not be done. Arthur Woods, formerly police commissioner in New York, put the case as follows: "Those who lightly advise that every law should be vigorously enforced cannot have in contemplation what such a policy would involve: police spies prowling around every household over which a scandal hovers, men and women shadowed by detectives, many respectable people accused unjustly by officious functionaries, immense sums of money spent in putting the entire community under police surveillance. All this would be necessary." [1] Whether it squares with our ideals or not, the police are forced by practical circumstances to determine where they shall put the emphasis in the enforcement of the law.

Under such circumstances, therefore, it is not surprising that they are disinclined to enforce statutes which lie in the region where public opinion is either uncertain or frankly antagonistic in its attitude toward the things sought to be required or repressed. Mr. Brand Whitlock defines the situation with admirable clearness: "When the act which violates the law is merely *malum prohibitum* and would not be wrong in itself, when large numbers of the people, or a majority of the people wish to commit that act or have no objection to others committing it,— such an act, for instance, as playing ball, going to a theatre, trimming a window, running a train, or having ice-cream delivered for the Sunday dinner,— then it becomes impossible to enforce the law without re-

[1] From a public address delivered in 1916, the manuscript of which lies before me.

sorting to violence, namely, by rushing policemen here and there in patrol wagons, and forcibly carrying away men and women to police stations, courts and prisons, and when they are out, doing the same thing over again. This process, when attempted on a large scale, is called a ' crusade,' and is invariably accompanied by disorder and tumult, sometimes by riot, and always engenders hatred and bad feeling. Its results are harmful and it being found to be impossible to sustain the high pitch of excitement and even hysteria which are necessary to conduct a crusade properly, the enthusiasm of crusading officials soon subsides, other duties are found to demand attention, and so the crusade dies out, is abandoned, and things are worse than before." [1]

Those who would push the enforcement of their ideas to such extremes as these overlook the fact so succinctly stated by former Mayor Jones of Toledo, that law in America is what the people will back up.[2] Its life is its enforcement. Victorious upon paper, it is powerless elsewhere. The test of its validity is the strength of the social reaction which supports it. " The true liberty of law," said Elihu Root, " is to be found in its development from the life of the people. The enforcement upon the people of law which has its origin only in the mind of a law-maker, has the essence of tyranny and its imposition is the mandate of a conqueror." [3] Said Emerson: " The law is only a memorandum. We are superstitious

[1] Whitlock, *loc. cit.*, p. 20, quotation slightly abridged.
[2] *Ibid.*, p. 55.
[3] From a speech delivered before the Harvard Law School Association of New York City, April 1, 1915, the stenographic transcript of which is before me.

and esteem the statute somewhat; so much life as it has in the character of living men is its force." [1]

One final adage is always hurled at this position. "The best way to repeal a bad law is to enforce it." This statement is largely fallacious. It is true only when those upon whom the obnoxious law is enforced have the power, through representatives that they themselves elect, to repeal it. When the case is otherwise it is not true. For years it has been the practice of state legislatures, largely representative of rural districts, to attempt the regulation by law of the customs, diversions, sports and appetites of city populations. The city police could enforce these statutes to the continuous discomfort and annoyance of all the inhabitants without effecting a repeal, because most city populations are represented in their legislatures by minorities. Only too often have these minorities sought in vain to obtain release from laws that are not adapted to the life and habits of the city and that in the nature of things cannot be adapted to them.

Meanwhile our police are caught in an embarrassing dilemma, and there is little hope of a sound and healthy basis of police work until our law-making bodies face the fact that men cannot be made good by force. The attempt to coerce men to render unto Caesar the things that are God's must always end in failure. The law cannot take the place of the home, the school, the church and other influences by which moral ends are achieved. It cannot be made to assume the whole burden of social control. Permanent advance in human society will not be brought about by night-sticks and patrol wagons, but

[1] Essay on *Politics*.

The American Problem

by the cultivation, in neighborliness and sympathy, of a public opinion which will reflect its soundness in the laws it enacts and in the approval it gives to their enforcement.[1]

[1] See Newton D. Baker: *Law, Police and Social Problems, Atlantic Monthly*, July, 1915; Chap. IX of Havelock Ellis' *The Task of Social Hygiene*, London, 1913; Chap. VIII of Fuld's *Police Administration*, New York, 1910; and Chap. VII of Woods' *Policeman and Public*, Yale University Press, 1919.

CHAPTER II

THE DEVELOPMENT OF AMERICAN POLICE CONTROL

The early beginnings: Boston, New York, Philadelphia, Cincinnati.— The intermediate period.— Opposition to uniforms.— Mob rule.— The rise of police boards.— The development of state control in police systems.— The New York example of 1857.— The extension of state control systems.— The bi-partisan board.— The passing of the police board.— The character of the development.— The search for mechanical perfection.— Politics in the development of the police.

BEFORE considering the present organization of our police machinery it is necessary to trace its development in some detail through the many changing forms it has assumed. From no other approach can the different types of control which we find in American municipalities to-day be understood.

The Early Beginnings.

The beginnings of police organization in America are traceable in the colonial period. Bringing with them the methods of local administration which existed at that time in England, the colonists on the Atlantic seaboard appointed their parish constables [1] and their civilian

---

[1] On January 1, 1634, Joshua Pratt was "chosen to the office of Constable for Plymouth and sworne to faithfulnes in the same." (Plymouth Colonial Records, 1, 21.) This officer not only served as jailer but executed punishment and penalties and gave warning of marriages approved by civil authority. He furthermore acted as Sealer of Weights and Measures and Surveyor of Land. For an

watch. As early as 1636 a night watch was established in Boston,[1] and thereafter hardly an important settlement existed in New England that did not have, in addition to its military guard, a few ununiformed watchmen.[2] In New York the *Schout*[3] and *Rattle Watch*[4] of the Dutch Colonists were superseded by the Constables' Watch of the English regime, and the complete English system of local government, including a High Constable, sub-constables and watchmen, was imposed by the Dongan Charter of 1686.[5] In Philadelphia a night watchman was appointed by the provincial council in 1700 and the system was begun by which all citizens were obliged to take their turns in the duty of watch and ward.[6]

excellent article on early constables in New England and their functions see *Norman Constables in America* by Herbert Baxter Adams, Johns Hopkins University Studies in Historical and Political Science, No. 8, Baltimore, 1883.

[1] By town meeting held February 27, 1636. See *Police Records and Recollections* by E. H. Savage, Boston, 1865.

[2] In 1699 the Province of Massachusetts standardized the custom by passing an act " for keeping watches in Towns," which provided that " in cases where no military watch is established justices of the peace acting with selectmen of the Town, or in case the Town has no justices of the peace, the selectmen alone, shall have authority to appoint and regulate the watch and preserve a ward." (Province Laws, Chap. 65.)

[3] An official whose duty it was to watch for infractions of laws and ordinances.

[4] *Ratelwacht:* So called from the rattles which the watchmen carried to warn of their approach. Rattles were subsequently used in many towns. The Rattle Watch of the Dutch regime was formed in October, 1658, and placed under the control of the Burgomasters. A description of this Watch is found in *Our Police Protectors* by A. E. Costello, New York, 1885, Chap. 1, and in *Memorial History of the City of New York* by James Grant Wilson, New York, 1892, Vol. 1, Chap. VII.

[5] Under this system the watchmen were supervised by the constables elected from the wards.

[6] See *Philadelphia, 1681–1887, A History of Municipal Development,* by Allinson and Penrose in the Johns Hopkins Studies in Historical and Political Science, Extra Volume II, Baltimore, 1887.

By the early part of the eighteenth century the " night watch " as an institution was well established in the existing towns and cities. Thereafter for nearly a century and a half it continued as a feature of the urban community and became in time a distinct branch of municipal administration.[1] Its function was simply the patrol of the streets. " Watchmen are required to walk their rounds slowly and silently and now and then stand still and listen " were the orders issued in Boston.[2] In many towns the watch was charged with the additional duty of crying the time of night and the state of the weather —" in a moderate tone," according to the Boston regulations.[3] In some towns, such as Philadelphia and Baltimore, it had the care of the street lamps. From the beginning it appears to have been no more efficient than the Dogberry and Verges type on which it was modeled. As early as 1642 the town government of New Haven issued a proclamation as follows : " Itt is ordered by the court that, from henceforwarde, none of the watchmen shall have liberty to sleep during the watch." [4] The town

[1] Under the Montgomerie charter of 1730 the common council of New York was given power to appoint watchmen "and to displace all or any of them and put others in their room, and to add or diminish the number of them as often as the said common council, or the major part of them, shall think fit." In 1762 the town of Boston petitioned the general court for authority to appoint its own watch, and an act was passed giving the selectmen the right to choose a number of the inhabitants, not exceeding thirty, to serve as watchmen. This was re-enacted in 1801 and remained in force until Boston became a city in 1822. (Savage, *loc. cit.*)

[2] *Ibid.*, p. 24.

[3] *Ibid.*, p. 26.

[4] New Haven Town Records II, 31. Quoted in *The Republic of New Haven,* by Chas. H. Levermore in the Johns Hopkins University Studies in Historical and Political Science, Extra Volume, Baltimore, 1886.

records of Boston tell a story of similar difficulties. A report of a committee of the Selectmen made in 1819, reads as follows:

"January 12: Find too many watchmen doing duty inside. Feb. 3: At one o'clock visited South Watch: constable asleep. One and one-half o'clock at Center Watch found constable and doorman asleep. Two o'clock at North Watch found constable and doorman asleep and a drunken man kicking at the door to get in." [1]

In Philadelphia the difficulty experienced in inducing the citizens to serve their turn as watchmen led to frequent grand jury investigations and presentments.[2] In New York the professional watchmen of the early nineteenth century were objects of constant ridicule; no orgy among the young men of the town was complete which did not end in upsetting a watch-box and its sleeping occupant or in lassoing an unwary "Leatherhead" as he dozed on his beat.[3]

As the nineteenth century progressed and urban populations grew in density the inadequacy of the night watch became increasingly apparent. The character of its personnel and its organization by wards and districts, each more or less independent of the other, prevented its adaptation to the growing needs of the time. Its ranks were made up for the most part of men who pursued regular

[1] Quoted in Savage, *loc. cit.,* p. 58.
[2] Allinson and Penrose, *loc. cit.* The watch became a paid body early in the nineteenth century.
[3] Costello, *loc. cit.,* p. 72. The term "Leatherhead" was given on account of the leather helmets worn by some members of the watch.

occupations during the day and who added to their incomes by serving the city at night. " Jaded stevedores, teamsters and mechanics" comprised the New York force.[1] No standards except those of a political nature were applied in selection. One Matthew Young was appointed watchman in Boston " in order that he and his children do not become a Town charge."[2] An investigating committee of the Board of Aldermen in New York made the finding that the incumbents were selected for political opinions and not for personal merit and that the term of service of the incumbent was uncertain and often very brief, depending on the change of political party.[3] Another investigation in 1838 showed that watchmen dismissed from one ward for neglect or drunkenness found service in another.[4] Moreover, such police protection as the watch system afforded was provided only by night — generally between the hours of nine o'clock in the evening and sunrise. At all other times there was no police service of any kind. Even the hours of night service were not uniform for a whole city. In New York the captains of the watch in the different districts interpreted the word " sunrise " as varying between three o'clock and five o'clock in the morning.[5]

This situation was first met in several towns and cities by the formation of a day police force independent of the night watch. Boston adopted this plan in 1838, establishing a force of six men for day duty. By 1846

[1] Costello, *loc. cit.*, p. 72.
[2] Quoted from Savage, *loc. cit.*, p. 26.
[3] Documents of the Board of Aldermen, 1843-44, Doc. No. 53.
[4] Documents of the Board of Aldermen, 1838, Doc. No. 62.
[5] Costello, *loc. cit.*

this force had grown to thirty men, of whom eight were on duty at night, although there was no connection, direct or indirect, with the night-watch.[1]   Similar arrangements were made in New York.   In 1844 the day force in that city consisted of sixteen officers appointed by the mayor, in addition to 108 Sunday officers.[2]   The night watch was a separate institution, consisting of twelve captains, twenty-four assistant captains and 1096 watchmen, under the control of the city council.[3]   In Cincinnati a day watch was created in 1842, consisting of two persons selected by the council.   Eight years later the council provided for the election by popular vote of six day watchmen for each of the wards of the city.[4]   In Philadelphia the will of Stephen Girard, in which he left a large sum to the city to provide for " a competent police "[5] stimulated more than usual interest in the subject,

[1] Savage, *loc. cit.,* pp. 77–87.   The night watch at this time consisted of 150 men.

[2] There was also a force of 100 " mayor's marshals " who, with the thirty-four constables (two elected from each ward) acted as general peace officers, serving in the courts and doing whatever detective work was done at that time.   This force was also independent of the night watch.

[3] Documents of the Board of Aldermen, 1843–44, Doc. No. 53. New York City at this time was divided into six districts, each in charge of a captain and two assistant captains.   These men, however, and the force of watchmen under them, served only on alternate nights, one complete company following another, with the acknowledged intent of distributing the patronage as widely as possible. Thus one-half the full force was on duty every night.   The watchmen patrolled in two-hour shifts, so that only one quarter of the force was on duty at a given time.   Watchmen were paid $1.00 a night in summer and $1.25 in winter.   The captains received $2.25 a night.

[4] *Centennial History of Cincinnati* by Charles Theodore Greve, Chicago, Biographical Publishing Co., 1904, p. 664.

[5] The clause in the will representing this peculiar bequest read as follows:

" Second.— To enable the corporation of the city of Philadel-

with the result that in 1833 an ordinance was passed providing for 24 policemen to serve by day as well as 120 watchmen by night.[1] This ordinance represented a distinct advance over previous police legislation in any city. It placed the appointing power in the hands of the mayor and provided that vacancies in the higher ranks should be filled as far as practicable " by promoting those who have distinguished themselves by diligence, integrity and skill in an inferior grade." Moreover, it centralized the control of the police force in a single officer known as the " captain," thus eliminating the chaotic district autonomy which had prevailed up to that time.[2] In 1835, however,

phia to provide more effectually than they now do for the security of the persons and property of the inhabitants of the said city by a competent police, including a sufficient number of watchmen really suited to the purpose; and to this end I recommend a division of the city into watch districts of four parts, each under a proper head; and that at least two watchmen shall in each round or station patrol together."

To illustrate the way in which this money was applied, the following transcript from the police budget of 1838 is illuminating:

Budget for the year .... $149,266.
Amount payable from the Girard Estate...... 33,190.

Amount required from the City Treasury.... $116,076.
(From the Journal of the Select Council, 1838, Appendix No. 20.)

[1] Ordinances, 1833, Chap. 552.

[2] Five years later a similar endeavor was made in New York to end the chaos resulting from the independence of the watch in the separate districts and an ordinance was passed putting the entire department under a superintendent. (Ordinances of 1838.) This attempt at centralization met with no greater success than in Philadelphia, and 18 months later the position of superintendent was abolished and the old system of twelve independent captains re-established. The report of the council committee, upon which this step was taken, is significant of the political influences which lay behind it:

" The change recommended by your Committee appears to be in accordance with the wishes of the Department, a consideration of no small importance to the prosperity, union and harmony of the

this ordinance was repealed and the old system of district independence was re-established. Thirteen years later, following the example that had been set in Boston and New York, an independent day police force was established, consisting of 34 policemen, while the old night watch was maintained in its original form.[1]

It was soon found that a system of two police forces, one for day and one for night, was from every point of view an impossible arrangement. It not only led to friction and conflict but it failed to correct the conspicuous evils which had developed in the night watch. In message after message the mayors of Boston, New York and Philadelphia called attention to the need of a new system. This need was emphasized by the increasing disorder of the times and the evident inability of the existing police forces to cope with it. Beginning in 1835 a series of mob riots swept the country. A fight in Boston in 1837 between the fire companies and the Irish involved 15,000 persons and was suppressed only by drastic action of the militia.[2] In Philadelphia the negro riots of 1838 resulted in the burning of Pennsylvania Hall and the death of many citizens.[3] These riots again broke out in 1842 and negro churches and meeting places were burned. In 1844 the native American riots lasted for three months, during which large numbers of people were

city Watch." Documents of the Board of Aldermen, 1839, Doc. No. 16.

[1] Ordinances, 1848, Chap. 1157. Providence, R. I., adopted a separate day police force in 1851 (Ordinance of December 23, 1850); Newark in 1852 (Ordinance of August 6, 1852).
[2] Savage, *loc. cit.*, p. 77.
[3] Philadelphia Journal of the Select Council, 1838 — Appendix No. 61.

killed and wounded and much property, including churches and public buildings, was destroyed by the mobs.[1] Riots of a similar nature were of continuous occurrence in Baltimore and New York. In the latter city mob violence due to racial and political differences frequently necessitated the presence of the militia. The Croton riots and the flour and election riots were typical of the lawlessness of the time.

In the face of such difficulties the police machinery went utterly to pieces. A handful of unorganized " day policemen " or a few ward watchmen could not hope to contend with serious conditions of disorder. New York took the first practical step to remedy the situation. In 1844 the legislature passed a law creating " a day and night police," which forms the basis of modern police organization in America. This act abolished the watch system altogether and established a force of 800 men under the direction of a chief of police appointed by the mayor with the consent of the council.[2] The example set by New York was followed by Boston in 1854 when the old organization of the Watch Department, after an existence of over 200 years, was consolidated with the

[1] The Journal of the Select Council contains much information bearing on these riots.
[2] Laws of 1844, Chap. 315. The act was put into effect by ordinance on May 23, 1845. During the interim the state act was ignored by the mayor and common council, whose authority was necessary to give it legal effect, and an ordinance was passed providing for a " night and day watch " of 200 men under a superintendent. This ordinance did not affect the original night watch, which was allowed to continue its existence as a separate institution. Mayor Harper's insistence on this new arrangement earned for the " night and day watch " the name " Harper's Police." Their career, which lasted but five months, was terminated when the common council finally agreed to the state act of the previous year.

day police force, and an organization of 250 men created under the control of a chief appointed by the mayor and council.[1]   In the same year the police forces of Philadelphia and the districts included within the county were consolidated under a marshal elected by the people for two years.[2]   Similarly, police forces under a single head were organized in Chicago in 1851,[3] in New Orleans [4] and Cincinnati in 1852,[5] in Baltimore [6] and Newark [7] in 1857, and in Providence in 1864.[8]

The Intermediate Period.

The movement toward consolidation and the creation

[1] Ordinance of May 17, 1855, printed on p. 391 of *Laws and Ordinances, Boston, 1856*.

[2] Laws of Penn., Acts of Assembly, 1854, No. 21. Two years later an act was passed abolishing the office of marshal and investing his powers in a chief of police appointed by the mayor with the approval of the select council (Laws of Penn., 1856, No. 587.)   The first attempt to consolidate the police forces of Philadelphia was made in 1850, when an act was passed (Laws of Penn., 1850, Acts of General Assembly, No. 390) creating an elected marshal of police for the "Philadelphia police district," which included the separately incorporated districts within the county of Philadelphia, to wit: Northern Liberties, Spring Garden, Kensington, Richmond, Penn, Southwark and Moyamensing. The marshal was given power to appoint policemen from the lists of nominees submitted by the select and common councils of the city and the commissioners of each of the incorporated districts. The act was faulty in that it failed to give the marshal control of all police bodies within his jurisdiction. The city of Philadelphia still insisted on maintaining its old day and night police. This fault was corrected by the thoroughgoing consolidation act of 1854, above cited.

[3] Charter of 1851, Private Laws of Ill., 1851, p. 132.

[4] Laws of La., 1852, No. 71.

[5] Laws of Ohio, 1852, p. 223.

[6] Ordinances: 1857, No. 4. It provided for the amalgamation of the night watch and the day police under a marshal appointed annually by the mayor with the consent of the councils.

[7] Revised Ordinances, 1857, Chap. XII, Sec. 3.

[8] Ordinance of August 12, 1864.

of an executive head in the person of the chief or marshal marked a long step forward in the development of municipal police organization. Many difficulties, however, were still to be overcome in shaping the police forces thus formed into effective instruments for public protection. The spoils system had taken a firm grip on popular imagination, and the legislation of the period reflected its sordid point of view. In New York under the Law of 1844 the captains, assistant captains and policemen were appointed for one year only, upon the nomination of the aldermen and assistant aldermen of the wards in which they belonged. In other words the police department was still a *ward* affair, used to satisfy the demands for district patronage, and the chief of police was a figurehead with no authority and little honor. Said the district attorney of New York County: "There is really no head of police at all, but each captain is a head in his own district, and discipline varies in different wards according to the attention or skill and tact." [1] It is small wonder that the new force was the object of vicious attack and that some despairing if misguided citizens sought the return of the old watch system.[2] In Baltimore the new force organized in 1857 became the prey of the Know-Nothing party and was employed principally as an instrument of the political faction in power to control elections. "Ruffianism" and "bloody tyranny" were among the milder offenses charged against the force.[3]

[1] From a letter quoted in New York State Assembly Document 127, 1857.
[2] The records of the common council during this period are filled with reports of charges and investigations.
[3] Baltimore *Sun,* November 14, 1859.

Development of American Police Control

Similar use of the police was made in Cincinnati. Even in Boston, where the spoils system was late in developing, it was not without its early disciples in the police department. An officer on the force wrote the following significant paragraph in his published memoirs:

> "The Marshal seemed to think that things looked a bit squally, and under his direction we very quietly dabbled a little in politics at the election. Our choice was successful and we were in very good spirits at the close of the year, in anticipation of a longer job." [1]

That the police force under such conditions should develop into an undisciplined, untrained group of place-seekers is not to be wondered at. Indeed, perhaps the most serious difficulty encountered by the police executive was the attempt to apply the regulations of the department to its own members. The departmental reports of the time indicate a condition of utter lawlessness on the part of the police themselves. Assaulting superior officers, refusing to go on patrol, releasing prisoners from the custody of other policemen, drunkenness, extorting money from prisoners — these were offenses of daily occurrence, committed often with impunity under the protection of a political over-lord. [2] Mayor Fernando Wood of New York in his message to the common council in 1856 emphasized the lack of discipline in the department. "A recollection of former prowess," he said, "or of successful political combats with the laurel still green pre-

[1] Savage, *loc. cit.*, p. 91.
[2] For example, see list of complaints against the police force for the year 1852. Documents of the N. Y. Board of Aldermen, Doc. No. 53, pp. 1047 ff.

vents that submission to the rules and regulations necessary in a well organized police corps." [1]

In nothing was the undisciplined attitude of the police
more clearly shown than in their refusal to wear uniforms. Although by 1855 a beginning had been made
by a few communities in the shape of regulation hats and
caps, no city had at this time a completely uniformed
force. " Un-American," " undemocratic," " militarism,"
" King's livery," " a badge of degradation and servitude,"
" an imitation of royalty "— ideas of this kind formed
the basis of opposition to putting policemen in uniform.[2]
In New York the policemen were simply guards in citizen's clothes, armed with 33-inch clubs. " Every watchman "— so ran the regulations —" shall wear a medal
inside his clothes, suspended round his neck, both day and
night when on duty, and shall expose the same when
about restoring peace, or on making an arrest, or when
performing any duty of that kind." [3] Said a writer in
1853, referring to the New York police: " If you want
one suddenly by night or by day, where will you look
for him? And look at their style of dress, some with

---

[1] Documents of the Board of Councilmen, 1856, Doc. No. 5.
[2] See Mayor Fernando Wood's address to the police of New York
in 1855, in which he tried to win them over to a uniform. Among
other arguments was the following:

" You draw from the city treasury as pay in the aggregate
nearly one million dollars per annum, besides what is given to individuals as presents, which last year amounted, according to the
books in the Mayor's office, to about $15,000, and so far this year
to about $4,000, not including many valuable presents not to be
estimated by money."

(Address of May 26, 1855, printed in the council reports of that
year.)

[3] Documents of the Board of Aldermen — New York City, 1844-45,
Doc. No. 30, Sec. 14.

hats, some with caps, some with coats like Joseph's of old, parti-colored. If they were mustered together they would look like Falstaff's regiment." [1] Even when the New York police finally adopted a uniform early in 1856, it was not standardized for the whole force. Each ward had its own uniform as it saw fit. The summer uniform in some wards consisted of white duck suits; other wards adopted colors; some wore straw hats and some felt. [2] In Philadelphia in 1856 the attempt to make the police even wear badges outside their coats met with bitter opposition. Only after much persuasion did Mayor Conrad induce them to adopt regulation caps, and not until late in 1860 did they put on complete uniforms.

With such lack of discipline the police could hardly be expected to make much impression upon the disorderly conditions which so characterized city life in the decade preceding the Civil War. "They inspire no respect, they create no fear," said a writer in 1853 in relation to the New York police. "Hardly a day passes but the thief or felon turns round and attacks the policeman." [3] Indeed, in many of the larger cities a state of terrorism existed, due to the inability of the authorities to curb the gangs and "clubs" which existed at that time. The mob riots which characterized the forties increased in fury and violence during the fifties. In Philadelphia organized bands of ruffians and thieves were associated under such names as "The Blood Cubs," "The Rats," and "The Schuylkill Rangers," and rioting was of con-

[1] *London and New York: Their Crime and Police,* a pamphlet by J. W. Gerard, New York, 1853, p. 17.
[2] Costello, *loc. cit.,* p. 129.
[3] Gerard, *loc. cit.,* p. 18.

71

tinual occurrence. In some cases houses were fired for purposes of pillage, and the firemen were forcibly prevented from attending. Sunday was given over to constant street fighting, in which the volunteer fire companies played a prominent and generally provocative part. Similar conditions existed in Baltimore. In 1859 the Baltimore *Sun* commented guardedly as follows:

> " The ' club ' organization in this city . . . can concentrate a formidable demonstration in any quarter against unorganized individuals and peaceable citizens. It is known to possess a variety of arms, such as muskets, revolvers, ' bob-tails,' billies and knuckles, including everything serviceable in the roughest and deadliest conflict. . . . The reproach to which our citizens are exposed is that of cowardice. . . . Why, if ruffianism is confined to a few, do not the many drive it out or destroy it? " [1]

In Cincinnati the Bedini riots of 1853 were followed by the Know-Nothing riots of 1855. In New York conditions were even worse. The composition of the local police force, largely Irish, provoked deep antagonisms, which were enhanced by the bitterness with which local political campaigns were waged.[2] The city was becoming increasingly cosmopolitan, and racial differences were set-

[1] Baltimore *Sun*, November 10, 1859.
[2] In 1855 Chief of Police Matsell of New York reported to the Board of Aldermen that 305 out of 1,149 policemen on the force had been born in Ireland. This was probably an understatement, as Matsell was at that time under fire for "Irishizing" his force. (See Documents of the Board of Aldermen, 1855.)
Strong feeling developed against the foreign composition of the police force in many cities. In Cleveland in 1872 an investigation

Development of American Police Control

tled in vicious and often fatal gang fights. The Astor Place riots of 1851, due to jealousy between the followers of the actors Forrest and Macready, resulted in the death of scores of people. Gangs known as "The Bowery Boys" and "The Dead Rabbits," centering in a district called "Five Points," terrorized the city. In 1858 a mob attacked and burned the public hospitals at the quarantine station, with no interference from the police, despite the fact that the intentions of the mob had been openly advertised.

Conditions such as these were common, to a greater or less extent, in all American cities in the middle of the nineteenth century. The strong hand of a well organized police was required, but in no city had the difficulties in the way of creating such an organization been overcome. Indeed, there seemed to be little appreciation of the nature of the difficulties or of the elementary steps to be taken in building up an effective police force. The citizens of that day were groping in the dark. No precedents existed to serve as guides or warnings. City populations had grown like magic. Municipal government had suddenly become a complex mechanism with no one skilled enough to handle it or even to grasp its implications. The task of creating rational municipal arrangements was obscured by the social and political movements which swept across the middle decades of the nineteenth

showed the force to be made up of the following nationalities (Cleveland *Daily Herald*, Feb. 5, 1872) :

American	46	English	9
German	35	Scotch	3
Irish	31	Bohemian	1
Austrian			1

century with peculiar force. Democracy was rising in a new strength, conscious of power, but vague and uncertain as to program and method. The early reaction from the doubt and conservatism of the Federalists had been continued and accentuated by the political theories of Jackson and his followers, and was now reaching its culmination. Universal suffrage without property qualifications had become an established fact; religious and property requirements for office holding had been abandoned; terms of office had been shortened; the principle of " rotation in office " had been accepted; even the judiciary had not been spared in the triumphant progress of the newly awakened democratic sentiment.

Among the many changes wrought by this tidal wave was the increased participation of the people in the direct election of their officers. Where hitherto the city council had chosen the mayor and other executive officers of local government, they were now chosen by popular election. This movement, which swept rapidly over the entire country, did not spare the police department. As early as 1840 members of the night watch of Cincinnati were elected by citizens of the ward in which they served.[1] In 1850 day watchmen were similarly chosen.[2] In the same year, as we have seen, the principle of a popularly elected marshal at the head of a police force was established in Philadelphia.[3] In 1850, also, San Francisco provided for an elective city marshal[4] and six years later

[1] Local Laws of Ohio, 1839, p. 157.
[2] Greve, loc. cit., p. 664.
[3] See ante, p. 67.
[4] Laws of Cal., 1850, Chap. 98.

for an elective chief of police.[1]   These examples were
followed in Chicago in 1851,[2] in Cleveland in 1852 [3] and
in many other towns and cities.   Brooklyn elected not
only its chief of police but its captains of police as well.[4]
These arrangements were not evolved as relating particularly to the police department.   They represented a phase
of the political philosophy of the time.   The charter of
the city of Cleveland of 1852, which provided for the
election of a city marshal, provided also for the election
of a civil engineer, a fire engineer, a treasurer, an auditor,
a solicitor, a police judge, a superintendent of markets,
trustees of the board of water works and three street commissioners.   The pure democracy of a New England
town meeting became the ideal of local government [5] and
the widening scope of popular elections represented the
attempt to adapt what had proved successful in small,
homogeneous villages to rapidly growing cosmopolitan
cities.

It would be difficult to overestimate the marked effect

[1] Laws of Cal., 1856, Chap. 125.
[2] Private Laws of Ill., 1851, p. 132.
[3] Laws of Ohio, 1852, p. 223. A marshal was elected as early as
1827 in Cincinnati under the city charter that went into effect at that
time, but the principle was given up some years before its initiation
in Philadelphia.   25 O. L. 40.
[4] N. Y. Assembly documents of 1857, No. 127, p. 3.
[5] Jefferson's influence contributed to this end.   He recommended
for Virginia a system of local government modeled on the New
England plan. (See his *Works*, VII, Washington edition, p. 357;
also V, 524.)   Naturally, he did not foresee the extraordinary
growth of city populations which followed later in the century.   He
insisted that the Americans would continue to be virtuous and retain
their democratic form of government as long as they remained an
agricultural people, but "when they get piled upon one another in
large cities, as in Europe, they will become corrupt, as in Europe."
(*Works*, IV, 479.)

of this movement upon police organization and municipal government generally. For years it retarded the natural growth of police function in many sections of the United States. Developing into the idea that the choice of administrative heads of specialized departments can wisely be left to the exigencies of popular elections, it became increasingly difficult of application as city populations grew larger and more complex; and while today its influence has been for the most part spent, its results are still visible, as we shall see in a later chapter, in the form and structure of many police forces throughout the country.

Meanwhile, attention must be turned to another development of the middle nineteenth century, whose effect upon police organization today is even more pronounced.

The Rise of Police Boards.

Prior to the formation of modern police forces, initiated, as we have seen, in the decade between 1845 and 1855, police arrangements were largely in the control of city councils. The office of mayor had not yet been associated with broad executive powers, and appointments, as well as administrative responsibilities were lodged in the common council. The decade just referred to, however, witnessed a pronounced decay in these wide powers and the waning influence of the council as an administrative body. This change was undoubtedly due in part to the rising democratic sentiment which brought with it a pronounced distrust of the legislative departments of the government, both state and local. It was due, too, to the growing complexity of municipal functions and the increasing difficulties of supervision through committees of council. Whatever the cause, council control gave way to an institution which came into instant and widespread favor and which has characterized American local government to the present day — the independent administrative board.

The origin of this novel experiment, particularly in its relation to police organization, cannot be exactly determined. School boards and poor relief boards had existed prior to this period and it is possible that the new movement was merely a wider application. It is just possible, too, that the English municipal reform bill of 1835, with its provision for " watch committees " of the local council, may have suggested a special board of police administrators. Again, it may be that the old council committee which for years had been practically responsible for the police, was the pattern for the new form of control. Apparently the earliest reference to such an arrangement was contained in an ordinance proposed in New York in 1844, to effect a reorganization of the police department. This ordinance, which subsequently failed of passage,[1] provided for a " board of police " consisting of the superintendent, the two sub-superintendents and the four directors, one for each of the subdivision districts. The board was charged with general administrative functions.[2] Somewhat similar arrangements were carried through in Philadelphia in 1850, when under the police act of that year [3] the marshal and the several

[1] Instead, an ordinance was passed providing for " Harper's Police." (See note 2, page 66.)
[2] The text of this proposed ordinance is noted in the Proceedings of the New York Board of Aldermen, 1843–44.
[3] Laws of Penn., 1850, No. 239.

77

lieutenants formed a board of police to "make such useful rules and regulations as may be required and to keep a chief police station in the city of Philadelphia." Later in the same year another act was passed providing that the police board should consist of the marshal of police, and the presidents of the respective town boards of the communities within the police district.[1]

This arrangement was copied in New York in 1853.[2] An administrative body was created, called the "board of police commissioners," consisting of the mayor, the recorder and the city judge. Apart from the fact that the chief of police was selected by the mayor with the board's approval, the board had full powers of appointment and dismissal of all members of the force and was charged with general administrative duties. Thereafter for forty-eight years the police department of New York was in the hands of some form of police board.

As the example set by New York in 1844 of consolidating the day and night police under a single head had been followed by all the large cities in the country, so now the Philadelphia board of 1850 and the New York board of 1853 became the general patterns which many communities took pains to copy, although the idea was subjected to endless modification. New Orleans adopted the plan in 1853, creating a board consisting of the mayor and the recorders of the city.[3] Cincinnati adopted it in 1859 providing for a board of four appointed

[1] Laws of Penn., 1850, No. 240. This arrangement lasted until 1854. (See note 2, on page 67.)
[2] Laws of N. Y., 1853, Chap. 228.
[3] Acts of La., 1853, No. 115.

by the mayor, the police judge, and the city auditor.[1]
In the same year San Francisco established a board of
three, consisting of the police judge, the president of the
board of supervisors and the chief of police [2] serving
ex officio. Detroit's board was established in 1861, made
up of the mayor and two persons appointed by the common council.[3] Boards were established in St. Louis [4]
and Kansas City [5] in 1861, in Buffalo [6] and Cleveland [7]
in 1866, in Richmond,[8] Atlanta [9] and other southern
cities in the decade beginning 1870. In the years that
followed, with the exception of Philadelphia, there was
hardly an important city in the country but that experimented in some fashion or other with a police board.
The modifications of the plan were of infinite variety.
Boards were made up of local officers serving *ex officio*
or of outsiders. They ranged in size from boards of
two, as in Cleveland [10] to boards of twelve as in Atlanta.[11]
They were chosen by popular elections, by district elec-

[1] Laws of Ohio, 1859, p. 48.
[2] Statutes of Cal., 1859, Chap. 135. This board was given no
real functions except to act as a check upon the members of the
force in receiving presents and following other professions.
[3] Laws of Mich., No. 136. Under this act the board was
given disciplinary powers over the members of the force. The chief,
however, was appointed and removed by the common council.
[4] Laws of Mo., 1861, p. 446.
[5] Local Laws of Mo., 1861, p. 63 (Called Session).
[6] Laws of N. Y., 1866, Chap. 484. This was the so-called " Niagara
Frontier Police Bill," which incorporated Buffalo, Tonawanda and
La Salle under the control of a board of police commissioners.
Tonawanda and La Salle, however, refused to enter the arrangement
and the act took effect for Buffalo alone. It lasted until 1872.
[7] Laws of Ohio, 1866, p. 104.
[8] Acts of Va., Ses. 1869–70, Chap. 101.
[9] Local and Private Laws of Ga., 1874, No. 111, Sec. 72.
[10] Municipal Code of 1902: Laws of 1902, Extraordinary Session,
pp. 68 ff.
[11] Laws of Ga., 1908, Part III — Title I, Act No. 515.

tions, by council elections, and by appointment at the hands of mayors, governors, judges, or groups of officials. Occasionally the law named the specific persons to serve on the board, as in New York in 1864 [1] and Detroit in 1865.[2] In political complexion, boards were partisan, non-partisan, or bi-partisan. In some cases they constituted· an integral part of the city government, rising and falling with an administration; in other cases they were independent of any municipal official or their terms of office were not coincident with an existing political regime. The powers of the boards ranged from mere advisory duties to absolute authority. In some cities these powers were measured by the responsibilities imposed; in others, full responsibility was exacted, while powers were shared with different branches of the municipal government.

In the kaleidoscopic variations and adaptations which followed upon the adoption of the board plan of control, it is difficult to trace the line of police development. A clue presents itself, however, in a movement, initiated in New York in 1857, to introduce in America Sir Robert Peel's method of police control which had been adopted for the metropolitan district of London in 1829.

The Rise of State-controlled Police Systems.

The law of 1853, as we have seen, gave to New York a board of police commissioners consisting of the mayor, the recorder and the city judge. In taking this step the legislature had hoped to eliminate the political favoritism

[1] Laws of N. Y., 1864, Chap. 41.
[2] Laws of Mich., 1865, No. 78.

and ward control which prior to that time had dominated the department. This hope, however, was justified only in part. The recorder and the city judge, serving *ex officio,* took little interest in the affairs of the force, and control was gradually assumed by the mayor. Policemen were still appointed for one year only and political faithfulness was the single standard imposed. " There is no incentive to promotion," wrote the district attorney of New York County in 1857. " On the contrary, captains are taken from citizens and placed over lieutenants and sergeants of ten years' experience." [1] The newspapers of the time were filled with similar expressions. " Vicious and inefficient " was the characterization of the New York *Times* in regard to the police force.[2] Said the New York *Tribune:*

> " We all know that at present the police seem powerless for good; that bold and dangerous criminals were never so bold and dangerous; that life and property were never so insecure; that gambling and prostitution and illegal trade were never so open and shameless; that the public sentiment of danger from violence was never so acute, nor with so much reason. And why is it? Because the policemen are politicians, getting the places as the reward of political service; because they dare not or will not offend the fellows who have fought shoulder to shoulder with them at the polls." [3]

In 1856 a legislative investigating committee — the

[1] Assembly Documents of 1857, No. 127, p. 2–3.
[2] New York *Times,* February 28, 1857.
[3] New York *Tribune,* February 5, 1857.

first of a long line of such committees to overhaul the municipal affairs of New York — reported on the scandalous practices existing in the department and recommended that the board of police commissioners be reorganized so that the mayor as *ex officio* member would serve with four to six competent persons to be elected by the people.[1] This recommendation, which was in line with the democratic sentiment of the time, was not adopted. In 1857, however, the legislature passed the so-called Metropolitan police bill, modeled after " the world renowned Police Act of London and its suburbs." [2] This act [3] consolidated the police districts of the cities of New York and Brooklyn and the counties of Kings, Westchester, and Richmond [4] under a board of five commissioners appointed by the governor — three from New York, one from Kings, and one from Richmond or Westchester, together with the mayors of New York and Brooklyn. It represented an attempt, more or less induced by partisan considerations, to do what the English parliament had done twenty-eight years before when it created out of a number of small, separate local constabula-

[1] Senate Documents of 1856, No. 97.

[2] Report of Assembly Committee on Cities and Villages, Assembly Documents of 1857, No. 127, p. 4.

[3] Laws of N. Y., 1857, Chap. 569. The bill as reported from the Assembly Committee provided for seven police commissioners — one from each of the counties of Richmond and Westchester, two from Kings county, and three from New York, with the mayors of New York and Brooklyn *ex officio,* " placing the great city in a minority, where her wealth and increasing importance may well permit her to be without injury, and which may be useful to check any tendency to extravagant expenditure." (Report of Assembly Committee on Cities and Villages, Assembly Document No. 127.)

[4] The towns of Flushing, Jamaica and Newtown, in Queens County, were added to the Metropolitan district by Laws of 1860, Chap. 259.

ries the Metropolitan police force of London.[1] As that force had been placed under the control of a state official, the Home Secretary, so the legislature of 1857 made the governor the appointing power, modifying the grant in characteristic American fashion by requiring the consent of the senate to the appointments. In other respects, however, the analogy between the two laws breaks down. The board form of control had by this time taken a firm hold on official imagination in America and Sir Robert Peel's provision for two commissioners, later changed to a single headed commission,[2] was abandoned in New York for a board of seven members. The New York act, too, reflected the democratic sentiment of the period in limiting the terms of the commissioners to three years, either in fear of the bugaboo of " an office-holding class," or in frank acceptance of Jackson's theory that offices should be " passed around." In Peel's act, on the other hand, no term was fixed for the commissioners, and that parliament intended the administrative head of the force to remain during good behavior was evidenced by the fact that the first incumbent, Sir Richard Mayne, served 39 years as chief of the metropolitan police, building up by his own initiative and statesmanship what is probably, even today, the most efficient police organization in Europe.[3]

In still another important respect did the New York act of 1857 differ from the English act from which it

[1] 10 Geo. IV, Chap. 44. See the author's *European Police Systems*, Chap. II.

[2] In 1856. 19 and 20 Vict. c. 2. The heads of police under Peel's original act were called " justices." The title " commissioner " was not used until the act of 1839. (2 & 3 Vict. c. 47.)

[3] See *European Police Systems*, Chap. IV.

was patterned. It provided that all policemen to be eligible for appointment must have lived at least five years within the limits of the metropolitan district. This clause, which remains to the present time one of the guiding principles of American municipal civil service, was written into the act in the interests of party patronage, on the theory that " the jobs belong at home." Sir Richard Mayne, on the other hand, was left free to develop his force as he saw fit, and early in his regime he established the principle which has effected so vitally the development of the London force of recruiting the major part of his men *outside* the metropolitan district.

One further dissimilarity between the two acts remains to be pointed out: the widely different spirit in which they were conceived. The English act of 1829 was a non-partisan attempt, scientifically based, to remedy an inefficient system. The New York act, on the other hand, represented the manoeuvering of a Republican legislature to obtain control over the affairs and particularly the patronage of a Democratic city.[1] To be sure, the situation in New York was desperate and cried for relief. " Murders have increased," said the report of the Assembly Committee. " Highway robberies have multiplied. The escaped convicts of other states and cities and countries and foreign lands have been allowed to congregate together and agree upon schemes to plunder." [2] At the same time a law conceived in a spirit of party advantage

[1] The Republicans had swept the state in the elections of 1856, when Governor King was chosen. They repeated their success in 1858 in electing Governor Morgan.

[2] Report of Assembly Committee on Cities and Villages, Assembly Documents of 1857, Doc. No. 127, p. 2.

can seldom become an instrument of permanent public benefit. Whatever the merit of the law of 1857, its usefulness in the development of New York's police force was handicapped by the crass partisanship to which it owed its birth. Of the five members whom the governor appointed on the first board, four were strong Republican party men, while the fifth belonged to the American party.[1]

The adoption of state control of local police aroused a storm of bitter protest in New York City. " It is abhorrent to our pride, adverse to our well-being and good government, and an insult to our intelligence," cried the mayor.[2] " The state authorities treat us as if we were an ignorant province with no rights which they are bound to respect," was the declaration of the board of aldermen. " When will the legislature at Albany cease to consider the functions of our municipal government as mere spoils to satiate the greediness of the followers of a temporary political majority? " [3] Mass meetings were held and suits were brought to test the constitutionality of the new act.[4]

[1] See New York *Times,* April 16, 1857.
[2] Mayor Fernando Wood in the New York *Times,* February 19, 1857.
[3] Board of Aldermen Reports, Vol. 134, p. 456.
[4] The act was held constitutional in 15 N. Y. 532. The opinion of Justice Shankland reads in part as follows: "How has the local authority of that great city (New York) discharged its duty of local government to its citizens of the state at large in protecting them in their liberty, life and property? Let the statistics of crime answer and convict that authority either of remissness in duty or the system of police hitherto in force as radically defective. But let the cause be what it may, which has paralyzed the arm of criminal law, the state is bound to protect the citizen in his life and property irrespective of locality; and if in the judgment of its representatives the local authorities have failed to accomplish this object, it was their duty to substitute another system more effectual in execution." (P. 556.)

" It lays the axe to the great principle of self-government "; " it poisons the very springs of our democratic
institutions "; " it is the invention and device of an unscrupulous political party "— these were the charges
brought against the plan by the indignant citizens of New
York.[1]

Especially incensed was the electorate that a foreign
pattern had been followed in framing the law. " The
originators of this act," said one of its critics, " cast their
eyes toward the British metropolis and there . . . found
the desired example for enslaving American citizens." [2]
Even the titles " superintendent " and " inspector," which
had been adopted in the new act from the London force,
came in for savage criticism. The minority report of
the assembly committee stated the case as follows:

> " As yielding to a desire entertained by many per-
> sons to copy the exploded ideas of English aristocracy,
> and who constitute in themselves a bad imitation of the
> same class of society in Europe, the minority of the
> Committee cannot permit this opportunity to pass of
> protesting against the adoption of the worn-out and
> peculiar official names borne by officers in England and
> other portions of Europe, as indicative of the par-

[1] Assembly Documents of 1858, No. 40, and Senate Documents, No.
46. In a petition presented to the legislature in 1858 the repeal of
the law was demanded in the following words: " The people of the
Metropolitan police district appeal to the legislature to restore to
them their ancient rights. They have been deprived of them against
their earnest remonstrance and without cause — rights which have
been enjoyed without interruption for a period beyond the memory
of living men have been taken away for no higher purpose than to
swell partisan triumph and gratify partisan ambition." (Senate
Documents of 1858, No. 46, pp. 12 and 13.)

[2] Assembly documents of 1858, No. 40, p. 4.

tiality of such persons to degrade the simplicity of the straightforward and honest use of the English language by our forefathers, and characteristic of republican institutions." [1]

Despite the protests of New York, which culminated in rioting and bloodshed,[2] the metropolitan police force was organized. Thereafter for thirteen years the state controlled the policing of New York and Brooklyn and the territory in the surrounding counties. The unhappy political auspices under which this method of control was launched continued for some years a source of friction and misunderstanding. In 1859 a special committee appointed by the senate reported that the force was organized "less with regard to its public duties than to its efficiency as a political machine." [3] The commissioners appointed by the governor were found to be "distinguished above their fellows as biter partisans." [4] During the first half of the following decade, however, the

[1] Assembly documents of 1857, No. 149, p. 7. Similar feeling was aroused in Boston when a Metropolitan police measure for that city was introduced in the Massachusetts legislature in 1863. "The proposers of this measure," said one of its opponents, "hold up for our example the system of London. In monarchies, however, the police force is less the watchdog of the cottage than the bloodhound of authority, ever ready to strike its fangs into the feeble and needy." (Argument of Thomas C. Amory before the Joint Committee of the Legislature, March 15, 1863 — a pamphlet.)

[2] Mayor Wood refused to recognize the authority of the commissioners appointed by the governor and insisted on maintaining his own municipal police. A series of serious clashes between the two police bodies ensued and it became necessary to call out the militia to put down the riots. The mayor finally submitted to the metropolitan board. A vivid picture of this period is shown in George W. Walling's *Recollections of a New York Chief of Police,* New York, 1887, Chap. 4.

[3] Senate documents of 1859, No. 113, p. 4.

[4] *Ibid.,* p. 7.

new appointments to the police board made by New York's war governor, General Morgan, raised the force to a level of efficiency which it had not previously reached. In 1863 the district attorney of New York county wrote of the police as being "entirely popularized, all local jealousy having subsided." [1] In his annual message of 1862 Governor Morgan spoke of the metropolitan force as a "system of police which has proved itself under trying circumstances and careful scrutiny equal to the objects sought in its establishment." [2] In 1864 Recorder Hoffman in a charge to the Grand Jury of New York County expressed himself as follows: "We have one of the most complete police forces in the world — a force that is approaching as near to perfection as ever can be attained in this city and county of ours." [3] The newspapers of the time reflect similar opinions. The New York *Tribune* said in 1864:

"The police force is loyal to the commissioners because the commissioners are faithful to their duties, without fear or favor. Every man among them knows that his political character has nothing to do with his standing, which depends solely upon the way in which he discharges his duty as a policeman. . . . The commissioners are respected without regard to their politics

[1] This, with other letters, was printed in Massachusetts Senate Documents of 1865, No. 171, at the time when it was proposed in the legislature to adopt state control for Boston's police force. Two years earlier a similar but equally fruitless attempt had the support of Wendell Phillips. (See his speech "On a Metropolitan Police," printed in pamphlet form from the Boston *Traveller*, April 5, 1863.)
[2] Journal of the Senate of the State of New York, January 7, 1862.
[3] Mass. Senate Documents of 1865, No. 171.

Development of American Police Control

because they are devoted to the duties of their office and are fearless and energetic in their performance." [1]

Despite this favorable situation a change in the organization of the board was made in 1864. In 1860 the membership of the board had been reduced from five to three and the *ex officio* participancy of the mayors of New York and Brooklyn had been eliminated.[2] The new law of 1864 increased the membership to four and took the appointing power out of the hands of the governor altogether, vesting it in the entire legislature. This change was due both to the desire of a Republican legislature to curb the power of a Democratic governor [3] and to the growing feeling that the political complexion of the board should be bi-partisan. In this latter respect this act marked the beginning of a movement which spread throughout the United States wherever the board form of control had been adopted. The act itself did not directly specify, as was later done in so many cases, that the board should be bi-partisan in membership; it was, however, a gentleman's agreement, thoroughly understood by both political parties, and from that time until state control of police was abolished in 1870 [4] the board was composed of two Republicans and two Democrats elected by the legislature. "The satisfaction at this result is very general," said the New York *Tribune* when

[1] New York *Tribune,* January 4 and 12, 1864.
[2] Laws of N. Y., 1860, Chap. 259.
[3] Governor Seymour. He attempted to remove the appointees of his predecessor, Governor Morgan, alleging as justification the failure of the police properly to handle the draft riots of 1863.
[4] Laws of N. Y., 1870, Chap. 137.

the act was passed. " Both parties are represented . . . and the organization of the police will be used, we hope and believe, for the purposes for which it was created, uninfluenced by partisan bias, and for the protection of the life and property of citizens." [1]

The Extension of State-controlled Systems.

The development of the state-controlled police force in New York City has been shown in considerable detail because of its pronounced influence upon police organization and municipal government generally throughout the United States. Following the precedent established in 1857 the state legislature invaded function after function of New York City's government. The park commission, the fire brigade, the health department and other branches of local service were placed under state boards and the example was widely followed in all parts of the country, so that in many cities the duties and powers of the mayor and council were materially circumscribed and reduced.

State control of local police bodies became especially popular. The plan was adopted for Baltimore in 1860, with a board of four commissioners chosen by the state legislature.[2] With the exception of an interregnum during the Civil War, when the city was under martial law,[3]

[1] New York *Tribune*, March 16, 1864.

[2] Laws of Md., 1860, Chap. 7. The mayor was also a member *ex officio*. The act provided among other things that "no Black Republican or endorser or approver of the Helper Book (*The Impending Crisis* by Hinton R. Helper) shall be appointed to any office under said board." The constitutionality of the act was upheld in Baltimore *v.* State Board of Police, 15 Md. 376.

[3] In June, 1861, General Banks of the Federal forces arrested the police commissioners and the marshal of police, Colonel Kane, and himself appointed a board of nine commissioners to manage the force of the department. This condition lasted for more than a year.

Development of American Police Control

the police department has ever since been controlled by a
state board, although the form of the board has several
times been altered.[1] A similar arrangement was made
for St. Louis in 1861, when the police force was placed
under the management of a board of four commissioners
appointed by the governor with the consent of the senate.[2]
Kansas City's board of three commissioners under similar control was instituted in the same year.[3] In the case
of both cities the step was influenced by the necessity,
arising from the location of Missouri as a border state
during the war, of maintaining a strong, centralized control over the forces of order. This arrangement of 1861
has remained practically unaltered to the present day.[4]
In the same year, too, the legislature of Illinois provided
Chicago with a board of three police commissioners appointed by the governor with the consent of the senate
for terms of two, four and six years respectively, their
successors to be elected by the citizens of the city.[5] This
act was prompted solely by partisan politics. The Repub-

[1] A board of two citizens elected by the legislature, serving with
the mayor *ex officio,* was established in 1862 (Laws of Md., 1862,
Chap. 131). In 1867 a board of three commissioners was established,
elected by the legislature, the participancy of the mayor as an *ex
officio* member being omitted (Laws of Md., 1867, Chap. 367). In
1900 the law was amended so as to provide for a board of three, appointed by the governor with the consent of the senate, not more
than two of the three being allowed from the same political party
(Laws of Md., 1900, Chap. 15).
[2] Laws of Mo., 1861, p. 446.
[3] Laws of Mo., 1861 (Gen. Laws, p. 446; Local Laws of Called
Session, p. 63). In both St. Louis and Kansas City the mayor was
ex officio a member of the board.
[4] The St. Louis law underwent slight amendment in 1899 (Laws
of Mo., 1899, p. 51) but the principles remained the same. The
Kansas City act was amended the same year (Laws of Mo., 1899,
p. 65), the board of three being changed to two, with the mayor
ex officio.
[5] Public Laws of Ill., 1861, p. 151.

91

licans controlled the state government while the city of Chicago was in the hands of the Democrats. The board appointed by the governor in compliance with the act was entirely Republican in complexion and the force for the next two years was managed entirely in the interests of the party. In 1863, however, the Democrats gained control of the legislature and the police act was amended, reducing the terms of the commissioners from six to three years and providing for their election at large by the voters of Chicago.[1] Under this arrangement the board passed into the hands of the Democrats and state control in the shape of gubernatorial appointment was eliminated.[2]

Detroit was the next important city to which a state controlled police board was given. In 1865, against the protests of a large section of the city, a Republican legislature passed an act creating a board of four commissioners appointed by the governor with the consent of the senate.[3] " There is no necessity of any such law as is asked for by some of our Republican politicians," said the Detroit *Free Press*. " We think the people of the city of Detroit are quite as competent to manage their own affairs as the people of any of the cities and villages of the interior (of the state)." [4] State police control, how-

---

[1] Private Laws of Ill., 1863, p. 40.

[2] In 1865 the Republicans regained control of the legislature and the police act was again amended, so that the members of the police board were chosen by the electors of Cook County rather than by the electors of the city of Chicago, on the theory that Cook County would be less likely to return a Democratic board. The six-year term was restored. (Private Laws of Ill., 1865, p. 284.)

[3] Laws of Mich., 1865, No. 78.

[4] Detroit *Free Press*, January 12, and January 20, 1865. A vigorous attack was made on the metropolitan bill in the state legislature, on the ground that " such legislation as this is a fatal assault upon

ever, was instituted and continued in effect in Detroit for twenty-six years.[1]

This example was followed by Cleveland in 1866.[2] The Cleveland law, however, grew out of a wide-spread dissatisfaction with existing police conditions and appears to have been warmly supported by the city's electorate. "The Police Department was a huge political machine," said the Cleveland *Herald* ten years later in reviewing the history of the force. "The chief of police was elected by popular vote. With the election canvass dawned the halcyon days of the thieves and bummers who had votes to give or who could control votes. They were the masters of the police instead of the police being their masters."[3] To correct these conditions the metropolitan system was instituted. It lasted, however, but two years. Skilfully engineered by a political clique, popular prejudice rose against "government from Columbus," and with a change of party control in the legislature, local management of police was re-established in the shape of a board of four commissioners elected by the people.[4]

the great principle of American freedom." (Detroit *Free Press*, January 20, 1865.)

[1] It was superseded by a board of four commissioners appointed by the mayor. (Local Acts of Mich., 1891, No. 349). In 1871, as a result of a political quarrel, the legislature amended the act so as to take the appointments out of the hands of the governor temporarily by specifically designating four men to serve as commissioners. This act provided, however, that vacancies thereafter were to be filled by the governor as before. (Laws of Mich., 1871, No. 479.)

[2] Laws of Ohio, 1866, p. 104. The act provided for a board of four commissioners appointed by the governor with the consent of the senate, serving with the mayor *ex officio*.

[3] Cleveland *Herald*, Jan. 17, 1876.

[4] Laws of Ohio, 1868, p. 45. This law provided for the election

American Police Systems

By this time state control of police forces had become a popular principle of government. There was scarcely an important city in the country in which this system was not tried or its adoption strongly urged. Following the example of the northern cities the plan was instituted in New Orleans in 1868 and was maintained for nine years.[1] Cincinnati's force was controlled by a state board from 1877 to 1880[2] and from 1886 to 1902.[3] Indianapolis had a similar system from 1883 to 1891.[4] Omaha's state board plan was established in 1887 and with some modifications lasted for ten years.[5] San Francisco had what virtually amounted to state control through the creation in 1877 of a board appointed by the three judges of the 4th, 12th and 15th judicial districts of California.[6] The

of a police commissioner from each of four districts to be established by the city council. The city council, however, failed to establish the districts, and for the next four years the mayor assumed temporary charge of the force. In 1872 a law was passed providing for a board of four commissioners elected at large (Laws of Ohio, 1872, page 28). Thereafter until 1891, the Cleveland police force was managed by an elective board.

[1] Acts of La., 1868, No. 1, as amended by Acts of 1869, No. 92. This law which was drawn by a Republican legislature to control the city of New Orleans enabled the governor to appoint a board of five police commissioners. The police district included not only the city of New Orleans but the parishes of Orleans, Jefferson and St. Bernard. The commissioners were given broad powers of subpoena and the right to call out the military.

The metropolitan police force created under this act was splendidly manned and equipped and organized as a military body. Its members were armed with rifles. Growing out of the conditions arising from the Civil War, its evident intent was to over-awe the people of New Orleans. It gave way in 1877 to a police board of four commissioners appointed by the mayor. (Acts of La., 1877, E. S., No. 35.)

[2] Laws of Ohio, 1876, p. 70.
[3] Laws of Ohio, 1886, p. 47.
[4] Laws of Ind., 1883, Chap. 74.
[5] Laws of Neb., 1887, Chap. 10.
[6] Statutes of Cal., 1877–78, Chap. 558.

failure of this law to provide for vacancies on the board threw subsequent appointments into the hands of the governor [1] who exercised the power until the "eternal board," as it was called, was superseded by municipal control under the San Francisco Charter of 1900.[2] The police force of Charleston, S. C., was under the control of a state board for one year, 1896–1897.[3] A similar system was in force in fourteen cities of Indiana during the years 1897–1909.[4]

Of the large cities in the United States with state appointed police commissions Boston was among the last to adopt the system. It was instituted in 1885 under the belief — frankly avowed at the time — that the laws against the illegal sale of liquor could in no other way be impartially executed.[5] Since 1878 Boston had had a board of three commissioners appointed by the mayor with the approval of the council.[6] To this board was given the right to license liquor saloons under a law which limited the number of such places in Boston. As licenses were for one year only it was possible to confine them to those applicants who, through campaign contributions or otherwise, stood well with the administration. So close was the relation between the politicians and the police department that a nominee to the board of commis-

[1] Under Article V, Sec. 8, of the state constitution, giving the governor power to fill offices for which no other provision was made.
[2] Statutes of Cal., 1899, Concurrent and Joint Resolutions, Chap. II.
[3] Acts of S. C., 1894, No. 533.
[4] Laws of Ind., 1897, Chap. LIX. The cities were Anderson, Elkhart, Elwood, Hammond, Jeffersonville, Kokomo, Lafayette, Logansport, Marion, Muncie, Michigan City, New Albany, Richmond, Vincennes.
[5] See Boston *Evening Transcript*, Feb. 6, 1885.
[6] Acts of Mass., 1878, Chap. 244.

sioners could not be confirmed by the common council without an exact understanding of his attitude toward the liquor interests.[1]   This situation gave rise to a demand for a board of police appointed by the governor, and through the instrumentality of a Republican legislature the measure was introduced.   Democratic Boston met the proposal with bitter opposition.   " To say that Boston has not the intelligence and the will to regulate her own immediate concerns is an insult to her citizens," cried the *Globe*.   " The metropolis of the Commonwealth is robbed of one of the most important functions of self-government in order to gratify the malice of some, the fanatical notions of others, and the political interests of many more." [2]   Despite the opposition which was largely political in character the measure was passed [3] and Boston's police department has ever since been under state control.   In 1906 the board of three was reduced to a single commissioner [4]— a significant step representative of a broad tendency throughout the country.   This development will be discussed in a later section.

The Decline of State Control.

In the foregoing survey we have traced the development of the boards of police appointed by state authority,

[1] My authorities are the *Evening Transcript* for January, February and March, 1885, and the testimony before the Joint Committee of the legislature on the subject of the state board.   (See *Testimony upon Petition of Amos A. Lawrence and others to establish a Metropolitan Police Commission* in the State House, Boston.)

[2] March 20 and April 17, 1885.   The Boston *Evening Transcript* supported the measure.

[3] Acts of Mass., 1885, Chap. 323.   This provided for three commissioners appointed by the governor and confirmed by the executive council.

[4] Acts of Mass., 1906, Chap. 291.

noting the subsequent abandonment of the plan which followed in many communities. Of the twenty-three cities in the United States whose populations exceeded 250,000 according to the census estimates of 1915, state controlled police systems had at different times been tried in twelve.[1] In only four of these twelve cities do such systems survive to the present day.[2] The rejection of this type of police management was due in nearly every case to one of two factors: political manoeuvering for party advantage or a belief, more or less sincerely held, in the principle of home rule. Often these two factors were combined, as in Cleveland, for example, where, as we have seen, the cry for home rule was skilfully incited by the local Democratic machine in 1868 to further its own interests. New York's experience with a state board was abruptly terminated in 1870 by the charter through which Tweed fastened his grip on the city's treasury. The state-controlled police force stood in his way and so supine was the public opinion of the time that despite the attacks of the newspapers he swept it aside with an arrogance unsurpassed in American municipal history. "Our independent police department," said the New York *Times,* "which has given us a disciplined and uniformed force in place of a vagabond band of ragamuffins, will yield obedience to that power which demands free rum and votes and gives us police justices who regularly set free fully one-half of all the villains the police properly arrest."[3] "By the passage of the Tweed charter," said

[1] Baltimore, Boston, Chicago, Cincinnati, Cleveland, Detroit, Indianapolis, Kansas City, Mo., New Orleans, New York, San Francisco, St. Louis.

[2] Baltimore, Boston, Kansas City and St. Louis.

[3] Feb. 9, 1870.

American Police Systems

the *Sun,* "New York has become a free city — that is to say, free to be plundered more than ever by Tweed, Sweeny and their chosen friends." [1]   Under such circumstances, New York returned to a municipally controlled police force.

Detroit's change from state control to local control after an experience of twenty-six years was due largely to the dissatisfaction which tends to accumulate against any kind or form of governmental mechanism.   The irresistible temptation of the state authorities to use the police force for political purposes, the occasional weaknesses which the department displayed, the unpopularity which it incurred in many quarters in its attempts to enforce the sumptuary laws — all these things, consciously and unconsciously, were laid to the *form* of control. Moreover, the feeling was growing that home rule represented the better principle of municipal management and the new law of 1891 which eliminated a number of state appointed boards was welcomed as an intelligent effort to give the people of Detroit an effective and symmetrical system of self-government. [2]

In New Orleans, the metropolitan police force was from the first deeply resented as a Republican measure to overawe a conquered city, and more than one armed clash occurred between its members and the citizens. [3]   On several occasions the Republican legislature was obliged to come to the rescue of the department when the local au-

[1] April 8, 1870.
[2] See Detroit *Evening News,* June 3, 1891.
[3] A monument in New Orleans commemorates the pitched battle between the metropolitan police and the citizens which occurred Sept. 14, 1874, in which the former were put to flight.

98

thorities of the city or the parishes included within the police jurisdiction failed to supply the necessary funds which the law had assessed.[1]   On at least one occasion the protest of the local officers on the question of expense was so vigorous and determined that the legislature passed an act directing the board of commissioners " to reduce the metropolitan police force in such manner and to such extent as economy and the limitations of expenditures empowered by law may require." [2]   With the Democrats once again in full control of the legislature short work was made of the metropolitan system.

Cincinnati experimented twice with a state-controlled board, the first period covering three years and the second sixteen years.   The first experiment was rejected in 1880 without fair trial for reasons which were purely and openly political.   The mayor of Cincinnati, under the guise of home rule, sought control of the police to carry the primaries and elections for his party.[3]   Once re-established under municipal management the police entered upon a career of graft and peculation which has made vivid the recollection of the " Boodle Board " even to the present time.   The return to state control represented the reaction against the conditions which left so black a page in Cincinnati's municipal history.   The second experiment with a state board, therefore, beginning in 1886, was given a far better opportunity to prove itself.   The end, which came in 1902, was due to circumstances not immediately connected with Cincinnati.   The political

[1] See Acts of La., 1873, No. 64; Acts of 1874, No. 33; Acts of 1875, No. 16.
[2] Acts of La., 1874, No. 60.
[3] See Cincinnati *Enquirer* for January and February, 1880.

manoeuvering resulting from the fight against the traction interests in Cleveland, together with the attempt to saddle a state police board on the city of Toledo, had led to the revolutionary decision of the Supreme Court of Ohio under which the old mechanical classification of cities was done away with, and almost the entire legal foundation of local government in the state destroyed.[1] The legislature, hastily summoned to meet the extraordinary situation, passed a uniform charter applicable to every city in the state.[2] Under this charter the police department of Cincinnati passed again into the hands of the municipal authorities. In other words, the question of the advantages or disadvantages of a state-controlled police force in a particular city was lost sight of in the demand for a uniform system of local government.

In this manner it would be possible to show in city after city the abandonment of the plan of state-controlled police boards. Never popular at any time, the system fell before the demand of the cities that they be allowed to handle their own affairs even if they handled them badly. Whatever its merits — and we shall try to appraise them in the next chapter in connection with those cities in which the plan still survives — the discrimination which it marked in powers of self-government as between

[1] State *ex rel.* Knisely *v.* Jones, 66 Ohio State, 453.
[2] Laws of Ohio, 1902. Extraordinary Session, pp. 66 ff. The new law called " The municipal code," provided for a police department under two or four " directors " as the local council might determine, not more than half from the same political party. They were appointed by the mayor with the consent of two-thirds of the council for a term of four years. The Cleveland council chose a board of two; the Cincinnati council, a board of four. The law which was palpably designed to keep the police of the cities of Ohio in Republican hands represented a perversion to low partisan ends of a great opportunity in municipal reform.

city and country districts created in the former a rankling sense of injury. Not even the increased efficiency of the police, when it followed under the state-controlled plan, could overcome the stigma which attached to a form of control based, impliedly at least, on the theory that city populations could not be trusted by country legislators to run their own affairs. This idea, not always expressed perhaps, was the underlying objection which in the end proved fatal to the wide adoption of state-controlled boards.

But it is by no means certain that state control of local police in those cities where it was temporarily tried accomplished what its sponsors professed in advance to believe, that is, the elimination of politics in the management of the force. Indeed the evidence indicates just the reverse. The police department was merely lifted from one set of political influences into another. Title was transferred to a new group of political overlords. Control of the police was a prize to be fought for and owned — the legitimate spoils of victory. As we shall see in the next chapter, political considerations can enter through state management as readily as through municipal management, and no mechanical organization or form of administrative machinery can be made proof against partisan practices if partisans themselves are set to run it. When the Denver department was under state control in 1893 the governor of Colorado removed the commissioner of police for the openly avowed reason that " the good of the Populist party in Colorado demanded it." [1] Den-

[1] See *History of the Government of Denver* by Clyde Lyndon King. Denver, 1911, pp. 211–213.

American Police Systems

ver had long been irretrievably Republican and little sympathy existed between the city and the state administration. In the bitter struggle which subsequently developed the governor was obliged to call out the militia to enforce his decrees. State control of police in Providence, Rhode Island, was marked by continuous political skirmishes between the Democratic governor and the Republican senate over the appointments to the police board. Similarly, under state control in Minneapolis from 1889 to 1891 political bargaining and party advancement were the chief factors in the administration of the force.

In other words, there was little to choose between state board and municipal board. One was as permeated with politics as the other. The question was a matter not of principle but of party victory. State control represented the tactics employed by one party to seize the elections, and municipal control, the tactics of the other party, and, as in Cincinnati for example, the type of board see-sawed back and forth as party victory alternated. The matter was never fought out on its merits, never tested from an unbiased, disinterested standpoint. Seldom if ever were the people of a city given an opportunity to pass fairly and directly upon the question of retaining after trial the state controlled form of organization. In most cases, as we have seen, the question was complicated by political cross-currents and obscured by extraneous and irrelevant controversies, and changes were made from state control to local control without adequate discussion and with no attempt to ascertain whether the former system had or had not proved a success.

Development of American Police Control

The Bi-partisan Board.

The state controlled board was ostensibly a method for taking the police department out of politics. Another method, devised for the same end and applied alike to state and municipal boards, was the so-called bi-partisan principle. This principle was instituted, as we have seen, in New York in 1864 when the state board of police was increased from three members to four members on the understanding that two should be appointed from the Republican party and two from the Democratic. This arrangement was continued through the Tweed charter of 1870 until 1873 when an act was passed increasing the board to five members.[1] The following year, however, the number was restored to four,[2] and thereafter for 27 years this form of control was in effect. Until 1895 no mention was made in the law of the bi-partisan principle, although, with the exception of two or three instances,[3] it was rigorously adhered to as an unwritten understanding. Upon the recommendation of the Lexow Commission in 1895, however, the bi-partisan theory was written

[1] Laws of N. Y., 1873, Chap. 335. The provision was savagely assailed by the New York newspapers. "The only defense for the provision," said the New York *Times,* "is that it will afford places for additional dependents on political patronage." (April 2, 1873.)

[2] Laws of N. Y., 1874, Chap. 300. "As for the 'fifth commissioner,'" said the New York *Times,* "he is only a battle ground for parties, and it will be an excellent plan to get rid of him altogether. . . . To insure equal justice for both sides let both be equally represented." (April 23, 1874.)

[3] In 1892, for example, when the term of a Republican police commissioner expired, Mayor Grant filled the vacancy by the selection of a Democrat, and until 1894 the commission consisted of a Republican commissioner, an Independent Democrat commissioner, and two Tammany commissioners. (See report of the Lexow Commission, page 66.)

103

into the law,[1] remaining in effect until the present single commissioner system was adopted in 1901.[2]

The bi-partisan principle was eagerly seized upon throughout the country wherever the board form of control was in force. Based upon the theory that politics can never be eliminated from the management of the police department it was adopted as a fair and practical arrangement of minimizing the effects of politics by setting one partisan administrator to watch another. The fact that the machinery of elections was largely under the jurisdiction of the police gave the argument for the bi-partisan system additional force. It was hoped that natural distrust of each other by the different party representatives on the board would breed a vigilance fatal to the political manoeuvering of any one of them, and that from this condition a genuinely non-partisan management of the force could be secured. As the report of the Lexow Commission in New York expressed it: " A bi-partisan board conveys a distinct declaration to its subordinates that they must conduct themselves upon non-partisan lines, and that neither favor, reward, nor promotion may be expected from aggressive partisanship." [3]

Upon this theory, therefore, the bi-partisan principle was widely adopted — at first, in the form of a tacit understanding not recognized by law, as in New York and Baltimore, but later written into the law itself. Such an

[1] Laws of N. Y., 1895, Chap. 569. Section 1 read as follows: " At no time shall more than two such commissioners belong to the same political party, nor be of the same political opinion on state and national issues."
[2] Laws of N. Y., 1901, Chap. 33.
[3] Report of the Lexow Commission, p. 58.

act was passed for Indianapolis [1] in 1883. Boston,[2] Milwaukee,[3] and Newark [4] followed in 1885. Cincinnati's state board of 1886 [5] was bi-partisan and the plan was continued in the municipal boards established in all the cities of Ohio by the general code of 1902.[6] Similarly the bi-partisan principle was adopted in Minneapolis in the municipal board of 1887 [7] and the state board of 1889.[8] Omaha adopted the system in her state board of 1887.[9] San Francisco's bi-partisan board was inaugurated in 1899 [10] and Baltimore's in 1900.[11]

The bi-partisan principle proved in most cases an unsuccessful experiment. Indeed the theory that police administrators are to be selected not on the grounds of fitness but because they are party favorites had far-reaching and often disastrous consequences. Under this system the boards were composed of extreme and often unscrupulous representatives, chosen equally from the two dominant parties, and subservient to the bosses to whom they owed their appointments. Representing on the board not the public but their political organizations they were regarded as under obligation to gain for their parties all possible advantages in the way of patronage and power. When Mayor Van Wyck of New York in 1898

---

[1] Laws of Ind., 1883, Chap. 74.
[2] Acts of Mass., 1885, Chap. 323.
[3] Laws of Wis., 1885, Vol. II, Chap. 378.
[4] General Public Laws of N. J., 1885, Chap. 250.
[5] Laws of Ohio, 1886, p. 47.
[6] Laws of Ohio, 1902, Extraordinary Session, p. 66.
[7] Special Laws of Minn., 1887, Chap. 9.
[8] Special Laws of Minn., 1889, Chap. 51.
[9] Laws of Neb., 1887, Chap. 10.
[10] Statutes of Cal., 1899, Concurrent and Joint Resolutions, Chap. II.
[11] Laws of Md., 1900, Chap. 15.

appointed on the police board two Tammany district leaders and two Republican district leaders he followed a custom well established not only in his own city but wherever the bi-partisan principle was in effect. It was the logical outcome of the theory that non-partisan administration can be secured only through conflicting partisan interests. The chaos and corruption which followed in the New York police department during the Van Wyck administration were directly traceable to the fact that the police commissioners had been appointed not to cooperate for public advantage but to fight each other for party gain.

The bi-partisan board failed in its principal object. It aimed to eliminate politics by taking the police department out of the hands of a single party; it actually strengthened the grip of politics on the department by turning it over to the keeping of *both* parties. Instead of a non-partisan administration it resulted in a pooling of interests and spoils by the party representatives on the board and a subsequent division highly advantageous to both political organizations. In many cases the commissioners did not hesitate to combine against public interests for party gain. For years in New York under the bi-partisan system appointments and promotions were officially " credited " to the commissioners responsible for them and no one commissioner was allowed to have more than his share.[1] The glamor of justice about the arrangement hid its vicious aspects and concealed the obvious truth that there is essentially no Republican way and no Democratic way of managing a police department.

[1] Personally communicated.

Development of American Police Control

The bi-partisan plan of police control has been largely discarded throughout the United States. New York, Boston, Cleveland, Toledo, Cincinnati, Minneapolis, Buffalo, Albany and Omaha have all relinquished it, and at the present time it is retained in only four of the larger cities: Baltimore, San Francisco, Milwaukee and Indianapolis.

The Passing of the Police Board.

The abandonment of the bi-partisan system of control, which we have discussed in the preceding section, was due not alone to the glaring weaknesses which it developed. The whole plan of administrative control through special boards fell gradually into disuse and the bi-partisan principle as a phase or outgrowth of that system shared the same fate.

The conception of a multiple-headed executive, to which the board method of management easily lends itself, was foredoomed to failure. In its attempt to make a group of people jointly answerable for the supervision of exacting details of administration, it violates the cardinal principle of effective control. Ultimate executive responsibility is not readily divisible among officers of equal rank and authority, nor can the burden of leadership be distributed among a group. This is the point of weakness in the board plan as related to municipal enterprise. Resulting from a confused attempt to apply legislative analogies to executive functions, it fails to develop the responsible leadership essential to successful management. Divided in its counsels, decentralized in its authority, with no unity of policy or solidarity of action, it has gradually given place to a more effective method of control.

In its adaptation to police departments the board form of management has shown perhaps its greatest faults. The function of police administration is seldom deliberative in the sense in which the word is used to denote the legitimate activities of a board of directors or other policy-forming organ of control. On the contrary, proper police management involves a degree of initiative, decisiveness and vigor which can be displayed only in single-headed leadership. " It is a matter of historical and governmental experience," said Governor Guild of Massachusetts, in his message to the legislature advocating a single police commissioner for Boston, " that inefficiency, if not disaster, follows divided responsibility in the control of any organized body of men, where discipline and *esprit de corps* must be the mainspring of success." [1]

The growing belief in the effectiveness of single-headed leadership has gradually undermined the board system of management in American police departments. In only 14 of the 52 cities over 100,000 population which at one time had the board form of police control does that form exist at the present time. In all other cases the one-man-control system has been substituted, generally in the shape of a commissioner or chief appointed by local authority, or, in the case of commission-governed cities, elected by the people. New York [2] and Detroit [3] abol-

[1] Massachusetts Senate Documents of 1906, No. 1, p. 28. It cannot be denied that political considerations may have had some influence on this opinion.
[2] Laws of N. Y., 1901, Chap. 33.
[3] Charter of 1901, Chap. 227.

ished their police boards and adopted the one commissioner plan in 1901, Boston in 1906,[1] Cleveland in 1908,[2] Cincinnati in 1908,[3] Birmingham, Alabama, in 1911,[4] Omaha in 1912,[5] St. Paul in 1914,[6] Buffalo in 1916.[7] Philadelphia as we have already seen, is the one large city which, with the exception of a nondescript type of board from 1850 to 1854, has consistently clung to the principle of single-headed leadership in the management of her police department.[8] A similar plan of control has been maintained in Chicago since the adoption of the present charter in 1875.[9]

The Character of the Development.

The history of the development of American police organization which we have briefly discussed in the foregoing sections presents one characteristic of outstanding prominence: the machinery of management and control has been subjected to endless experiment and modification. Change rather than stability has marked its course. With the exception of one or two cities, no carefully thought out plan of supervision has been fixed upon and maintained as a type most likely to meet legitimate de-

[1] Acts of Mass., 1906, Chap. 291.
[2] Laws of Ohio, 1908, p. 562. Cleveland previously had single-headed management under the so-called "Federal" plan which went into effect in 1891 (Laws of Ohio, 1891, p. 105) providing for a "Director of Police" appointed by the Mayor. This arrangement was superseded by the board form of control which the ill-advised Municipal Code of 1902 made necessary. (See *ante*, p. 100.)
[3] Laws of Ohio, 1908, p. 562.
[4] General Laws of Ala., 1911, No. 163.
[5] Laws of Neb., 1911, Chap. 24.
[6] Charter of 1912, Chap. 18.
[7] Laws of N. Y., 1914, Chap. 217.
[8] See *ante*, pp. 77–78.
[9] Laws of Ill., 1875, p. 43.

mands for years to come. Instead, American cities, as if in panic, have rushed from one device to another, allowing little or no time for the experiment last installed to prove itself, apparently under the belief that somewhere or in some fashion a form of machinery could be found or developed which would ensure perpetual efficiency and guarantee the lasting integrity of its operators. With this idea, cities have tried partisan boards, bi-partisan boards, and non-partisan boards; they have lodged the appointment of their heads of police in the hands of governors, legislatures, mayors, common councils, boards of public works, attorney generals, judges of the circuit court, probate judges, state auditors, state commissioners of public buildings, and the people themselves; they have laboriously written into their laws elaborately devised checks and balances, covering every possible contingency of administration and every item of probable expense; they have borrowed the plans of other cities which happened at the time to have honest police executives, or they have combined the plans of a number of communities in fanciful arrangements of their own, in which, as likely as not, an elaborately chosen board of commissioners with full responsibility and no powers was superimposed on a chief of police with wide powers and no responsibility. For some years in Dayton, Ohio, the police department was administered by a bi-partisan board of four police directors appointed by a bi-partisan board of six tax commissioners, who in turn were appointed by the judges of the circuit court, these last officials being elected by the people! [1]

[1] 89 O. L. 106.

Development of American Police Control

In this blind search for the " ideal system," this belief in the efficacy of checks and balances, if only the proper combination can be discovered, continuity has been sacrificed, and the existing arrangements have again and again been overturned. In the 91 years in which the Metropolitan police organization of London has been in existence, but one substantial change has been made in its machinery of control, and that was in 1856, when, after six years of trial with a single-headed commission the act of 1829 providing for two commissioners was altered to fit the new condition. In the 75 years in which New York City may legitimately be said to have had a regular police force nine fundamental changes, involving distinct breaks with the past, have occurred in the framework of her organization. Aldermanic control gave way to local board-control which in turn was superseded by a state board of seven; the membership of seven was reduced to three and then increased to four; the board was returned to municipal control and later its membership increased to five; the following year it was reduced again to four; later still, it was made bi-partisan and finally the single commissioner plan was adopted.

Comparisons of this kind could be drawn without number. Amid all the vicissitudes of empire, kingdom and republic, the control of the Paris police organization has remained practically without change from the hour it was established by Napoleon over a century ago. Its prefect is today appointed by the Ministry of the Interior with the approval of the head of the state as he was in Fouche's time. The same principle of continuity holds for Berlin and Vienna. Similarly the machinery of police control in the provincial cities of England — Liverpool, Manchester, Birmingham, Bristol — has been left substantially without modification since the Municipal Reform Act of 1853. In Cincinnati, on the other hand — to pick out an American city at random — ten fundamental organic changes have occurred in a little over fifty years. Their nature is shown in the following table:

Prior to 1859 — Police under control of mayor.

1859 — Board of four commissioners appointed by mayor, police judge, and city auditor.

1860 — Board abolished — chief of police appointed by mayor.

1873 — Board of four commissioners elected by people.

1874 — Control by mayor re-established.

1877 — Board of five commissioners appointed by governor.

1880 — Control by mayor re-established.

1885 — Board of three commissioners appointed by local Board of Public Works.

1886 — Board of four commissioners appointed by governor.

1902 — Board of four commissioners appointed by mayor and council.

1910 — Director of Public Safety appointed by mayor.

New Orleans, another typical city, shows the following changes in the frame work of the police management:

Prior to 1868 — Police under control of mayor.

1868 — Board of five commissioners appointed by governor.

1877 — Board of four commissioners appointed by mayor.

Development of American Police Control

1888 — Board of six commissioners elected by common council.

1898 — Board of seven commissioners elected by common council.

1904 — Board of two commissioners appointed by mayor, serving with mayor.

1912 — Board of three commissioners consisting of mayor, commissioner of public safety and civilian chosen by common council.

For this continuous alteration of the police machinery, this willingness to experiment with new forms and devices, one factor, as we have already suggested, is in part responsible — the apparently ineradicable belief of the American people that in the right mechanical arrangement of a municipal department, if only it can be discovered, lies the solution of the ills that trouble us. If scandal occurs in the police department, if the force becomes the tool of the politician in carrying elections, if headquarters is remiss in enforcing laws against crime and vice, the belief gains ground that something is wrong with the machinery of organization, some necessary check missing, some element of responsibility inaccurately placed. The law makers, therefore, under public pressure, begin to tinker with the mechanism. A patch is added here, a cog-wheel inserted there. If the force has been under the control of the municipal authorities it is handed over to the governor; if under the control of the governor, it is given to the municipal authorities. If the board has had large powers, they are taken away and shared with the chief, or *vice versa* the chief's powers are conferred exclusively upon the board. If the common council is under suspicion its authority over the police is given to the board of public works or to the judge of the circuit court or to any other body or officer temporarily possessing public confidence. The reports of investigating commissioners the country over, notably the Lexow Commission in New York in 1895, furnish striking examples of this kind of thinking. Whatever the arrangement of the police machinery, it is wrong and must be changed, and an ideal new system installed.

This belief in the occult qualities of mechanical organization leaves strangely out of consideration the character and ingenuity of *men*. It is a trite remark, but it must be repeated, that no form or arrangement of organization is proof against corruption or inefficiency if corrupt or inefficient men are allowed to operate it. The character of the administrator is of far greater consequence in the upbuilding of a police force than the kind of administrative machinery through which he works. A dishonest or incompetent police executive will ruin the best of organizations just as an able executive will make his effectiveness felt in spite of the handicaps of poor mechanism. State control of police generally works well in Baltimore and wretchedly in Kansas City; at this moment municipal control is a success in Los Angeles and a disgrace in Chicago.

It must not be forgotten, of course, that there are both good and bad forms of organization. As we have already seen in this chapter, responsibility may be dissipated and power and authority lost or scattered through ineffective administrative machinery. It is, indeed, highly important that leadership be established and responsibility definitized, and constructive thought is necessary to build a machine in which these ends are accomplished. But in the long run it is the quality of leadership that counts. No system of control is guaranteed to produce adequate results without relation to the men who operate it. No automatic type of organization exists through which competency and effectiveness are assured. In our continued search for such a self-regulating arrangement we have been chasing a will-o'-the-wisp.

Another factor, perhaps more important, is responsible for the constant alteration in our police machinery. It is summed up in the word *politics*. Enough has been said of it in this chapter, doubtless, to disclose its relation to our phenomenon of change. There is scarcely a city in the United States in which the police department has not been used as the ladder by which political organizations have crawled to power. Obstacles in the way of complete dominance by party machines have been overcome by the easy processes of law, and police departments have been revamped and reshaped, not in the interests of public service, but to facilitate the operation of the spoils system or strengthen the grip of some political machine. Examples of this are legion; no state in the country has been free of it. Of the nine fundamental changes in New York's police organization in 75 years scarcely half were made in good faith. The struggle for party dominance, the desire of "jobs" for the faithful, the determination to control the machinery of elections were the contributing motives in the principal alterations. This remark is equally true of Chicago, San Francisco, New Orleans, Cincinnati, Indianapolis, Omaha, and a dozen others. In many cities, indeed, no attempt has been made to conceal the real purpose of proposed changes, and violent alterations have been carried through on the open and acknowledged basis of party interest. Of this kind not a dozen but literally scores of instances could be cited, gathered from every city visited. In many of these instances, the cities have been perhaps more sinned against than sinning; they have been victims of party rivalry in the legislature, pawns in the clash of party interests for the control of the state. Our political history discloses nothing more sinister than the continuous legislative interference in municipal arrangements for partisan advantage. On the theory that what the state has given the state can take away, the administrative machinery of city government has periodically been pulled apart and rearranged, as party interests have dictated. The effect of this treatment on police organization has been peculiarly disastrous. The department has been stunted and dwarfed, with no opportunity for rational development. It has been shaped as a tool of party success rather than an instrument of public service. Regarded as the legitimate spoils of victory at the polls, it has been prostituted to base and selfish purposes.

One looks in vain for parallel conditions in the cities of England, France, or Switzerland. In these countries the mechanism of the police department is the product not of political expediency but of painstaking care and deliberation. It has been thoughtfully put together as an instrument of vast public usefulness. The best brains obtainable have been devoted to the task. When the growing needs of the department have indicated the necessity for change it has been brought about carefully and conscientiously, with the single idea of producing a better machine.   As a result we find such admirably articulated organizations as Scotland Yard in London, and the *Praesidium* in Vienna, with years of efficient police service to their credit.   No tinkering patchwork has checked their development; no sacrifice to political necessity has interfered with the orderly operation of their administrative machinery.   Planned deliberately on a basis of efficiency, the product of excellent workmanship and unselfish ideals of public service, they have run for years without hitch or breakdown.

The contrast between the old world and the new in respect to the evolution of local government leaves little to the credit of America.   One turns from the history of our municipal development with the wish that most of its sordid story could be blotted out.

CHAPTER III

THE PRESENT STATE OF POLICE CONTROL

State versus municipal control.— Successes of state control.— Failures of state control.— State control in relation to home rule problems.— Applicability of state control.— Board control versus single-headed control.— Weaknesses of board control.— Board administration a part time task.— Lack of unity in board administration.— Conflict of authority in board administration.— Politics in board administration.— Elective boards.— Bi-partisan boards.— The development of single headed control.

In the foregoing chapter we have followed the development of police organization in America from the simple night watch of early days to the elaborated forms of administration which were evolved during the latter half of the nineteenth century. We have seen the rise of that anomalous instrument of supervision, the executive board, with its many and often capricious modifications, superseded in part within recent years by the responsible leadership of single-headed management. We have observed the wide popularity of direct state control of local forces and its subsequent abandonment, except in a few instances, in favor of home rule. The line of progress has led toward concentrated responsibility under local rather than state supervision.

This development, however, has been by no means uniform or consistent. Rather, the cities have straggled along unsymmetrically and without plan, following first

The Present State of Police Control

one path and then another, undiscouraged in attempting new courses by the previous failures of other municipalities. While, therefore, it is possible to perceive a general trend in the evolution of police control, one cannot classify the development according to sharply defined periods. The progress has been too irregular and distorted for orderly cross section analysis. Today police organizations are to be found in every stage of growth. Archaic and modern forms exist side by side in the same state and reversions to older types are often encountered. The historical survey which we have been making has shown us something of the relation and development of these forms of control. Our present task is to examine their practical working and operation in the cities in which they are now in effect.

I. STATE VERSUS MUNICIPAL CONTROL

Of the ten largest cities in the United States, the police departments of three — Boston, Baltimore, and St. Louis — are under direct state control and their heads are appointed by the state governors. Kansas City and St. Joseph in Missouri, Fall River in Massachusetts, Lewiston in Maine,[1] and a few cities and towns in New Hampshire[2] and Rhode Island[3] are under similar control. In Montgomery, Ala., the police department is administered by a board of public safety elected by the State Senate of Alabama.[4] In none of the larger of these cities does

[1] Private and Special Laws of Me., 1917, Chap. 37.
[2] Berlin, Dover, Exeter, Laconia, Manchester, Nashua, Portsmouth and Somersworth. Laws of N. H., 1913, Chap. 148.
[3] Cumberland (Acts and Resolves of R. I., 1913, Chap. 993).
[4] General Laws of Ala., 1915, Act No. 29, sec. 27.

the arrangement represent an experiment recently undertaken. It has been in effect in Baltimore, St. Louis and
Kansas City since the outbreak of the Civil War; in Boston since 1885.

The theoretical argument for state control has been
many times repeated. The police are engaged primarily
in the enforcement of laws enacted by the legislature and
intended to operate uniformly throughout the state. In
the performance of this function, therefore, they are
agents not of the municipality which hires them but of
the state whose laws they are sworn to execute. This
point has been made repeatedly by our courts. " Police
officers can in no sense be regarded as agents or servants
of the city," said the Supreme Court of Massachusetts.
" Their duties are of a public nature. Their appointment
is devolved on cities and towns by the legislature as a
convenient mode of exercising a function of government." [1] In other words, the interest of the state in
efficient police administration is vital and permanent and
its right to see that its mandates are enforced is of fundamental importance.[2]

Back of this theoretical justification of state control
lies the consideration of necessity. Officers under local
supervision have been easily reached by local influence.
State control is more detached and inaccessible and pres-

[1] Buttrick v. The City of Lowell, 1 Allen (Mass.) 172. See also
Culver v. Streator, 130 Illinois, 238, and Prather v. Lexington, 13
B. Monroe, 559. These cases are discussed by Dr. Goodnow in his
Municipal Home Rule, New York, 1906.

[2] The argument is admirably expressed in *The Control of Police,*
by A. R. Hatton, printed in Western Reserve University Bulletin,
Vol. XIII, No. 3. See also *Principles and Methods of Municipal
Administration* by William Bennett Munro, New York, 1916, pp.
268–273.

sure cannot be so immediately or directly applied. The very propinquity of the law-enforcing machinery to the people affected by its operation has often been a source of weakness. Moreover, city populations have in many cases been apathetic and contented, and municipal administrations have consequently remained in unwise and dishonest hands. Under such circumstances, anything approaching effective police arrangements has been impossible. Mismanagement and corruption have left life and property inadequately protected. The excise laws to which greater importance has generally been attached by country than by city legislative representatives have been dishonestly enforced or unenforced altogether and other sumptuary statutes have been disregarded. The state, therefore, has been obliged to supersede its derelict agents and through direct control to insure the execution of its will. Such, at least, is the argument by which those in favor of state control have supported their claims.

Successes of State Control.

That the application of this principle has in a number of instances proved successful — at least that it has brought about more satisfactory police conditions — cannot be disputed. Of this point Boston furnishes a striking example. The Boston force has recently been discredited by the unfortunate strike which terminated the careers of most of its members. It must not be forgotten, however, that for many years Boston maintained a police department, under state control, which in point of personnel and the general satisfaction which its operation afforded stood well in the lead of police organizations throughout the country. During thirty years it was practically alone among American police departments in its freedom from scandal. Particularly after the creation of single-headed management in 1906, the administration of the police force was conducted with a disregard for political considerations rarely encountered in American cities. " In my ten years of service (as commissioner) under five governors representing the two leading political parties," said the police commissioner in 1916, " I have never received from any of them a request or an intimation designed to influence my official action, through favor towards them or their friends, on any subject whatever. On the contrary, they have uniformly assured me of their desire that I should maintain the independence of judgment and conduct which was the basic condition of my acceptance of office." [1]

That such conditions could have been achieved under municipal control in Boston is difficult to believe. The city administration has for years been dominated by partisan politics and marked by many of the unhappy features too often typical of our municipal government. Under such control the police department could not have maintained the public confidence which it long enjoyed.

The condition of the Boston police force in this environment is explicable simply on the basis of the average superior quality of the state government. Whether due to a large foreign population, or some condition of civic

[1] Boston Police Department, General Order No. 1,063, June 5, 1916. Issued by Stephen O'Meara upon the completion of ten years of continual service as police commissioner.

inertia, or factors peculiarly local — whatever the cause may be — the government elected by the city of Boston has generally been below the level of the government elected by the state of Massachusetts. For many years men of larger capacity have been secured for the administration of the state than of the city. As a result, better appointments have been made to the police commissionership and political interference is less pronounced than could have been expected under local supervision. The matter centers entirely around the character of the appointing officers, and state control is acquiesced in, even with its somewhat invidious implication, because in the long run the chances seem better of electing good governors of Massachusetts than of electing good mayors in Boston.

The case is even more strikingly illustrated in connection with the police department of Fall River, in the same state, which has been under state control since 1894. Only thirteen per cent of the population of this city of 120,000 are native born of native parentage; the balance, attracted by the textile industry to which the city owes its rapid growth, is made up of French Canadians, Irish, Poles and Portuguese. Prior to 1894, under the control of the mayor and an aldermanic committee, the police department was corrupt and disorganized. Politics ran riot. Gambling dens and disorderly houses were shielded, the liquor laws were habitually violated, and the city was plagued with a disproportionate amount of crime. With a police board of able men appointed by the governor, however, under the Act of 1894, the situation was rapidly changed and for over twenty years the de-

American Police Systems

partment has been effectively administered. In spite of a forty per cent increase in population, largely foreign born, crime has been reduced below the figures of 1894;[1] disorderly houses have been eliminated; and the police force is held in public confidence to a degree rarely encountered. " I have had many pastorates in many cities," said a clergyman to the writer, " and I have never seen such a clean and orderly city as Fall River." This testimony was widely supported.

Baltimore is another city in which good results are obtained from a state-controlled police force. Since 1900, when the right to appoint police commissioners was taken from the legislature, where it had lodged for forty years, and given to the governor, the department has been in the hands of men of excellent repute. Prominent representatives of the bar and leading business men have held places on the board, and the administration of the force has been characterized by an absence of political manoeuvring and intrigue. Under such control the department has made marked progress and has gained for itself the respect and support of the citizens of Baltimore.

In this case, as in the other cases which we have cited, the merit of state control depends upon the probability of securing better appointments from the governor than can be secured from local officers. Baltimore has enjoyed the advantage of having her affairs administered by high-minded, public spirited men because the governors making these appointments have acted upon their obligation to choose the best men available for so important a task.

[1] See the annual reports of the police department for the years 1894, 1895 and 1915.

The Present State of Police Control

No guarantee exists, however, that future governors will see the obligation with equal clarity. Nothing about the present arrangement warrants the forecast that the police department of Baltimore will always be free from partisan politics. A governor could alter the situation any time he chose. A board composed of unfit men, appointed perhaps for reasons of political expediency, would shortly plunge the department into the old conditions when political expediency was its ruling principle. Similarly in Fall River a designation by the governor of commissioners unsuited for their tasks might undermine in a week the public confidence which it has taken years to establish. At best, the situation is one of chance, and the practical question which confronts these cities and others contemplating a similar form of control is whether appointments by state officers are of higher character and less attended by political considerations than appointments by local officers.

Failures of State Control.

That this question is one to which a ready answer cannot be given for all cities or even for a single city, is shown by the situation in St. Louis, where, as we have noted, state control has long been in operation. The police administration has been both good and bad, but recently more good than bad. The appointments to the police board by Governors Folk and Hadley ten years ago were particularly creditable, and hard, conscientious work was done to make the organization effective. Prior to 1905, however, under exactly the same method of control, a far different situation existed. The Democratic boss of the city was president of the board. Two of his fellow commissioners were brewers. The city was wide open and corruption and politics ruled the department. Citizens of outlying counties without qualification or merit were placed on the force through the influence of the governor. The police were the tools by which victory was enforced at the polls. In the investigation by the prosecuting attorney which marked the end of the notorious "Hawes board," four police officers committed suicide rather than face the results of their acts.[1] In other words, ten to fifteen years ago state control in St. Louis was a complete failure. Obviously, the explanation must lie in the changing character of the state government. Police administration under state control encounters the same pitfalls as under municipal control. The ideals and wisdom of the governor or mayor determine the level of the administration.

Another example may illuminate the point. Probably no large police department in the country is so permeated with politics, and consequently so demoralized, as the department in Kansas City, Missouri, where state control has been in effect for over fifty years. Always an adjunct to the political party in power, the police boards appointed for this city by the various governors have been strictly partisan in character — sometimes fairly good, never first class, often downright bad. The department has for years been the center of the perennial feud existing between the two factions of the local Democratic party. The chief, with the backing of the gover-

---

[1] See speech of ex-Governor Joseph W. Folk before the City Club of St. Louis, printed in the St. Louis *Star*, December 19, 1912.

nor, is often the creature of one faction, while the board with its constantly shifting personnel is often representative of the other. The various governors, out of touch and out of sympathy with local conditions, have assumed no positive leadership, with the result that the rank and file of the force have aligned themselves with one of the two political " bosses " whose backing seemed to promise the greater security. Under such conditions demoralization has been wide-spread.

Similarly in St. Joseph, Missouri, a city of 77,000 population, state control of the police force has been attended with unhappy results. At the time of my visit, the board appointed by the governor consisted of a dentist, a baker and a lawyer, and the department was the creature of the dominant political faction. With no civil service system the appointments to the force were notorious, and suspicions existed of more serious conditions. Two of the commissioners were under indictment by a grand jury for oppression and malfeasance in office; [1] and the charge was openly made that licenses were withheld from saloons whose proprietors criticised the governor or the political party he represented, and that breweries were forbidden to advertise in a newspaper antagonistic to the department, under penalty of drastic action against the saloons which they controlled.

State control as a supervisory method possesses no inherent superiority. Without relation to the quality of the state government it guarantees nothing in the way of effectiveness. As a bare arrangement of organization it

[1] These indictments were subsequently quashed, but the commissioners in question were later removed from office.

contains no greater promise of integrity than municipal control. The efficiency or inefficiency of a police force depends largely — one might almost say exclusively — upon the character and ability of the men who run it, and governors, like mayors, can make bad appointments. If this were the only angle from which the subject could be approached, therefore, the problem would involve, as I have pointed out, merely the determination in a given state of the source from which better appointments could in the long run be reasonably expected.

State Control in Relation to Home Rule Problems.

The problem, however, is not so easily disposed of. Indeed, it is vastly complicated by the troublesome questions involved in the principle of local self government. The inevitable friction and discord arising from a situation in which the public functions of a community are partly under state and partly under local control; the conception of absentee management and responsibility implied in a system of state supervision; the requisition by state authorities of funds raised by municipal taxation without vote or check on the part of local officers; the invidious inference attaching to state-controlled police that in respect to this one function at least the people of a locality are unfit to govern themselves — considerations of this kind, often more intangible than practical, must be carefully weighed even against the efficient results which state management may in some instances make possible.

Many of these considerations, which militate against the public satisfaction that state control of police is in

The Present State of Police Control

some quarters expected to afford, are bound up in the question of finance. In establishing metropolitan police systems the legislatures have generally found it necessary to make the requisitions of the state appointed police executives mandatory upon the local councils. Otherwise by refusing to grant funds or by granting them in insufficient amounts the communities might nullify the purpose and operation of the acts. Thus in St. Louis the law provides that the board of police commissioners appointed by the governor shall annually prepare and certify to the municipal assembly an estimate of monies necessary for the ensuing year and the latter body is " hereby required to set apart and appropriate the amount so certified, payable out of the revenue of said city." [1] Any member of the municipal assembly resisting the enforcement of this provision is liable to a penalty of $1,000, and may further be disqualified " forever " from " holding or exercising any office or employment under the mayor or municipal assembly." [2] Similarly, in Baltimore the board of police commissioners appointed by the governor makes an estimate of expense for the current fiscal year and certifies it to the mayor and city council, " who are required without delay specifically to assess and levy such amount as shall be sufficient to raise the same, clear of all expenses and discounts, upon all the assessable property of the City of Baltimore." [3] To cover in-

[1] Laws of Mo., 1899, p. 57, Sec. 13.
[2] *Ibid.*, Sec. 14. This provision was inserted in the law to prevent the practice of members of the municipal assembly of holding up the police appropriation while they bargained with the commissioners for " jobs " for their henchmen.
[3] Laws of Md., 1898, Chap. 123, Sec. 747.

sufficient estimates the police board is empowered to issue certificates of indebtedness not to exceed $50,000 in any one year, the amounts of which are added to the municipal tax levy for the year next ensuing.[1] In Boston, where the police commissioner is also appointed by the governor, the law provides that all the expenses of the department shall be paid by the city " upon the requisition of said police commissioner." [2] In Kansas City under similar arrangements the common council is obliged to set aside, as its initial appropriation, the amount of money asked for by the police board. Additional expenditures for extra police work, unforeseen at the time of the first estimate, must be granted by the municipal authorities as requested by the board.[3]

The effect of these acts, to be sure, is often tempered by further provisions fixing the approximate numbers to be employed in each rank of the police force, so that a state-appointed police executive can not arbitrarily add to the municipal budget by greatly extending his department. In Boston, indeed, the commissioner may not employ additional patrolmen, " except as authorized by the mayor," nor may the salaries of the force be increased except by the concurrent action of the mayor and commissioner.[4] There still remains, however, a large margin of expense, over and above the mere salary budget, the necessity for which is not debatable by local fiscal officers, but rests entirely in the discretion of men in no way responsible to the municipal government.

[1] Laws of Md., 1898, Chap. 123, Sec. 747.
[2] Acts of Mass., 1906, Chap. 291, Sec. 8.
[3] Laws of Mo., p. 68, Secs. 15–16.
[4] Acts of Mass., 1906, Chap. 291, Sec. 13.

The Present State of Police Control

Such a situation inevitably breeds resentment and even bitterness. Other city departments must take their chances in their requests for funds; their appeals must be weighed with other appeals and the issue settled on the basis of comparative urgency. The police estimates alone go unchallenged. As a result, health, charity, public works and a score of other municipal functions are subordinated to the unquestioned and unanalyzed needs of the police. In St. Louis considerable feeling on this point has frequently developed. In 1899 the common council refused to pay the claims of the police board involving the salaries of extra policemen until forced by a decision of the Supreme Court.[1] In Boston, in 1914, the police commissioner successfully defied the mayor and the Finance Commission in a contest over increased rates of pay for officers of rank. The increases in question had been made on the basis of a small unappropriated balance in the remaining days of the former city administration, and the new mayor's appeal to the commissioner to consent to a restoration of the former rates of pay so as not to impair the efficiency of other branches of the municipal service was disregarded on the ground that such a step would work injury to the morale of his department.[2] Whatever the merit of the commissioner's position, it served not only to emphasize the lack of unity in the governmental functions of Boston but to throw into relief the rankling implication of the law that in respect to the man-

[1] 153 Mo. 23: People *ex rel.* Hawes *v.* Mason. The entire police force went without pay for three months while the case was in the courts.
[2] The reports dealing with this case are printed in the annual report of the Boston police department for 1914.

agement of the police force the citizens of Boston must be protected against themselves. Fuel such as this keeps home rule agitation continually smoldering.

The financial detachment of state-controlled police forces shows in their expenditures. In the cities in which such control exists, a larger proportion of the municipal budget is given to the police departments than in cities of the same class in which the police are under local management. This fact is shown by a comparison of the ratio of police cost to total municipal cost, in St. Louis and in Philadelphia, the city next larger in size. In the former city in 1915, 14.8% of the annual municipal appropriation, exclusive of public service enterprises, went for police purposes; in the latter, with a population nearly a million greater and hence with police functions relatively more complex and expensive, 13.8% of the budget was devoted to the police during the same period.[1] Similar comparisons for the years 1910, 1911 and 1912 bear out the same divergence.[2] Equal results are obtained by comparing ratios of cost in Boston and Baltimore on the one hand, representing state-controlled police forces, with Cleveland and Pittsburgh on the other, representing municipally controlled police forces. The latter cities are chosen because in population they most closely approximate the former. The following table embodies the fiscal year of 1915:

[1] Figures obtained from the U. S. Census publication, " Financial statistics of cities having a population of over 30,000 — 1915." New York and Chicago, because of their vast size, cannot fairly be compared with St. Louis. The same remark holds true of the smaller cities. It is obvious that the larger the city the greater must be the relative cost for police purposes.

[2] Figures for 1913 and 1914 are not obtainable.

The Present State of Police Control

	City	Population	Ratio of police cost to total municipal cost [1]
State Police	Boston ...	734,747	11.3%
	Baltimore .	579,590	13.
Municipal Police	Cleveland .	639,431	9.2
	Pittsburgh .	564,878	7.8

The comparatively greater expense of state-controlled police forces is shown by an examination of the costs per capita of population, as follows: [2]

	City	Cost per capita of population
State Police	St. Louis	2.90
	Boston	3.47
	Baltimore	2.20
Municipal Police	Philadelphia	2.68
	Cleveland	1.59
	Pittsburgh	1.78

If figures were lacking, the superior material equipment of the police departments of St. Louis and Baltimore would substantiate the point that more money is spent by a city for police under state control than under municipal control. In the former city particularly, the physical property of the department is indicative of uncramped financial conditions. The station houses are models of their kind, splendidly built and equipped. The headquarters building is perhaps the most complete in America; and throughout there is every evidence that

[1] Figures obtained from the U. S. Census publication, "Financial statistics of cities having a population of over 30,000 — 1915."
[2] *Ibid.*

133

the department has not been obliged to compete with other departments in a scramble for funds. What the police want they are legally bound to obtain. " For four years," said a former member of the municipal council of St. Louis, " I was obliged by law to vote unquestioningly the requisitions of the police board. We had to cut down on health, on parks, and on public improvements. For the sake of economy we slashed a hundred public needs that should never have been slashed. But our economy measures could not touch the police department." [1]

That under such circumstances home rule sentiment smolders constantly beneath the surface is scarcely to be wondered at. Of the four large cities with state-controlled police, Boston is perhaps most committed to the plan. Even the recent police strike apparently did not shake her faith in this method of management, which has become too firmly established in public estimation to be easily overthrown. " It 's a habit," said a prominent citizen of Boston. " We are used to it and it *works*." The same opinion was encountered in Baltimore. In St. Louis and Kansas City, on the other hand, dissatisfaction

[1] Personally communicated. That larger expenditure inevitably follows state-controlled police departments is shown in the experience of German cities. When the burgomasters and local authorities are in control, economy is the guiding rule because of the immediate presence of the taxpayers. Economy is not, however, so pressing a matter with the officials of a state-controlled force, for the taxpayers are far removed from the scene of action and the incentive is not so direct or compelling. In Saxony, for example, Dresden annually spends 20% more for its state police force than Leipzig does for its municipal force, although the population of Leipzig is larger by 40,000. For further discussion see *European Police Systems*, pp. 72–73 ff.

is continually expressed, and the feeling for home rule will not down. In St. Louis, indeed, in 1914, a home rule police bill, passed by the legislature and submitted to the entire state on referendum, received in the city a majority of 7,000 votes, although in the remainder of the state the measure was buried under an avalanche of 175,000. The Democratic rural districts of Missouri are suspicious of any bill conferring larger powers on the Republican cities. The situation is complicated, too, by the fact that the home rule movement, at least in St. Louis, has not been discussed from the point of view of more effective enforcement of law and the selection of better police officials. It has been largely a protest, more or less sentimentally founded, against rural domination. Oftentimes, too — as in the case of the 1914 measure — home rule has been merely a partisan movement, decorated to attract the unwary, and engineered by special interests. " Last summer when these measures were first proposed," said ex-Governor Folk in an address before the City Club of St. Louis on the home rule police bills, " it was freely stated in the public press that the object was to make St. Louis a wide-open city. Without imputing these motives to those who now advocate these measures, I believe it is clear that they were born of that desire." [1] In the struggle which culminated in the final overthrow of the proposition at the polls, St. Louis was treated to the spectacle of the better civic elements of the city fighting the home rule which theoretically at least they approved, while the brewery interests were listed as its

[1] Quoted in the St. Louis *Star*, Dec. 19, 1912.

chief champions. " Real home rule and not brewery rule — this is the issue," said ex-Governor Folk.[1]

The Applicability of State Control.

In the last analysis the choice between state and municipal control as a method of police administration can be made only in the light of local conditions. Not only must the comparative average quality of the state and the municipal government be considered, but the genuineness and extent of the demand for home rule — however vaguely conceived — must enter into the solution as an indispensable element. Popular content or discontent is, in a democracy, of all forms of government, a factor of vital significance. A city accustomed to its own management in matters relating to its own well-being cannot readily be saddled with a form of exterior control. Moreover, the feeling of irresponsibility for police conditions, often bred in the local citizenship as a result of such absentee management, is a hurt not ordinarily compensated by any possible advantage in the greater efficiency of the force. Indeed, one might go so far as to say that only serious conditions of demoralization, denoting not only present but future inability effectively to manage its police department, would initially justify a state in superseding the police arrangements of a given city. On the other hand, he would be a hasty critic who would advise Boston or Baltimore to return to municipal control. The present method of police organization in those cities has been tested practically. The adjustment of public opinion has been made. The arrangement now

[1] *Ibid.*

meets with fairly constant popular support. To root it out merely to satisfy some abstract ideal of local self government would be the course of unwisdom.

Cities, like men, are shaped and controlled by different combinations of psychological and material circumstances. Only through the appreciation of its own special tastes and needs can a local government find its most effective form.

II. BOARD CONTROL VS. SINGLE-HEADED CONTROL

Of the 63 cities of the United States whose populations, according to the census estimates of 1915, exceed 100,000 seventeen have their police organizations under the control of boards of police commissioners or boards of public safety. The police departments of the remaining cities are under single-headed management, either commissioners or chiefs appointed by local or state authority, or in the somewhat anomalous guise of the commission form of government. The principal cities in which police boards are found are St. Louis, Baltimore, Los Angeles, San Francisco, Milwaukee, New Orleans, Kansas City, Indianapolis, Providence, Louisville, and Atlanta.[1] Single-headed police control is found in New York, Chicago, Philadelphia, Boston, Cleveland, Pittsburgh, Detroit, Buffalo, Newark, Cincinnati, Minneapolis, Seattle, Jersey City, and Portland, Oregon.[2]

[1] The other cities of the 63 over 100,000 population which have police boards are as follows: New Haven, Paterson, Fall River, Bridgeport, Hartford, Springfield (Mass.).
[2] The other cities of the 63 over 100,000 population which have single-headed management are as follows: Washington, Denver, Rochester, St. Paul, Columbus, Oakland, Toledo, Birmingham, Omaha, Worcester, Richmond, Syracuse, Spokane, Memphis, Scran-

American Police Systems

The boards of police commissioners vary widely as to source of appointment, size and functions. In St. Louis, Baltimore and Kansas City, as we have seen, the boards are appointed by the governors of the respective states; in other cases they are appointed by local authority, generally the mayor, with or without the confirmation of the common council. Often the mayor is himself *ex officio* an officer of the board. In Atlanta and other southern cities the board members are elected by the municipal council, one member being chosen from each of the wards into which the cities are divided.[1] New Orleans curiously combines a police board with a commission form of government, the board consisting of the mayor, the commissioner of public safety and a civilian member elected by the commission.[2] The size of the boards in the different cities varies from three members, as in Kansas City, Indianapolis, Baltimore, Los Angeles, Louisville and Providence, to twelve members in Atlanta.[3] St. Louis and San Francisco have boards of four; Milwaukee, a board of five; New Haven, a board of six.

The police boards are for the most part charged with complete responsibility for the enforcement of law. Most of them, too, are given full powers over the departments which they control, including the right, under oc-

ton, Grand Rapids, Dallas, San Antonio, Dayton, Salt Lake City, New Bedford, Nashville, Tacoma, Houston, Cambridge, Trenton, Lowell, Youngstown, Reading, Albany, Camden, Lynn. This list includes commission governed cities.

[1] See Laws of Ga., 1908, Part III, Title I.

[2] Laws of La., 912, No. 159.

[3] In Kansas City and Los Angeles the membership of three is inclusive of the mayor *ex officio*. In Atlanta the mayor and chairman of the police committee of the council are *ex officio* members of the board of twelve.

casional civil service restrictions, of appointment and dismissal of members of the force. This is true of such
cities as St. Louis, Baltimore, Indianapolis and Louisville. There are, however, one or two notable exceptions.
In Los Angeles the chief of police is appointed and removed not by the police board but by the mayor. Further — in the words of the act — " the chief of police
shall have the supervision and control of the police force
of the city and in that connection he shall be subject only
to the orders of the mayor." [1] As a result the board is
little more than an advisory body. [2] Because it has no
control over the chief it lacks contact with the department
and is obliged to confine itself to such perfunctory duties
as the issuance of licenses. In Milwaukee the police
board [3] is given no administrative powers whatever.
Indeed, it has little to do with the police department except to appoint the chief — and if necessary remove him
under charges reviewable by the courts — and act as a
civil service commission for the appointment and promotion of officers in the department. Having once appointed a suitable chief, it has no responsibility for the
enforcement of law. All powers as regards discipline,
transfer and removal are lodged exclusively with the
chief. [4] Even in financial matters the board has no functions whatever. In making up the departmental budget
the chief deals directly with the municipal council without the intervention either of the mayor or the police

[1] Los Angeles Charter as amended April, 1913, Sec. 53.
[2] The anomaly is accentuated by the fact that the police surgeon
is appointed by the common council.
[3] Called Board of Fire and Police Commissioners.
[4] In cases of actual removal, police officers may take an appeal to
the board of commissioners.

board. Further, he makes all rules governing the conduct of his force and is given " custody and control of all public property pertaining to said department and everything connected therewith and belonging thereto." [1] Throughout the act and in its operation emphasis is laid upon the conception of the chief as the " head " of the department, responsible to the public for its efficiency and general good conduct, while the board is relegated to a relatively obscure and insignificant position.

The Weaknesses of Board Control.

This curious arrangement in Los Angeles and Milwaukee, by which a board is created and then shorn of its powers, represents an attempt — crude, perhaps, and clumsily put into operation — to protect the police department against the excesses of board control. As was pointed out in the last chapter, police boards were established, not because they were fitted for police administration, but because the board system was supposed to be the proper form of municipal government. Los Angeles and Milwaukee, therefore, with the difficulties of other cities in mind, have erected bulwarks against possible abuses by their police boards, although they have somewhat naively accepted them as essential parts of their police machinery.

That the fears of these cities are justified not only by the history of past boards but by present conditions in municipalities which retain this form of control is obvious to any student. With the exception of Baltimore, where the high character of the appointees has often out-

[1] Laws of Wis., 1911, Chap. 586, Sec. 23.

weighed the inherent ineffectiveness of board management, most of the cities in the United States with police boards are experiencing difficulties traceable to no other source than the decentralization of authority which that form of control inevitably tends to develop.[1] The absence of individualized responsibility, the ready excuse with which a single member can shift blame for joint failure or neglect, the sense of protection furnished by mere corporate entity — these factors create an atmosphere in which shiftlessness is encouraged and personal rather than public ends are easily served. Even in Baltimore, among the members themselves of present and past boards, there is no little sentiment for single-headed management. " No business would attempt to conduct its affairs under the supervision of three heads of equal power," said one of the commissioners. Said another: " For the money spent on this board we could obtain the services of an excellent administrator who could give his entire time to the direction of the department and the study of its problems. Wherever we three commissioners have accomplished good results, one man might have done even better." [2]

Board Administration a Part-time Task.

This suggests one of the practical objections to board administration even at its best. It is a part-time task. Three or four estimable citizens, preoccupied with their own affairs, are asked to devote some fraction of their

[1] New Haven and Fall River should perhaps be mentioned with Baltimore as noteworthy exceptions to the general rule.
[2] Personally communicated. The members of this board have since been superseded.

attention to the management of an enterprise with which, except through newspapers, they have had no previous acquaintance. Often their acceptance of the appointment is conditioned upon the understanding that they will not be called upon to give more than a specific amount of time — perhaps only to attend board meetings. Otherwise commissioners of adequate calibre could not be obtained. With no appreciation of the fact that police management is a highly specialized business demanding an intimate and often technical knowledge of matters not common to other enterprises, the commissioners attempt, with the help of the clerks whom they find at headquarters but without really expert advice, to exercise some form of control. In most cases such control consists solely in the disposal of routine matters, such as appointments, transfers, and disciplinary trials at the stated meetings of the board. Policies looking toward the increased efficiency of the department, and the extension of its usefulness as an instrument of public good, are neglected. Indeed, they are not. thought of. The commissioners have no time to exercise the same degree and quality of initiative and imagination that would be necessary in the successful operation of a private business. Technical questions relating to the proper organization of a detective bureau, to the policy to be followed in the identification of criminals, to the method of determining the comparative efficiency of members of the uniformed force, are passed over without consideration, either because the board members have not had time to think of them, or because they do not feel themselves competent to pass upon them. The chief of the department, coming from the ranks, is seldom gifted with constructive ability; and in the absence of other expert advice no progressive steps are taken. In some cases the board does not meet often enough to give even routine matters more than a superficial and perfunctory oversight. In St. Louis and San Francisco it meets once a week; in New Haven and Paterson, twice a month.[1] Under such circumstances it is impossible for the commissioners to contribute anything of real value to a progressive management of the force. Of the many police commissioners whom I met and talked with, from California to Maine, scarcely half a dozen showed any thorough grasp either of the technique of police business or of the principles underlying the effective management of a police force. Indeed, in most cases they made no pretense of knowledge. They were very busy men, who devoted such spare moments as they could wrench from their own affairs to the more or less thankless task of "looking after" the police department. Their conception of police administration, often frankly expressed, was merely to maintain the *status quo* of things as they found them.

Lack of Unity in Board Administration.

Another difficulty attends the board form of management even at its best. The inevitable lack of unity in its

---

[1] The laws regulating some of the police departments obviously contemplate only a part-time participancy by the commissioners. In San Francisco, Los Angeles, and Kansas City they are obliged to meet "at least once a week." (San Francisco Charter, Art. VIII, Chap. II, Sec. 4; Los Angeles Charter, Sec. 96; Laws of Mo., 1899, p. 65.) The Atlanta ordinances provide that the board "shall hold a stated meeting each month and such other meetings as the public interest may from time to time require." (Ordinances of Atlanta, Sec. 400.)

opinions and decisions curtails its effectiveness as an administrative instrument. " We were so split in our interests and enthusiasms," said a former board member of a large city in explaining the disruption of a really excellent administration in which he had served, "that we never really centered on anything. I was interested, for example, in traffic regulation, but the other two members cared little about it. When the superintendent (chief) saw how we were divided he did nothing." [1] Such a situation is the logical result of a multiple-headed executive. The lack of decisiveness creates an uncertainty in the uniformed force, and the fear of offending either party results in a policy of inaction. Moreover, the diverse membership of the board affords an opportunity, seldom overlooked by the force, to interest individual commissioners, either through their own efforts or the efforts of their friends, political and otherwise, in their grievances and claims. This gives rise to a situation in which, in the absence of any definite policy or standard, the recommendations of a commissioner are apt to be accepted by the board without reference to other claims of perhaps equal merit, on the principle of " courtesy " so often enunciated in legislative bodies. A commissioner voting against the recommendation of another member might find his own suggestions vetoed at a future date.

Occasionally disagreements within the board produce results almost ludicrous. In the trial of two sergeants in Kansas City before the police board in 1915, one commissioner admitted certain questions in evidence which

[1] Personally communicated.

the other commissioner declined to admit. The proceedings degenerated into an acrimonious wrangle.[1] During the Ruef-Schmitz regime in San Francisco in 1905, the police board stood two to two on the question of licensing the notorious " French Restaurants," and Schmitz was unable to put through his vicious plans until he had removed one of the members. Before the recent change in Newark to commission government, the police board was deadlocked for many months over the appointment of an inspector and the question of recommending an increase in the force. Indeed, the " deadlock " has been characteristic of many boards throughout the country, particularly those with membership of even numbers. But even in those with odd numbers, the objections of the minority have often produced confusion and delay, and the departments have suffered from lack of definite leadership.

Conflict of Authority in Board Administration.

Another difficulty to which the police board lends itself is even more serious. The members of a board, in the absence of definite administrative plans, are continually tempted to encroach upon the proper functions of the chief. The theory of the board form of management, whether in business or government, is that it creates a deliberative council, presumably representative of various points of view, concerned primarily with policies of operation and procedure and the maintenance of general regulative oversight. In the application of its rules and policies to specific cases it has no direct or immediate in-

[1] Kansas City *Star*, January 30, 1915.

terest. These things are matters of detail for which its business executive or superintendent is solely responsible. This distinction in function between a deliberative or regulative body and its executive arm furnishes the only possible justification for the existence of a board. Without it nothing is left but an uncoordinated executive of many heads. When, therefore, a police board infringes upon the proper activities of the chief and attempts itself to handle the detail of administration, it undermines its only basis of support.

Unfortunately, most of the police boards in the United States are in this situation. Neither in law nor in practice has their true function been defined. Indeed, the laws have often loaded the boards with duties which by no process of reasoning can properly belong to any deliberative body. Even in those departments in which the prescriptions of laws and ordinances are not definite or detailed there is little attempt at clear-cut differentiation, and the distinction between the board's duties and the chief's duties is a vague, uncertain line, varying from week to week and even from day to day, dependent largely upon the activity and attention of the commissioners and their interest in particular cases. Often the chief's proper functions are deliberately raided by the board because, ignorant of the formulation of constructive policies or the principles of administration, it hastens to lay hands upon certain routine affairs whose nature it understands. While holding the chief responsible for the management of the department, it nevertheless appropriates enough of his functions to render him practically powerless. The most trivial details of police business come before it for determination. It spends hours in deciding whether a given patrolman was off his beat as charged by his sergeant. It will take days to determine whether the chief's recommendation for the dismissal of a drunken officer is justified. Most of its time is given to the consideration of details that would not be considered for a moment by the board of directors of a business concern. In some cities the police boards so far usurp the functions of the chief that they even exclude him from their deliberations, as if what they did with his men was none of his affair. In Newark, during the life of the board, it handled all transfers, promotions, and special assignments of policemen, occasionally without the knowledge, often without the recommendation, of the chief of police.[1] A situation largely similar prevails in other municipalities, notably in Kansas City. "I am not consulted on such matters," said the chief of police of an important southern city in talking to me confidentially of his work. "I hear of the orders of the commission through the secretary of the board. I have very little to do. The board decides all."[2]

This frank statement is significant of a wide-spread condition. There are but few chiefs in the United States serving under a board, who will not in confidential moments admit the continual interference on the part of board members in matters properly within the functions of the uniformed force. "I really do not know what my duties are," said the chief of a large city. "On paper I have a great many, but most of them are per-

[1] Personally communicated.
[2] *Ibid.*

147

formed by the board." [1]   So flagrant did this situation
become in Atlanta that the following ordinance — more
forceful than grammatical — was passed by the general
council: "The board shall discharge hereafter the
duties of an administrative board and shall not be permitted nor shall they designate any of their members to
carry out the orders or direction of the board as to matters over and about which the city has selected officers or
patrolmen to cover or perform, and compensates them
therefor." [2]   This failing to correct the evil, another
ordinance was passed to the effect that the head of the
police department (meaning the chief) "shall be not
only the nominal but the actual executive head." [3]   Even
this ordinance had little result.   At the time of my visit
to Atlanta the board was attempting to determine what
disorderly houses should be raided and what clubs closed.

The police boards of the United States have practically
ceased to be deliberative, policy-forming bodies, if indeed they ever were.   The difficulty of drawing practical
lines of differentiation, the mandatory provisions of the
law, and above all, the limited scope for the deliberative
function in police administration, have driven them into
other fields, and they perforce have become simply multiple-headed executives.   In some cases, undoubtedly this
is what the law intended them to be.   It is, moreover,
their true status as many people conceive it.   Indeed, if
the boards did not usurp some of the proper duties of
their chiefs they would have little to do.   For police

[1] Personally communicated.
[2] Ordinances of Atlanta (Compilation of 1910), No. 1,931.
[3] Ordinance of June 2, 1913.

management, as I have previously pointed out, is a matter not so much of deliberation as of initiative, decisiveness, and vigor. There are but few broad general policies arising and none that one responsible man cannot determine. There is little need of a council to consider and discuss. Even the judicial aspects of the board's work, the trial of offenses and the determination of punishments, can be handled by the head of the department, as in Milwaukee, or by a disciplinary tribunal within the force itself, as in Boston and elsewhere. This function alone does not justify the existence of a separate administrative body. In brief, a board, unless scrupulously limited in its function, is a fifth wheel, an incumbrance rather than a help. The essential qualities in police administration are those which a single-headed executive can best bring to the task.

Politics and Board Administration.

Thus far I have spoken of the operation of the police board at its best — on the supposition that with all its inherent administrative weaknesses its personnel represented the ablest citizens obtainable. Unfortunately, except in a few cities, this supposition is without foundation in fact. Because of its multiple membership the board seems to lend itself peculiarly to the unhappy incidents of American municipal politics. " Give him a place on the police board. Any harm that he can do will be counterbalanced by the other members." This principle has led to more than one evil appointment, even by executives above the usual average. One can go through the list of commissioners of all the board-controlled de-

partments and find but few who on the basis of education and general ability alone, not to mention technical
qualifications, are even moderately fitted for the task.
Too often, indeed, the boards are composed of political
hacks to whom the post is a " job," bestowed without regard for fitness, as a reward for party service.   In some
cities appointments of such a character constitute an established tradition, supported by a public opinion apathetic
and quiescent.   " Police business is nothing but politics
anyway," said a cynical citizen of Kansas City when I
expressed amazement at the unperturbed public attitude
with which the political appointments to the police board
were received.   A furniture dealer who subsequently
used his position to advertise his private business and a
" personal appointee " of the governor, allied with one
of the warring political factions — this was the police
board unquestioningly accepted by the citizens of Kansas
City because it seemed neither better nor worse than its
predecessors.   It was barely ten years ago in San Francisco that the president of the police board was one of
the Democratic bosses of the city, a saloon-keeper by profession, whose principal official act was " to open up the
town," so that San Francisco might become " the Paris
of America."   Even today, politics plays no little part in
the constitution of San Francisco's police board.   St.
Louis, as we have already seen, has suffered severely
from the character of its police administrators, and the
" spoils " idea has too often marked the appointments.
In recent years there has been considerable improvement
in this city, but as late as 1916 an attempt was made by the

governor to appoint as commissioner a man previously convicted of murder.

Elective Boards.

Conditions appear even more discouraging when, as in Atlanta and other southern cities, the police boards are elected by the common councils rather than appointed by executive authority.[1] In the latter contingency there is at least the hope, justified by occasional experience, that a governor or mayor will act upon his public obligation to appoint effective and intelligent police commissioners. In the former contingency there is no such hope, for the very method of selection, at least in the present stage of municipal development, vitiates the results. In Atlanta, as I have already pointed out, the members of the police board, to the number of twelve, are elected on the basis of district representation, one member from each of the wards into which the city is divided. The practice is for the two councilmen and the alderman from each ward to agree upon a candidate for police commissioner. The nomination is thereupon accepted by the general council without debate or discussion, because the representatives of the other wards wish the same privilege of choosing their candidates. Until recently, similar arrangements were in vogue in Richmond (Va.). While no such definite understanding existed, the elections to the police board were purely matters of ward politics, in which the man who had the most friends and could command the largest number of votes won the place.

[1] This is true in Durham, N. C., Greenville, S. C., and Macon, Ga.

151

This method of selection is based upon certain confused analogies which are not without defenders in some quarters in the cities above mentioned and elsewhere: first, that ward representation on the police board is desirable because ours is a representative government; and second, that election rather than appointment to a police board is in accordance with democratic principles. Municipal government in the United States has been wrecked by adherence to analogies of this kind. In the same class is the idea that city councils must be bicameral because the legislative branch of the federal government is bicameral, and that the town fathers must have the right to veto the appointments of the mayor because the consent of the United States Senate is necessary to the appointments of the president. In framing these analogies little thought has been given to the distinction in function between federal and municipal government. The former was organized primarily with a view to legislative efficiency; the latter is a matter of administrative efficiency. The peculiar activities of a city, involving the guardianship, health and education of a population stratified by racial, economic and religious lines, while compressed within narrow geographical limits, present a unique governmental problem comparable only to a limited degree with the problem of national organization. The test of a form of government to be applied to such a situation is its serviceability and not its resemblance to forms adapted to other purposes. The question to be asked is not whether it adheres to an eighteenth century political ideal, but *does it work?*

Under such a test as this, a police board of ward representatives becomes an absurdity. Instead of serving the interests of efficient police organization the boards of Atlanta and other southern cities serve the interests of ward politics, with all the elements of barter and trade which such an arrangement involves. Some years ago in Richmond the board passed a resolution under which appointments to the force were distributed evenly among the wards, each commissioner taking his turn (arranged on a basis of seniority in service with the board!) in naming his candidate. This resolution was later rescinded and not even a gentleman's agreement took its place. " They scrap it out among themselves," said one of the officials of the board, " each commissioner fighting for the candidates from his own ward." [1] In Atlanta, in 1914, against the bitter opposition of the chief, the police board reinstated three patrolmen who had been dismissed, one for habitual drunkenness, one for assaulting a citizen while drunk, and one for entering a house of assignation while drunk.[2] The only explanation for this step which I could obtain was that the three officers in question " had put the matter up to their ward representatives on the board and had been taken care of." Other examples of this kind were brought to my attention in both Atlanta and elsewhere.

When the elective method of choosing police commissioners is added to ward representation on the board, the results are peculiarly disastrous. In the scramble for office, ideas of administrative experience or personal fit-

[1] Personally communicated.
[2] So bitter was the opposition of the chief that the board put him out of the meeting before taking action. The chief was later dismissed on charges preferred by the board.

ness, not to mention expert service, are forgotten. The issue becomes a matter of " influence " and " trade " or is smothered by some larger political question. For years the boards of Atlanta and elsewhere have too largely represented not only less desirable but occasionally vicious elements. The better class of citizens holds itself aloof from the sordid give and take of ward politics, and the police department is consequently abandoned to those who want it. At the time of my visit to Atlanta and Richmond the police boards of the two cities were under grave suspicion. It was charged that one member was interested in the cigar business which had the contract for tobacco with the disorderly houses, and that another was the agent for the liquor concern that supplied these houses with liquor. One member had been warned by the courts for gambling; one had been under indictment for immorality and cruelty; another had at one time operated a bar-room; another engaged in the small-loan business and was known as a " loan shark "; against two others the charge was openly made that they were financially interested in houses of prostitution. These men had been chosen by a so-called " democratic " method to administer the police departments, and in both cities good citizens were asking why their police affairs should be so continually in a tangle!

Bi-partisan Boards.

Results equally unhappy if not so demoralizing are often found when boards are constituted on the bi-partisan principle.[1] This principle, as we have seen, is based

[1] Bi-partisan police boards are legally required in Baltimore, San

The Present State of Police Control

on the theory that the action of two opposing forces will create a sort of neutral zone favorable to the development of an adequate brand of administration. It is an elaborated check and balance system that sets one group of party representatives to watch another. The groups may be equal in strength, as in San Francisco, where the board is composed of an even number; or they may be unequal in strength, as in Baltimore, Fall River, and Indianapolis, where there are boards of three. In either case, the administration of the police department tends to become a matter of bargain and trade, and further, in odd-numbered boards, the minority is often ruthlessly overridden and the very purpose of the arrangement vitiated. In this latter case the results are apt to be peculiarly deplorable to the service, because the board members who have seized the reins have been chosen not because they were expert administrators but because they were party representatives.

The anomaly of the bi-partisan board as a scheme of administration is shown in the very laws creating it. Elaborate and often highly technical provisions are written into the statutes to keep the police department out of politics, while in the same paragraphs the commissioners are drafted from the political parties whose influence the law is avowedly attempting to destroy. Thus, in Baltimore the charter provides that the commissioners shall take oath before the Judge of the Superior Court that they " will in no case and under no pretext appoint, promote,

Francisco, Milwaukee, Indianapolis, New Haven, Fall River, and Bridgeport. Occasionally the principle is followed in other cities, on the basis of some political understanding or otherwise.

reduce in rank or remove any policeman or officer of police or detective, or any other person under them, for or on account of the political opinions or affiliations of such policeman, officer, detective, or other person, or for any other cause or reason than the fitness or unfitness of such person." [1] In the same section of the law it is provided that " two of said commissioners shall always be adherents of the two leading political parties of the state, one of each of said parties." [2] Similar provisions appear in other charters, and out of the attempt to make the contradiction work grow some of the most serious evils of board management.

Until it was recently abolished Newark's police board furnished perhaps the best example of the practical operation of the bi-partisan principle. It was composed of two Democrats and two Republicans, appointed by the mayor, with the consent of the city council. At the time of my first visit to the Newark department [3] the board consisted of a photographer, an architect, a contractor for steamheating plants, and an employee of a telephone company. This board had appointed as its administrative secretary an attache of a bowling alley. From the very first the board was deadlocked on matters of current business. For example, the rank of inspector in the uniformed force was created, and pending a civil service examination a Republican police captain was appointed *pro tem*. When the examination was held a Democratic captain headed the list, the Republican captain in question standing third. The Republicans on the board insisted

[1] Baltimore Charter, Revised Edition, 1915, Sec. 740.
[2] *Ibid.*
[3] In October, 1916.

on passing the first two names on the list and appointing
their own party man.   The Democrats, on the other hand,
with their belief in civil service principles stimulated by
visions of a Democratic inspector, refused to accede to
this plan, and the post was unfilled for over a year.   Ultimately the deadlock was broken by creating two places
and appointing both inspectors.   Again, the Democratic
commissioners estimated that twenty-five additional policemen were needed on the force.   This was agreed to
by the board as a whole and the necessary civil service
examinations were held.   When the matter had reached
the stage of appointments, however, the Republican commissioners refused to take action, charging that the motive of the Democrats in attempting to add to the force
was to embarrass the Republican city administration by
increasing the budget.   This deadlock was not broken
until the end of the administration.

Illustrations quite similar could be given of police
boards in San Francisco and Indianapolis.   The same
kind of bargaining, the same trading of support has characterized police management in these two cities at one
time or another.   For years in Indianapolis there was not
even a pretense of non-partisanship in the work of the
board.   Everything from the appointment of a patrolman to the dismissal of a chief was on a frankly political
basis.   It was a game in which the minority representative on the board got what he could for his own party.

Board Administration and the New Development.

Whether bi-partisan, uni-partisan, or professedly non-
partisan — whatever its form or arrangement — the

board plan of police control, with its divided powers and scattered responsibilities, plays into the hands of the most sinister influences in American politics. Occasionally, to be sure, the high character of the commissioners gives an appearance of effectiveness to board organization, and the results are credited in many quarters to the mechanical arrangement and not to the men behind it. But board organization in such cases reflects a glory not its own. Based on the principle of decentralized administration and designed to prevent an abuse of power, it exhausts the efforts of the best-intentioned commissioners and nullifies the positive qualities of leadership which constitute the secret of successful police management.

It is therefore encouraging to note the trend of contemporary opinion toward responsible leadership. The checks and balances of earlier days are being cast aside in the belief that men count more than machinery and that an arrangement to prevent arbitrary action serves only to impede positive action when public interest demands it. The application of this principle to police organization has resulted in single-headed leadership, now in effect, as we have seen, in many important cities of the United States, including the three largest. But single-headed leadership, as a bare arrangement of control, guarantees nothing in the way of better police methods. It means that responsibility for bad management is definitized, and that the public can more readily assess the blame for evil conditions; it means that a type of administrative machinery has been devised, which will secure the best results for a skilled administrator. Whether such an administrator has been found, and if found,

The Present State of Police Control

whether he has been permitted to manage his department without political hindrance, are questions for local determination. In the same breath in which we praise the accomplishments of the Boston department under Commissioner O'Meara and the New York department under Commissioner Woods, we would have to admit that under the same type of single-headed control the Chicago force reached a depth of demoralization seldom sounded even in American cities. Obviously, other factors than mechanical organization must enter into the solution of the police problem. Of these factors, the type of administrator is perhaps the most important, and to the consideration of this question we return in a later chapter. For the present we can only note the improving character of the framework of police control, which, in line with modern business organization, is based upon the proposition that responsibility cannot be centered without corresponding concentration of power.

CHAPTER IV

SPECIAL PROBLEMS OF POLICE CONTROL

SEVERAL incidental questions growing out of the general topic of police control and management remain to be discussed in this chapter. These include an examination of one of the factors of responsible leadership, a consideration of the proper jurisdiction of a police depart-ment, and an outline of the police problem as affected by the widely adopted commission form of government. For the sake of clearness these topics are discussed under appropriate heads.

I. THE PRINCIPLE OF RESPONSIBLE LEADERSHIP

The necessity of definite responsibility through single-headed leadership involves a further principle to which attention should be called. It is equally essential that the responsibility of the appointing agent in the selection of the police head should be clearly and sharply defined.

Special Problems of Police Control

If such responsibility is shared by some legislative body or council which otherwise has no jurisdiction over the administrative branches of the city government, the lines of control are confused and public opinion is consequently unable to establish accountability for unsatisfactory police conditions.

This point of view frankly clashes with the principle of legislative confirmation widely held in many parts of the United States. Copied along with other " check and balance " devices from the pattern of the federal government, the principle was applied to municipal affairs, not because of any need which it supplied, but because at the time it was supposed to be the " correct " governmental arrangement. It was predicated on a fear of the executive, a belief that leadership would develop into tyranny. It was an outgrowth of our early inhibitory conceptions of government and of the theory that charters of liberty could not at the same time be charters of powers. It was one of many expedients which, designed to guard against the abuse of authority in high places, has nullified the possibility of constructive action on the part of responsible officials, and by emphasis on limitations of power rather than on impositions of duty has often crippled the machinery of positive government service.

Whatever may be thought of the principle of legislative confirmation in higher governmental positions as a check upon the discretion of the executive, it is certainly superfluous and confusing in the compact administration of the city. Abolished in some municipalities as a relic of outworn political theories, it is still retained in many of our large communties, more, perhaps, as a concession to tradition and conservative influences than because of any conscious support behind it. The tradition is perhaps more tenaciously guarded in its relation to the police department than to any other branch of municipal activity, probably because of the belief that the right of life, liberty, and property can be seriously affected by the police authorities and that adequate barriers should be erected against a possible abuse of their powers. It is common, therefore, to find the appointment of the police head conditioned upon confirmation by the legislative council. This is true under both state and municipal control of police organization. Thus, in Baltimore, St. Louis, and Kansas City, the governor's appointments to the police boards must have the concurrence of the state senate. In Boston and Fall River the governor appoints the police heads with the approval of the governor's council. In cities like Chicago, Minneapolis, Los Angeles, Providence, Pittsburgh, Springfield (Mass.), Worcester, and Cambridge (Mass.) the police heads are appointed by the mayor with the consent of the city council. Similarly in many of the commission governed municipalities, as we shall see, such as Buffalo, Memphis, Nashville, and Dallas, the appointments of the director of public safety must be confirmed by the commission.

In some few cities the nominations of the appointing officer are accepted without question. In others, by far the greater number, the theory that the council refuses its confirmation only in cases of unfitness is frankly thrown aside, and the power is used for partisan purposes, either to embarrass or coerce the executive, or as a basis for political trade. The situation is especially confused and the results particularly demoralizing when the mayor represents one political party and the council another. In Newark in 1915 the two Democrats nominated for the police board by the Republican mayor were turned down by the council because, in the words of the mayor, " Nugent (the 'boss' of Essex County) said they were not good Democrats." [1] Thereupon two others more acceptable for their faith were appointed. In 1917, in the same city under the same circumstances, confirmation was refused by the council to seventeen out of eighteen names submitted by the mayor as members of the police, fire and health boards. No reason was given for the summary action, but the mayor's attempt to force an investigation of the council was undoubtedly responsible. The one nominee successful in obtaining confirmation was a collector for a brewery, whose brother was a member of the council.

Examples of this kind could be multiplied at length. The departments of many cities are today suffering from the lack of definite responsibility for police management. It is doubtful whether the confirmation principle has ever proved an effective check upon the exercise of the mayor's discretion or has in any way safeguarded the cities against the selection of incompetents. In too many cases, indeed, it has served as a cloak to allow the mayor to escape with inferior appointments.

The same conditions of confused responsibility follow the principle of legislative approval of *removals*. I am here referring not to the separate powers of removal sometimes lodged in different agencies of government —

[1] Personally communicated.

American Police Systems

as, for example, the right of removal of New York's police commissioner by either the mayor or the governor — but to the *joint* responsibility in this matter of executive and legislative branches. Thus in Cambridge " the mayor may, *with the approval of a majority of the members of the city council,* remove any head of a department or member of a board before expiration of his term of office." [1] Similar provisions affecting members of the police boards are found in Providence [2] and in Springfield (Mass.).[3] In Chicago, the council can, by a two-thirds vote, restore to office any official, including the superintendent of police, removed by the mayor.[4] In Worcester (Mass.) the head of the police force can be reinstated by a three-fourths vote of the board of aldermen.[5] In Hartford (Conn.) the concurrence of four members of the board of aldermen is necessary to removal.[6] In Boston [7] and Fall River [8] the removal of police commissioners by the governor requires the consent of the council.[9]

Cambridge (Mass.) furnishes an excellent illustration

---

[1] General Acts of Mass., 1915, Chap. 267, Part III. This provision is uniform in all Massachusetts cities having *Plan B* charters.
[2] Acts of R. I., 1906, Chap. 1379.
[3] Ordinance of August 2, 1902.
[4] Laws of Ill., 1875, p. 41.
[5] City Ordinances, Chap. XXXI, Sec. 1.
[6] City Charter 1907, Chap. 9, Sec. 101.
[7] Acts of Mass., 1906, Chap. 291, Sec. 7.
[8] Acts of Mass., 1894, Chap. 351.
[9] The executive council has not hesitated to interfere with the governor's management of Boston's police force. In 1891 the governor's attempt to remove a police commissioner on serious charges was thwarted by the council, the vote being unanimous against the proposal (Executive council records for 1891, p. 45). Again in 1897 the council prevented the removal of a commissioner against whom charges had been filed (Records for 1897, p. 6).

of the practical operation of this principle. Without warrant in necessity, the position of director of public safety was created in 1912; its subsequent history completely demonstrated the uselessness of the post. The efforts of a new mayor, elected in 1916 on a reform ticket, to abolish the position were thwarted by a majority of the council representing another political party. The council itself assumed no responsibility for the management of the force, and did not hesitate to criticize the mayor in his struggles to reorganize it; on the other hand, the action of the council effectively prevented the mayor from exercising his responsibility for the efficient administration of an executive department.

It is, of course, an open question how far a mayor or governor or other executive officer should be allowed to go in removing at will the heads of departments. As we shall see in a later chapter, administrative efficiency is largely predicated on continuity of service, and there is little hope for a specialized function of government like health or police so long as it is under the direction of a periodically shifting body of officials, drawn for political motives from an inexperienced public. Whether the remedy for such periodic removals is to be found in legislation, or whether it is a matter that must be left to the slow processes of education is beyond the limits of this present discussion.[1]   One principle, however, can be definitely stated: If removals are to be made, the responsibility should not be scattered; it should be sharply defined, single and not joint. Our too frequent assumption that

[1] The matter is discussed in Chap. VI, under the heading: THE CHIEF AND CIVIL SERVICE, p. 259.

an executive, obliged to share his powers with an entirely separate branch of government, can be held solely answerable for administrative results, is an irreconcilable paradox.

II. THE JURISDICTION OF THE POLICE DEPARTMENT

Policing in America, as we have seen, has generally been regarded as a function of the municipality. Even when controlled by state authorities its operation has been confined to a particular city rather than to a district embracing perhaps a number of cities and towns. This policy was the natural development of a period when cities were widely scattered and when little was to be gained from combination and centralization.

Within two decades, however, radical changes have been wrought by the concentration of population in metropolitan districts or sections, irrespective of established city boundaries. Not only have cities enlarged their limits, but the intervening towns and villages have grown to fill in the gaps, so that what is in reality one vast city is often made up of a dozen or more municipalities, each with its own system of government and its own laws. This situation is illustrated, for example, by the condition in eastern Massachusetts. Within a radius of approximately twelve miles of the center of the business district of Boston are 38 cities and towns, all except six exceeding 5,000 in population, with a total population of over 840,000. That is, while the city of Boston has a population of 745,000, the metropolitan district of Boston, consisting of practically unbroken urban development, has a population of 1,588,000.[1] Within this territory which, geographically speaking, is not extensive, and which has already been consolidated into a single district for purposes of metropolitan park administration, are 39 different police forces, each with exclusive jurisdiction over a portion of the field, and each independent of any common superior authority.[2]

A similar situation is shown in connection with the vast, continuous population bordering on and stretching back from the western bank of the Hudson River opposite New York City. Here we have within approximately thirty square miles nine cities, towns, and townships: Jersey City with a population of 270,000, Hoboken with 67,000, West Hoboken with 38,000, Bayonne with 64,000, West New York with 22,000, Union with 21,000, North Bergen with 20,000, Weehawken with 13,000, and Guttenberg with 6,000. Altogether they comprise a composite city of 527,000.[3] Each of these places, separated from its neighbors by boundary lines long since outworn, maintains its own police force under standards good, bad, or indifferent.

Illustrations such as this could be multiplied at length. Most of the large cities of the country are fringed by

[1] These figures are obtained from the state census of Massachusetts, 1915.

[2] In 1917 a bill was introduced into the Massachusetts legislature, creating five police districts in the state, one of which was to include Boston and adjacent territory; each district was placed under the control of a district commissioner, who should have general supervision over all city and town forces within his jurisdiction, and be answerable for his acts to a state commissioner of police. The bill failed of passage. (See House Document No. 539, January, 1917.)

[3] These figures are obtained from the state census of New Jersey, 1915.

municipalities and townships separated from their common centers by fictitious boundaries rather than by any real divergence of interest or population.[1] In consequence, the function of policing, instead of being unified and coordinated under single management for a single people, is broken up and scattered in patch-work fashion among irregularly formed groups.

This criticism is of course true of other government functions, such as public works and the health service. It is particularly applicable, however, to the police and fire forces. The management of these forces is concerned primarily with the protection of lives and property. It is a matter of finding the factors which will promote the most efficient service. There are but few questions of broad general policy to be considered, such as relate to the management of local public works, for example, the determination of which must necessarily be left to the individual community. Rather, police and fire management is a distinctly technical problem offering little legitimate opportunity for differences of opinion based on local or parochial grounds. Policing in Hoboken demands the same intelligent methods and administrative oversight as in West Hoboken.

These two services, moreover, fire and police, gain much from coordination and amalgamation. The police and fire forces of Greater New York, each now under single management, are far more effective today than they were when Manhattan, Brooklyn, Long Island City,

[1] In Detroit three separate villages, Highland Park, Hamtramck, and St. Clair Heights are completely within the city limits. Each village, however, has its own distinct municipal government.

and the many scattered towns in Queens County had their own departments, each more or less self-sufficient and jealous of its own prestige. Standardization of method under single leadership has lifted both services to a degree of effectiveness impossible under diverse management. In not a few of the towns and cities in the neighborhood of Jersey City and of Boston, police conditions are distinctly inferior, sometimes demoralized, because of a lack of means adequately to maintain a separate establishment, with all the heavy overhead charges which such independence involves. Moreover, separation in management is a serious handicap to the effectiveness of police work, in that it renders impossible a single policy and a united front against crime. Under modern conditions of life the traveling professional criminal has come to play a predominant part in the police problem, and the success of any endeavor to counteract his work depends in large measure upon harmonious cooperation, over a wide area, of the forces of law and order.

London faced the question of divided police jurisdiction within a metropolitan area, when, in 1829, out of a number of boroughs and counties, supporting several ineffective and conflicting constabulary systems, she carved the metropolitan police district, which today embraces 700 square miles and supports the largest and undoubtedly the best local force in the world. Prior to 1829 the same combination existed of parochial jealousies, lack of cooperation, and general demoralization typical today of the situation in northern New Jersey and elsewhere in the United States.[1]

[1] See *European Police Systems*, p. 100.

Similarly in Berlin the district over which the police president presides was in 1900 enlarged to include the neighboring suburbs of Charlottenburg, Schöneberg, Neukölln and Lichtenberg.[1] In Paris the authority of the prefect of police extends over the whole department of the Seine, including the communes of St. Cloud, Sevres, and Meudon.[2]

Police consolidation for metropolitan areas would undoubtedly produce beneficial results in the United States. The increase of crime in urban districts, traceable in many cases to the isolation of small police departments in heavily populated sections would seem to make necessary some form of cooperation as yet untried. The difficulty of creating an administrative district for the exercise of a single government function is admittedly formidable although precedents for such action exist.[3] Where the police commissioner is appointed by the governor, as in Boston, it would seem that his jurisdiction could easily be extended by act of legislature, without violent wrench to principles of local autonomy. In the Jersey City district, however, where no state control of police forces exists, consolidation would involve either the creation of some new machinery of supervision, based perhaps on a federalized or representative system, or a frank return to the metropolitan police arrangement under state control. Either course would be fraught with difficulty. Of the growing need of some such action, however, there can be no question. In many urban cen-

[1] *Ibid.,* p. 109.
[2] *Ibid.,* p. 88.
[3] As for example, the Metropolitan Park Commission and the Metropolitan Water and Sewerage Board in Massachusetts.

ters, particularly where communities more or less parasitic have developed around the original city, the difficulty could be solved by extending the geographical limits of the municipality for the exercise not only of the police function, but of other local governmental functions as well.

We cannot leave the consideration of this subject without at least a passing reference to a perplexing problem which it uncovers. In all our populous states are literally scores of police forces, maintained not only by cities, towns and villages but occasionally by park area administrations and other governmental units. Except in occasional matters of insignificant detail, these police forces are independent of any common superior authority and uncoordinated by any single agency of supervision. Within a given state, therefore, it is possible to find police departments of widely varying degrees of efficiency, representing all sorts of standards, high and low. Effective cooperation between these forces is not only nonexistent but practically impossible, with the result that crime and lawlessness are difficult to prevent and still more difficult to punish.

The formation of state constabulary systems will in part remedy this condition by eliminating many of the village forces and by providing a single agency for the apprehension of criminals in country districts and in small communities. There still remains a large part of the problem, however, which the state constabulary system will not touch. Why in New York State, for example, should it be possible to find such marked variations in police efficiency, to say nothing of police practices and methods, as exist between the departments of New York City and Buffalo or of Rochester and Albany? Why in a state like Ohio should there not be some uniformity in police procedure, some standardization in the technique of police work, which will bring the weaker forces up to higher levels and make possible some degree of effective cooperation?

The experience of Europe in the solution of this problem is worthy of consideration. In England, after a long period of demoralization, similar to that which exists in many of our states today, Parliament passed, in 1856, the Rural Police Act which standardized the system of police administration for the entire country. This act provided for the appointment of Inspectors of Constabulary under the Home Office with authority to visit and inquire into the state and general efficiency of the police in the various towns and counties [1] of England and Wales. It further provided that on certificates from the Home Secretary to the effect that the police force of a locality is efficient in point of numbers and discipline, a sum not exceeding one-half part of the total cost of the pay and clothing of the force was to be contributed from the national treasury. Through the operation of this act there was established a complete system of national supervision over all the police forces of England and Wales, which, while it in no way robs the cities and counties of the right of local control, stimulates their efforts to main-

[1] Each county in England has its own police force with complete jurisdiction except in the municipalities that have their own forces; but municipalities with a population of less than 20,000 are debarred from having separate police departments. (See *European Police Systems,* pp. 61–64.)

tain an efficient standard and introduce uniformity into their organization and management. To be sure, the Home Office, particularly as far as the towns and cities are concerned, has no positive authority over the police force. It cannot remove an official or compel the adoption of any improvements. It acts only in the capacity of friendly guide. Its sole lever is the national subvention or grant in aid, which may be withheld if the report of the supervising inspector indicates unsatisfactory conditions.[1]

While it is probable that the English plan in its entirety could not easily be adapted to a state like New York or Ohio, it is nevertheless suggestive of a method of supervision and coordination in no way fatal to the principle of local autonomy. Some such plan would undoubtedly prove of great benefit to our states. It is encouraging, therefore, to note the report of the special commission on police appointed in 1916 by the governor of Massachusetts in which the establishment of a system of supervision through a state commissioner of police was strongly urged. It is possible that the particular method suggested by the commission was faulty and that the details of the proposed organization would not stand the test of practical operation. The idea underlying the plan, however, points the way toward a uniformity of police practice and method and a standardization of work without which no real progress can be made in the positive development of police effectiveness.

[1] For a discussion of the operation of this plan, see *European Police Systems*, pp. 48–64.

American Police Systems

III. COMMISSION GOVERNMENT AND THE POLICE
FORCE

The commission form of government has been so widely adopted and presents so many interesting administrative problems, that its relation to the police department deserves separate consideration. It is now in force in 27 of the 69 cities in the United States over 100,000 population,[1] and in 105 cities over 30,000,[2] while of cities of all classes it is installed in over 500.[3] It represents a reaction against the inefficiency of the mayor and council plan of city government, and its success in stimulating official effort and in creating a new and better civic spirit has been attested by competent observers.[4]

[1] According to U. S. Census publication, "Financial Statistics of Cities,"— 1917, there were 26 cities as follows: Birmingham (Ala.), Buffalo, Dallas, Dayton, Des Moines, Fort Worth, Houston, Jersey City, Kansas City (Kan.), Lawrence, Lowell, Lynn, Memphis, Nashville, New Orleans, Oakland (Cal.), Omaha, Portland (Ore.), Reading, St. Paul, Salt Lake City, San Antonio, Spokane, Tacoma, Trenton, Washington (D. C.). Since the beginning of 1917 Newark has adopted the commission form of government and Grand Rapids has adopted the commission manager plan, while Lynn has abandoned commission government.

[2] *Ibid.* The U. S. statistics show 91 cities but since 1917 East St. Louis, Ill., Jacksonville, Fla., Bay City, Mich., and Charlotte, N. C., have adopted commission government, and the commission manager form has been adopted in the following cities: Akron, O., Auburn, N. Y., Charleston, W. Va., Fresno, Cal., Kalamazoo, Mich., Lynchburg, Va., Norfolk, Va., Roanoke, Va., Waltham, Mass., Wheeling, W. Va.

[3] These figures include city manager and commission governed cities.

[4] See *City Government by Commission,* edited by Clinton Rogers Woodruff, New York, 1911; *Commission Government in American Cities,* by Ernest S. Bradford, New York, 1911; *Commission Government in American Cities,* printed in the *Annals of the American Academy of Political and Social Science,* 1911; *The New City Government,* by Henry Bruere, New York, 1912; *Municipal Freedom,* by Oswald Ryan, New York, 1915; *History and Analysis of the Commission and City Manager Plans of Municipal Government in*

174

Special Problems of Police Control

The Personnel of Commissions.

Our interest lies in the relation of commission government to the particular function of policing. Briefly, the commission consists of a board, generally of five members elected at large, combining in itself all the legislative and administrative functions of the municipality. Each commissioner assumes charge of a particular department of the city government; and ordinarily he is paid a salary which enables him to devote his entire time to the work.[1] He is thus not only a director in city affairs but an active administrator of a city department. In some cities the assignment of departments is a matter of board action, the commissioners themselves determining what department each shall head; in others, a candidate for election designates in advance the particular department he wishes to administer, and the electors at the polls are asked to pass upon his qualifications for the post. In twelve of the twenty-seven commission cities over 100,000 population, this latter method is in effect; and the choice of administrative heads of particular departments is thus left to the exigencies of a popular election. In Buffalo Portland (Ore.), Houston, Birmingham (Ala.), Nashville and other important municipalities, the director of public safety and his colleagues are chosen by a method which, as we have already seen, is utterly unadapted to

the United States, by Tso-Shuen Chang, University of Iowa, Iowa City, 1918.

[1] In Buffalo the mayor-commissioner's salary is $8,000 a year, and that of the other commissioners is $7,000 each; the commissioners in Birmingham (Ala.) receive $7,000; in Memphis the mayor-commissioner's salary is $6,000, and the others receive $3,000; in Spokane the salary is $5,000 to all alike; St. Paul pays $5,000 to the mayor-commissioner and $4,500 to the others.

the selection of trained administrators. Its results are shown by an analysis of the personnel of some of the boards. Barbers, undertakers, dentists, stone-masons, carpenters, and bakers have been elected to manage the affairs of city departments. In Elgin, Illinois, the commissioner of health was recently a harness maker. Ignorant of the meaning or significance of typhoid fever reports turned in by the doctors, he allowed them to accumulate on his desk until an epidemic swept the town. In Houston, Texas, the commissioner of streets and bridges was a horse-shoer, the commissioner of finance a machinist, and the commissioner of health a printer. In Topeka, Kansas, the commissioner of public utilities was a barber, and the commissioner of parks and sanitation a house-mover. Jersey City had an undertaker as a commissioner of health. Kansas City, Kansas, had a groceryman as commissioner of streets, and Lynn, Massachusetts, a pressman from a newspaper office as commissioner of finance. The point, of course, is not that these various employments ought not to be represented in municipal government, but that they do not fit a man for an occupation demanding technical, administrative ability.

Commission Government Wrong in Principle.

Even when the assignment to departments is left to the judgment of the board, the results are but little changed. A commissioner may be given a department for which he has no special talent; or his lack of training and experience may unfit him to serve as an administrator of any department. The difficulty with the situation is rooted in the very conception of the commission plan. It confuses the deliberative or policy-forming function of city government with its technical, administrative function. One is the determination of community plans in the light of public opinion; the other is the management of specialized lines of business by competent experts. The former in republican government must necessarily be based on some kind of representative principle; in the latter the representative principle has no proper place. It is quite possible that the carpenters or iron-workers or doctors of a community might feel that either their own professions or the broader interests they typify should be represented in the city's regulative machinery; on the other hand, it is impossible to conceive of a carpenter's way or an iron-worker's way or a doctor's way of managing a police force or a department of public works. The commission plan was framed with only the administrative necessities of a city in mind, on the theory that the people at the polls would choose their commissioners for administrative ability, and that these commissioners could incidentally be entrusted with the legislative, policy-forming functions of the city government. While the old idea of sectional or geographical representation was wisely omitted from the plan, no provision was made for the representation of different points of view in regard to city policy or of different groups or classes. By implication, at least, the commission plan limits the people in their selection of commissioners to men of the employer type, competent to hire and direct the labor of other men.

With an instinct, however, more deep-seated and far truer than the instinct of charter-makers, the citizens of most commission cities have elected their commissioners, not for their administrative abilities, but because they were representative of a group, a policy, or a principle. The basic administrative feature of the plan has been largely neglected or else, under the lingering spell of Jacksonian principles, the voters have argued that any honest man of average ability, regardless of his previous experience, is fitted to run a city department. In other words, although commission government fails to provide for the principle of representation, the public at the polls sweeps aside the intent of the charter and makes that principle its gauge and standard. When Wichita, Kansas, elected a railway switchman on its commission, or when Topeka, Kansas, elected a barber, it was not because these men were regarded as administrative experts, but because they were representative of particular groups with particular points of view. As members of the commission, their ideas were worthy contributions to the joint discussion of municipal projects. In one of these cases, indeed, no opinion on city policy of any of the commissioners was more anxiously awaited or more thoroughly respected. The absurdity of the situation lay in the fact that these two public servants, valuable in a representative capacity, should be called upon to reorganize and manage specific city departments — one a water department and the other a department of public works — without any qualifications whatsoever for the task.

This situation is clearly evident in the management of the police force. Prior to his election, the director of public safety in New Orleans was engaged in the insurance business; in Newark he was the business agent of the Stationary Firemen's Union; in Salt Lake City he was a city auditor. In Memphis the commissioner of fire and police was a manufacturer of mixed feeds; in Nashville, a merchant. These commissioners or directors are many of them men of character, and some have real administrative ability. In only a few cases, however, is their ability adapted to the highly specialized requirements of either police management or city management generally. They can maintain the status of their departments as they have inherited it, but they are seldom able to reorganize and reconstruct on new, progressive lines.

To meet the difficulties inherent in this situation, the apologists of the commission plan sometimes conceive the commissioner as a kind of supervisor whose function it is, not to assume direct administrative charge of the details of his department, but to hold himself responsible for its general policies, and advise with the permanent expert officials under him. This conception, however, does not square with the facts. Almost without exception, in the cities visited, the commissioners regard themselves as the actual administrators of their departments. All the intimate detail of departmental business, the means and methods by which ends are achieved, come before them for determination. Transfers, promotions, assignments, and questions involving technical points of organization and procedure are their immediate concern. Indeed, in most cases, this conception is in accordance with the intent of the commission charters. As we have seen, the commissioners are paid substantial salaries, and many of them are obliged to give full time to their tasks. Under such circumstances it is not practicable to have expert administrators of high grade serving under the commissioners. As President Lowell points out, such an arrangement would be playing false to the public by taking pay for work unperformed, even if the double charge of full salaries to both commissioner and administrator were not prohibitive.[1]

Commission Government and Transient Management.

Not only does the commission form of government introduce police administrators inexperienced and unfitted for their tasks, but, because of the recurrent elections naturally involved in the plan, it subjects the departments to the demoralizing influences of transient management. The value of permanence in high executive positions is ignored. Here again we see the confusion arising from the attempt to confer upon a policy-forming body, subject to the uncertainties of popular control, specialized administrative functions in which success is based alone upon security and continuity in office. In many commission cities the commissioners serve for two years; in some, for three; and in some for four. The elections, in cases of candidates standing to succeed themselves, are

[1] *Public Opinion and Popular Government*, New York, 1913, p. 287. In Newark, New Jersey, an effort has been made to provide expert administrators for the several divisions included in the department of public safety. The elected director of public safety appoints a board of three members known as the board of public safety. One member is given charge of administering the police department with the title of police commissioner, one serves as fire commissioner and the other as commissioner of licenses. In so far as the law defining the duties of elected city commissioners permits, administrative functions are delegated to the respective subordinate commissioners in charge of the fire, police, and license departments. They are responsible to the director for the management of their departments; their term of office is at the pleasure of the director.

seldom contested on the basis of administrative ability; the issue is formed by political questions or by controversies arising from the activities of the commissioners in their legislative capacities. In consequence, the director of public safety and his associates are not long enough in office to learn even the meaning or possibilities of their departments. In Omaha there have been three directors of public safety in eight years; in Dallas, Texas, six in thirteen years; in Memphis, ten in ten years. The tenure is so insecure that serious attention cannot be paid to policies which take time to develop. What new projects are initiated are often abandoned by a fresh administration, and the department, instead of sailing on a definite course carefully mapped out, merely drifts in vacillation and uncertainty.

The periodic elections of administrative heads often prove an incentive to political activity within the department. The members of a police force will work for the election or reelection of a " good " commissioner, while they will oppose the candidacy of one whose point of view they regard as hostile to their own interests. In Omaha in 1914, the commissioner of police, running for reelection, received the solid support of the entire department. " We worked our heads off for him," an officer of the force told me. " He had treated us square." Said the secretary of the department: " The police are more mixed up in the political game now, under commission government, than they were under the old regime." This situation, paralleled in some other commission cities, notably St. Paul and Birmingham, is the inevitable consequence of an elective, administrative head.

American Police Systems

Commission Government and Irresponsible Administration.

Another weakness of the commission plan, reflected in the management of the police force, lies in the fact that in many cities employees cannot be dismissed by the director in charge of the department without the approval of the commission. This is true in Buffalo, Jersey City, St. Paul, Birmingham, Omaha, Salt Lake City, San Antonio, and many other municipalities. In some cities all disciplinary fines and penalties and all appointments must have the sanction of the commission. In other words, in so far as this interference is prevalent, commission government represents in its relation to the police force nothing else than the multiple management and divided responsibility of the old type of police board.[1] With the commission exercising its right to check the director in the handling of his men, no one official can be held solely answerable for the conduct of the department — an arrangement productive of all the vicious results of scattering control. In Jersey City in 1915, the director of public safety attempted to remove the chief of police on charges of drunkenness and insubordination. By a vote

[1] In at least one city — East St. Louis, Illinois — the commission form of government has not eliminated the old system of board control. The law creating the commission provides that the boards of fire and police commissioners shall not be disturbed (Laws of Ill., 1910.) Consequently, in this city the elected commissioner of public health and safety, charged with the administration of the police department, yields his authority to a board of fire and police commissioners appointed by the mayor with the consent of the city commission, of which the commissioner of public health and safety is himself a member. To add to the chaos of this situation, removals from the police department are effected by a trial board consisting of the county judge, the circuit judge, and the county probate judge!

182

of three to two, the commission refused to sustain the director, and the chief was reinstated in full power. At the time of the investigator's visit to Jersey City, the director was manoeuvering to discipline a lieutenant of the force without incurring the disapproval of the board. " My colleagues are not concerned with me or my department," he said. " If it will bring them any votes to be lenient with ' John Brown ' of the police force when he is on trial, ' John Brown ' will undoubtedly get off easy. They will play the political game straight through and win as much favor as possible before concerning themselves with the discipline of my department."

Similarly, in San Antonio the attempt of the director of public safety to remove the chief of police was frustrated by the commission. In this case, to be sure, the commission acted in the public interest, for the director's move was prompted by his desire to secure the position for a friend — an iceman by profession. At the same time, the director of public safety had been elected by the people to manage the police department, and the interference by the commission tangled the lines of responsibility.

The Effect of Commission Government on the Police Force.

It is difficult to appraise the commission form of government in its relation to a particular branch of municipal service. Police duty in America has been to so large an extent an unimaginative, perfunctory routine that it would probably be the last phase of city government to feel the stimulus of a new movement. Certainly, of any

positive effect of commission government upon the work
and administrative mechanism of the police department,
little can be seen at the present time. Indeed, a survey
of a number of commission cities seems to justify the
conclusion that the plan has made no impression whatever
upon the business of policing. In some cities commission
government is little more than an ornamental device,
superimposed upon old methods and worn out practices
— a more or less elaborate machine of control, without
contact or connection with the real working of the department. In Omaha, for example, at the time of my
visit, the same political boss who ran the police force
under the old regime was running it under commission
government. Similarly in Jersey City the same political
influences that wrecked police administrations in other
years were in active operation. In St. Paul commission
government had not shaken the grip of the political ring
on the police department. Birmingham, Alabama, with
eight or nine years of commission government to its
credit, has perhaps one of the shabbiest police organizations of any large city in the United States. With no
civil service, with no standards for appointment or promotion, with no modern equipment, with nothing to stimulate effectiveness or punish slackness, its affairs throughout are governed by the petty politics of the commission.
In none of these police departments is there any knowledge of progressive methods in police work, or any genuine desire for change. Down-at-the-heel and contented,
with no vision and no constructive policies, they follow in
the rut of previous administrations. I asked a well-

known citizen of Omaha what effect commission government had had upon the police administration of his city. " It has not even made a dent in it," he replied. This remark could truthfully be applied to many of the commission cities visited.

I do not mean to imply, of course, that the police departments of commission cities are worse than those of the mayor and council type. Probably they are better. In some of the smaller cities, such as Cedar Rapids and Des Moines, Iowa, they are decidedly better. The stimulated civic spirit which brought the commission plan into being would necessarily be transmuted at least into a temporarily improved attitude on the part of public officials. Indeed, one is led to suspect that the good results credited to commission government are due not so much to any particular merit in the plan itself as to the " new broom " enthusiasm which accompanies the introduction of any civic novelty. Commission government is given the appearance of efficiency because in many cases the reins of control are in new hands. But without a program of administrative reorganization, without trained men as executives to manage the details of the work, without imagination in the development of departmental functions; — in brief, without constructive leadership to study and anticipate community requirements,— the results of the new plan, or of any other plan, cannot be permanent.. Commission government provides for none of these things. It is a mere reshaping of the governmental machine, with serious inherent defects. Unless it can bring to its service the effective, united leadership which its very construction seems to bar, it will go the way of other artificial arrangements, equally promising at the start.

City Manager Plan.

A word in conclusion is necessary as to the operation of the city manager plan — a modification of commission government. This plan has grown in recognition of the fact that the commission government scheme does not provide administrators trained in municipal affairs. Under the commission manager plan, the elected city commissioners constitute the city's legislative body, and are charged with the responsibility for laying down the general policies to be followed in the various branches of municipal administration. The city commission appoints the manager who takes over all purely administrative functions. The commission is simply a board of advisers or directors, devoting its energies to plans and policies, and maintaining its contact with the city government through its business representative.[1]

In Dayton the city manager appoints a director of public safety subject to the approval of the city commission.

[1] At the present writing, January, 1920, 165 communities, notably Dayton and Akron, Ohio, and Grand Rapids, Michigan, are operating under or pledged to the commission manager plan. Of the 165 cities and towns, 105 have approved city manager charters, ten have charters with some standard feature of the manager plan lacking, and in 50 communities the position of manager has been created by ordinance. (See *National Municipal Review,* January, 1920.) In the past seven years the plan has become effective in the following seven cities having a population ranging from 50,000 to 100,000: Akron, Ohio; Altoona, Penn.; Kalamazoo, Mich.; Norfolk, Va.; San Diego, Cal.; Springfield, Ohio; Wichita, Kan. Twelve cities from 30,000 to 50,000 have the commission manager plan at the present time.

Special Problems of Police Control

The director has immediate control of the police and fire departments and the bureau of weights and measures. In smaller cities having the commission manager plan, there is no officer between the city manager and the professional head of the police force.

The results achieved by the city manager scheme depend largely upon the skill of the manager and the presence or absence of politics in the board. Certainly in freeing the elected commissioners from the necessity of administering particular departments, the city manager arrangement contains a degree of promise which cannot be looked for in the regular commission form of government.

It is still too early to appraise the effect of this plan upon the police department. As we shall see in a later chapter, its installation in the largest city in which it is now in operation, Dayton, Ohio, has been attended with some administrative confusion. In other cities the vicious play of politics has not been eliminated in spite of the theoretic merits of the plan. Whether this scheme by itself offers any permanent solution of the evils with which our police departments have long been associated, has yet to be proven.

CHAPTER V

General organization.— Relation between supervision and work.— Examples.— Adjustment of the machinery to its task.— Examples.— Adaptation of the machinery to its work.— Faulty mechanism due to inelastic legal restrictions.— Illustrations.— European departments far more elastic.— Faulty mechanism due to unnecessary functions.— Faulty mechanism due to inadequate leadership.

I

THE organization of American police departments shows little divergence from a standard type. In most of the larger cities a civilian commissioner or director, or a civilian board, controls the force through a chief or superintendent. The same director or board may also control other municipal functions, such as fire and health.[1] In smaller cities the civilian administrative agencies are often omitted, and the chief as head of the

[1] In Philadelphia, for example, the director of public safety has under his jurisdiction the fire and police forces of the city as well as the bureau for the inspection of buildings. Arrangements largely similar prevail in Milwaukee, Louisville, Indianapolis, and in most of the commission governed cities. Sometimes a miscellaneous assortment of activities is brought under the control of a single administrator or board. In Louisville the charter provides that the board of public safety shall have exclusive jurisdiction of "the fire department, the police department, the health department, the department of buildings, of the pounds, and prisons, and market places, and of all the charitable, reformatory and penal institutions of the city." (Charter of Louisville, Sec. 2,861.) Mobile (Ala.) has a department known as the "Department of health, justice, sanitation, pounds, police, cemeteries, meat and milk, weights and measures."

force is responsible to the mayor or other appointing officer.

The structure of the department includes, as its two main branches, the uniformed force and the detective bureau. The cities are generally divided into precincts or districts in charge of a ranking officer, usually a captain. In larger cities the precincts are grouped into several territorial divisions under an inspector or other official, or occasionally they may have subdivisions of their own. The precincts have their " beats " for patrol purposes and their fixed posts, and there is the usual accompaniment of mounted men and bicycle squads, sometimes attached to headquarters, sometimes to the precincts. In larger cities an independent traffic squad, responsible to the head of the department or one of his representatives, covers important traffic points. Detective work is handled either by headquarters or the precincts, or both, or by specially arranged detective districts.

Such in barest outline is the internal organization of the department. The charts included in this book will, it is hoped, convey a general idea of local arrangements, for it is impossible to cover the subject descriptively within the limits of a chapter. It is scarcely less difficult to examine the arrangements critically. Their weaknesses are so complex and often so interwoven with factors of personnel that the dissection is neither simple nor easy.

Generally speaking, sound mechanical organization must fulfill three conditions: first, the relation between supervision and work must be well-balanced; second, the different parts of the mechanism must be adjusted to each other; and third, the whole machine must be adapted to its task. There are undoubtedly other standards that could be applied, but none more important than these. By their aid we are able briefly to examine some of the more obvious mechanical faults of our police systems.

Supervision and the Police Force.

In the first place, the relation between supervision and the police force is in many cities poorly balanced. Strangely enough this condition is as often the consequence of too much supervision as too little. Of recent years, indeed, the frequent attempts to reorganize the departments have resulted, in not a few cases, in the mere addition of supervisory agencies without sharp distinctions in function. Some departments, therefore, give the impression of being overloaded and top-heavy. The small, commission governed cities, with their directors of public safety and chiefs of police, are perhaps the best illustrations of this condition. The forces are small and the responsibilities in quiet communities are not onerous. There is nothing that one well-equipped executive could not adequately handle. Yet in such cities there are really two executives, with duties poorly defined or not defined at all, both of them under the more or less direct supervision of a board. In consequence, as we shall see in a later chapter, one of the executives, generally the chief, is often crowded into comparative obscurity, while the other manages the department.

The top-heavy condition of police supervision can be illustrated — perhaps in exaggerated form — by the situation in Dayton, Ohio, in 1916. Here we had, in sequence of authority, a commission, a city manager, a director of public safety, and a chief of police, governing a police force of 128 men. To be sure, Dayton is an industrial city of 125,000, with a rather large and constantly increasing foreign population. The duties of the force are not, however, such as make necessary an elaborate scheme of supervision. Indeed, between 7 A. M. and 3 P. M., in addition to the traffic force, there were but eight uniformed men on patrol to be supervised. Under such an arrangement, a considerable degree of crowding in the administrative branch could logically be looked for. The city manager is the general executive head of all the municipal machinery, responsible for the policies and effective operation of the departments. But why should there be two executives under him to carry out his wishes in regard to the police? A study of the situation in Dayton indicated that either the office of director of public safety or the office of chief could have been abolished without detriment to the force. The director was the official who really managed the department. At the time of the investigator's visit this official with the assistance of his secretary, who acted as a sort of deputy-director, was making assignments of men for a coming parade, and was handling the details of policing a strike then in progress. Uniformed men and detectives came to him for orders. The duties of the chief, meanwhile, seemed to be confined to opening such mail as was directed to him, and acting as a rubber stamp for his superior officer. He had no independent function whatever, and no assigned function which could not easily and quickly have been handled by the director. The impression created by

American Police Systems

the situation was that the office of chief had been retained out of respect to convention rather than from any dictates of necessity.

Poorly balanced relations between supervision and work show themselves with perhaps equal force in inadequate administrative machinery. There occurs no more glaring illustration of this than the Chicago police department, where for years the heavy administrative burdens attending the management of a force of 4,500 in a city exceeding two million population have been given to a chief of police customarily promoted from the ranks. The continuously demoralized condition of the force is undoubtedly due in no small degree to the city's failure to supplement the technically-equipped uniformed head of the department with a trained executive of broad administrative experience and social outlook. As we shall see in the next chapter, Chicago could profitably employ a civilian commissioner to whom the chief of police would be a subordinate officer.

A condition of under-supervision of a slightly different variety is shown in the Philadelphia department, where the civilian director of public safety, occasionally a man of wide training and genuine ability, is given too many diverse functions to control. His department embraces not only the bureau of police, but the fire department, the bureau of fire prevention, the bureau of buildings, the inspection of electrical service and other miscellaneous activities more or less related. In a smaller city such an arrangement might not prove ineffective; that is, a community of from 25,000 to 50,000, or even larger, might well group a number of functions or bureaus

The Organization of the Department

under the control of a single administrator, without loss of efficiency. Thus, the association in smaller cities of the fire department with the police department under the same supervision cannot be condemned off-hand as a faulty plan. In a city of Philadelphia's size, however, with its diversified population and its complex social and industrial organization, the function of policing needs the undivided attention of the best administrator obtainable. The director of public safety at present is so weighed down by his many administrative responsibilities that he cannot give the police department the continuous thought and oversight which its importance demands. Hundreds of papers and documents, relating to other activities and demanding perusal or signature, cross his desk every day; intricate questions of public safety regarding the fire-fighting force or the inspection of buildings consume much of his time and energy — with the result that there is not the close and intimate touch with police affairs from which alone successful management can develop. Under the Blankenburg administration, the director of public safety, a man of ideals and ability, was unable to effect the much-needed reorganization of the detective bureau, solely because of the pressure of other public business. Admitting that it was in critical shape, he was, to use his own words, " sheerly unable to get at it." [1]

This condition is true not only of Philadelphia, but of certain large commission governed cities where functions have been similarly grouped. In Buffalo, for example, a city of 400,000 population, the supervision of the director of public safety covers not only the police depart-

[1] Personally communicated.

193

ment, but the fire department and the bureau of health. Moreover, by charter the director is the mayor of the city, with the large executive responsibilities which the post entails. Consequently his time is absorbed in other duties to the exclusion of department matters. The chances are that the machinery for managing a city of 50,000 will be entirely unsuited to a city of 500,000. Difficulties in government increase with size. Cedar Rapids may successfully place its police and fire departments, and other miscellaneous functions, under the supervision of a single director. In the very nature of things, Buffalo cannot.

The Adjustment of the Machinery.

The second condition which good organization must fulfill is the harmonious adjustment of its various parts. The application of this standard to American police departments is distinctly discouraging. As we have seen in a preceding chapter, the departments are the products of haphazard growth — as often the result of expediency and circumstances as of deliberate counsel and plan. One seldom encounters, therefore, any considerable degree of orderly or systematic relationship between the various bureaus and divisions.

This condition shows itself, for example, in the manner in which in many departments a long line of specific activities is placed directly under the chief, instead of being broken up and grouped under subordinate officials. In Los Angeles — to pick out a police department almost at random — a number of small and relatively unimportant branches of the service, dignified in most cases

by the title of bureau, are appended to the office of chief
of police, with the result that the effectiveness of that
official as a general supervisor is hampered by the petty
details with which he is constantly confronted. The
property bureau, the accounting bureau, the municipal
farm, the printing and publishing bureau, the chain-gang,
the juvenile bureau, the metropolitan squad, the Chinatown squad, the probation bureau, and the identification
bureau are placed under his direct and immediate control. In other words, the department is not *organized* at
all, in the strict sense of the word. Its parts are merely
strung together like beads. There is no conception of
the organic relationship which one function or division
logically bears to another. The identification bureau, for
example, in any well-conceived organization would be a
branch of the detective division. Its purpose is to establish the identity of those arrested for crime, and in ful-
filling this mission it is at once the right arm and the
most effective tool of the plain-clothes service. No European police department has ever established its bureau
of identification in any other relation than as a definite
part of the detective branch. Indeed that relation would
suggest itself to any one familiar with problems of business organization. Yet in Los Angeles and in a dozen
other cities the mere fact that the identification bureau was
created subsequent to the detective bureau seems to justify its independent existence. It is admitted on an equal
footing with its fellow-bureaus, and in many cases is
even assigned office space remote from the detective
branch which it serves. In consequence, through friction
or disuse, it falls short of its possibilities, while the chief

of the department is burdened with additional detail, the nature or significance of which he may not be technically equipped to comprehend.

Similarly in the Chicago department until 1912, the telegraph bureau, the ambulance bureau, the detective bureau, the record bureau, the printing bureau, the bureau of identification, the matrons, the stables, the construction department, the dog pound, and the uniformed force were all considered independent units, each directly responsible to the superintendent of police.[1] Each branch jealously guarded its own separate existence and defied attempts at coordination. In an endeavor to remedy this situation and relieve the superintendent of some of the burden of administration, the reorganization ordinance of 1912 [2] clumsily grouped the bureaus under two deputy superintendents, with little regard to similarity or relationship in function; and while the rearrangement, on paper at least, was undoubtedly an improvement, it cannot be said that any substantial degree of coherency or cohesiveness was achieved. A plan which placed under a single specialized administrator such diverse activities as the construction and repair of police stations, the supervision of the vice squad, the bureau of records, the drill and inspection of the uniformed force, and the censorship of moving pictures, could hardly be expected to work harmoniously.

Faulty adjustment of the parts or branches of police

[1] See report of the committee on schools, fire, police and civil service of the city council of Chicago on the question of a reorganization of the police department, printed in the Journal of the proceedings of the city council, November 25, 1912, pp. 2,416–2,433.
[2] Ordinance of December 30, 1912.

The Organization of the Department

organization is shown not only in these bad arrangements for distributing the administrative burden, but in the opposite practice of giving the head of the force incomplete oversight of the work of his department. In guarding against the direct responsibility which often swamps a chief or commissioner with irrelevant detail, the fundamental necessity of *ultimate* responsibility should not be lost sight of. In too many police departments the nominal head is entrusted with only part of the oversight, while the remainder is shared by other officials of perhaps lesser rank. This situation is due as often to circumstances as to charter arrangements. An aggressive mayor, perhaps, eagerly seizes the reins of authority; the heads of bureaus or subdivisions begin to report directly to him, and the authority of the chief or commissioner is gradually reduced lower and lower. Examples of this are frequent. Perhaps the most illuminating is found in the relations of the uniformed force with the detective bureau. Between these two branches of the service the closest degree of cooperation should prevail. Experience both here and abroad has repeatedly shown that without the aid of the uniformed men substantial and permanent success is impossible for the detective force. The harmonious relationship essential to this cooperation is obviously the result of common management. In other words, the chief of police, as the head of the force, should be clothed with ultimate responsibility for the operation of the detective bureau. Yet in a large number of cities the detective bureau is run as an independent organization, apparently on the theory that the chief of police has no proper place in its counsels. In Pittsburgh, for example, the superintendent of police and the chief of detectives are independent of each other. They are equal in rank, appointed practically by the same authority,[1] and receive the same salary. At the time of the investigator's visit, friction and misunderstanding marked the relations between the two bureaus. The two heads were politically antagonistic, and in consequence the department was divided into rival camps.

Similarly in Cleveland the head of the detective bureau, designated by the director of public safety without consultation with the chief, managed his specialty as an independent unit. More and more the chief was relegated to the background as the responsible administrator of his department. Maladjustments of this kind, due to vague conceptions of the meaning of organization, are obviously fatal to effective police service.

The Adaptability of the Machine.

The third characteristic of good organization to which we called attention is the adaptability of the machine to its work. It is undoubtedly in this respect that the American police department shows its greatest weakness. As the community's instrument for the protection of life and property and the promotion of orderly relations, it seems primitive and crude. It has developed without plan or design, its purposes never accurately determined, often vaguely conceived. It has seldom been modeled from the point of view of what it was intended to accomplish.

---

[1] According to the ordinance of December 28, 1915, the chief of detectives is "the civilian aide to the director of the department of public safety." This official is appointed by the director of public safety, who also appoints the superintendent of police.

The Organization of the Department

Little exact study has been given, for example, to the relation between patrol duty and crime conditions. In city after city visited by the investigator no revision of patrol posts has occurred in years, in spite of constantly shifting populations. Old patrol arrangements sanctioned by time and tradition are accepted without examination. Because fifty men have been detailed by preceding administrations to patrol a given precinct it is assumed that fifty men are necessary today. That an analysis of patrol posts, based on present conditions, might show the necessity of seventy-five men or twenty-five seems seldom to occur to most police administrators. In Seattle the discovery was made that twelve square blocks in the heart of the city had for years been unpatrolled by day or night, while seven-eighths of the city was without police protection between four A. M. and twelve noon.[1] I was told by the chief of the Salt Lake City department that the residential section of his city never sees an officer during the 365 days of the year, unless one is specially detailed to a particular case. In cities like New York, Chicago, and Philadelphia little attempt has been made to vary the methods of patrol to suit the needs of different neighborhoods.[2] Not infrequently one finds an Italian section or a Russian Jewish section patrolled exactly as it was before the influx of the foreign population. Patrol arrangements originally planned for the business and

[1] Personally communicated by police officials.
[2] An examination in 1916 by Commissioner Woods showed that precinct boundary lines ran through the middle of streets, with the result that such streets were doubly patrolled by officers of the two contiguous precincts. By the simple expedient of running the boundary lines to a given street, instead of including one side of it, many patrolmen were released for other work.

populous residential districts have in many cases been extended, theoretically at least, to the suburban districts, regardless of the fact that the police problem is here radically different, while the very size of the territory to be covered makes the adaptation utterly impracticable. In Seattle at the time of my visit two patrol posts in the suburbs were respectively 49½ miles long and 90 miles long. On each post there were two signal boxes, at which the officer on beat had to report hourly, with the result that the well-marked path from one box to another constituted the extent of his actual patrol. In Denver at the time of my visit the patrol posts on well-lighted and busy thoroughfares were only two and three blocks long, while in the dimly lighted suburbs, where by night police protection is especially needed, they were often two miles long.

This lack of careful study and analysis of the task which the police are called upon to do makes it impossible to gauge the number of men needed on a force. The matter is apt to be judged by the existing size of the force rather than by a first-hand survey of requirements. The standard applied is simply traditional practice. One hears increases in the force advocated on the ground that " there has been no increase in five years," or that there are serious outbreaks of crime in particular neighborhoods. It is entirely possible even under these circumstances that the force is too large rather than too small. What is attributed to inadequacy of force may be ascribable to faulty methods of patrol or improper distribution. The fact-basis for judgment is missing. In consequence there are wide discrepancies in size between our police departments, which cannot be accounted for alone by divergent conditions of disorder. New Orleans and Birmingham have eleven policemen of all classes for each ten thousand of population; Cleveland, twelve; Milwaukee, fourteen; Boston and Philadelphia, twenty-three; New York, twenty; and Pittsburgh, sixteen. Little relationship appears to exist between the size of the police department in these cities and the general character of police work. Generally speaking, Cleveland, with one officer to every 796 inhabitants, is a better policed city than Philadelphia, with one to every 431; Milwaukee, with one to every 722, is certainly better policed than Pittsburgh, with one to every 626.

In brief, one gets the impression in many American cities that police organization is merely a conventional arrangement, sanctioned by usage and tradition, but with little relation to needs or neighborhoods. It looks too often like an importation — as if it had been wrenched from widely different surroundings and poorly fitted to its new environment. The admirable adaptation of means to end, of machinery to purposes, which one finds in many European departments, is conspicuously lacking. The Italian *Carabinieri* use a system of patrol adjusted to the peculiar crime conditions of Italian cities. The *arrondissements* and *quartiers* of the Parisian organization in charge of *commissaires de police,* represent a successful arrangement for handling the disorder and occasional turbulence of the French capital. The unique system of decentralization at Scotland Yard is adapted to the wide territory covered by the metropolitan police.

In American cities, on the other hand, the extraordinary crime conditions which confront us have stimulated little invention in the way of new and comprehensive police methods. With some notable improvements in equipment, Philadelphia and Chicago are patrolled today in much the same fashion as they were thirty years ago. Irish detectives still predominate in New York's detective bureau, in spite of the fact that the prevailing nationality of the criminal is no longer Irish. The police of Boston, Baltimore, and San Francisco follow the same general practices as regards the use of reserves and the publication of alarms that were in vogue before the influx of a complex foreign population. To be sure, modern appliances have greatly improved the technique of the departments in such matters as the identification of criminals and the control of traffic, but only occasionally does one observe a thorough-going adaptation of police methods and organization arrangements to social or criminal conditions. For the most part cities are content to copy the patterns of their neighbors, regardless of fit or suitability. Indianapolis, with a homogeneous population of 265,000, is policed in very much the same fashion as Chicago, with a heterogeneous population of 2,500,000. The police arrangements of Trenton (N. J.) and Bridgeport (Conn.) are shaped not by local necessities but by the conventional model furnished long ago by New York. Throughout the country there is little evidence of systematic plan or thought in adapting the police department to its work. To the construction of the police mechanism no real creative intelligence has been devoted.

The Organization of the Department

II

The faulty mechanism which we have just been discussing is the final outcome of many causes. We have space to comment upon only a few of them.

Inelastic Legal Restrictions.

Instead of being free to build their own municipal structures on the basis of their particular municipal requirements, our cities have been saddled by legislatures with stereotyped forms of organization ill-fitted to local conditions, and with methods of operation ill-adapted to local needs. In the determination of the framework of management the authorities immediately concerned have had little voice. I am here referring not to the distinction between state control and local control discussed in previous pages, but to the legislative prescriptions which have rendered immobile the internal arrangements of municipal departments. The state legislators rather than the local authorities have determined not only the general form of departmental organization, but the minutest details of the administrative machinery. One has only to look at the charters or special laws to realize how the inventiveness and imagination of local executives in framing administrative processes have been checked and thwarted, and their opportunities for wholesome experiment with municipal methods cramped in the straightjacket of detailed legislation imposed by the state.

In the police department this condition runs back to an early period. The law of 1857, creating a metropolitan police system for New York, established the complete administrative framework of the new department. .The method of listing stolen property, the kind of books that should be kept, the manner in which reports should be rendered, the precise circumstances under which gambling houses might be raided, the location of the superintendent's office, the number of police surgeons — in brief, the entire machinery of administration — was prescribed in elaborate detail.[1] This precedent was followed throughout the country. In 1866 the Ohio legislature decreed that Cleveland should have " a superintendent of police, a captain of police, and one captain in addition for each 50 patrolmen called into service more than the first 50, and a sergeant of police to each twelve patrolmen." [2] This same ratio, couched in identical language, was employed by the Michigan legislature for Detroit in 1867.[3] The form of police organization adopted by the Connecticut legislature for New Haven in 1881 is typical of limitations imposed by law-making bodies the country over. " There shall be a police department," said the law, " which shall consist of one chief of police, not more than two captains, not more than two lieutenants, not more than three sergeants (one of whom shall act as an inspector of licensed public vehicles), not more than three doormen, and not more than 50 supernumerary policemen." [4]

Inelastic restrictions of this kind still encumber the police organizations of most of the cities of the United States. In only a few has any appreciable freedom of

[1] Laws of N. Y., 1857, Chap. 569.
[2] Laws of Ohio, 1866, p. 104.
[3] Laws of Mich., 1867, No. 312.
[4] Special Acts of Conn., 1881, p. 294.

action been achieved. In New York the rigid provisions of the charter have for years been a handicap to efficient administration. So inflexible is the organization in this city that a former commissioner was obliged literally to take the stump and conduct a wide campaign of publicity in order to induce the legislature to give him the right to reduce to the rank of captain the police inspectors whom he knew to be notoriously unfit. Similar activity secured for the commissioner the power to appoint as first grade detectives the men whom he regarded best qualified for the positions. The request of the city administration in 1915 that it be allowed to appoint such additional deputy commissioners as the executive burdens of the department might make necessary was denied by the legislature at Albany, although after considerable delay and not a little opposition consent was given to the appointment of one additional deputy.

Yet in respect to the inelasticity of its organization New York is by no means in the worst position. The rigidity of the Baltimore charter is even more pronounced. It prescribes the number of officers in each police district, as well as the number of turnkeys and telephone operators. There shall be " two additional captains, one of whom shall be assigned to have charge of the detective office, and one . . . to have charge of the police patrol boats; five additional lieutenants, one of whom shall be assigned to have charge of the bureau of identification, one of whom shall be assigned to the said police patrol boats, one of whom shall be assigned to have charge of the police department horses, wagons, motor vehicles and stables, one of whom shall be superintendent of the police signal and telephone service, one of whom shall be assigned to night duty at police headquarters." [1]   Further, the methods of appointment, promotion, and dismissal, the salaries to be paid, and the precise duties and powers of the board of police commissioners are set forth in great detail.

In Buffalo the recently adopted charter provides that " the tours of duty of sergeants and patrolmen . . . on the streets or other public places of the city shall be changed at least once in each calendar month." [2]   It further specifies that " policemen while on reserve duty . . . shall not be required to render any service except in the case of an emergency, and shall be free to retire for sleep during reserve duty in their station house.[3] . . . Members of the police force shall not be required to wear a uniform when not on actual patrol duty." [4]   The charter also prescribes the number of platoons into which the force shall be divided, the hours of duty, and the length of leaves of absence.   Such leaves of absence must begin at six o'clock in the evening of one day and end at six o'clock in the evening of the following day.[5]   The provisions governing the detail of police management cover twenty-three pages of the charter, and show throughout the anxiety of the uniformed men to prevent possible encroachments upon their rights by their superiors.

Similarly in San Francisco the administrative methods of the department are prescribed at length, even to the

[1] Charter of Baltimore, Section 745.
[2] Buffalo Charter, Sec. 250 A.
[3] *Ibid.*, Sec. 250 B.
[4] *Ibid.*, Sec. 250 D.
[5] *Ibid.*, Sec. 250 D.

point of requiring the chief to keep in his office "the statutes of the state and of the United States and all necessary works on criminal law." [1] According to the Missouri law, the board of police commissioners of St. Louis "shall establish the Bertillon system of identification of criminals and others by means of anthropometric indications." [2] As illustrative of the folly of a legislative body assuming to determine administrative policies and details, it may be pointed out that at the time this provision was written into the law by the legislature of Missouri the Bertillon system of identification was being discarded in most European police departments.

Under limitations of this kind rational development of police organization cannot be looked for. The machine cannot be made to adjust itself to the widely contrasting social and economic conditions found in every city, while the constant flux and change in population and racial habit leave practices and methods soon out of date. The initiative and imagination of the average police administrator are strangled at the start. Experimentation with new ideas is practically impossible. Innovations calculated to increase the quality of the service are barred. Official activity is so curbed and hedged about that the new administrator, with perhaps a genuine desire to serve the public, soon finds himself little more than a machine, doing the things the law tells him to do in the way the law prescribes. Under such circumstances, unless possessed of unusual force and originality, he soon settles

[1] Charter of San Francisco, Art. VIII, Chap. IV, Sec. 4.
[2] Laws of Mo., 1899, p. 51, Sec. 479.

back into the old rut, content to maintain his department as he inherited it. Meanwhile the city's necessities develop while the police force stands still.

This rigid predetermination by statute of police organization and methods is in marked contrast to the flexibility of European police legislation. Police executives in England and on the continent are given wide powers in shaping their instruments of control and in adapting administrative processes to local conditions. Instead of the minute charter prescriptions which one finds in such cities as New York, Buffalo, and Baltimore, the statute governing the municipalities of England and Wales, for example, leaves the local authorities free to develop their own police departments. "The Watch Committee," according to the terse provision of the law, "shall from time to time appoint a sufficient number of fit men to be borough constables." [1] The special laws governing London's police force are equally free of regulative detail. Sir Robert Peel's act of 1829 begins with this simple declaration: "A sufficient number of fit and able men shall from time to time, by the direction of one of his majesty's principal secretaries of state, be appointed as a police force." [2] In the words of the act the commissioner of police, with the approbation of the Home Secretary, is given power "to frame such orders and regulations as (he) may deem expedient relative to the general government of the members of the police force; the places of their residence; their classification, rank, and particular service; their distribution and inspection; . . .

[1] Municipal Corporations Act of 1882, Part IX, Sec. 191.
[2] 10 Geo. IV. c. 44.

and all such orders and regulations as (he) shall deem expedient for preventing neglect or abuse or for rendering such force efficient in the discharge of all its duties; and (he) may at any time suspend or dismiss from employment any man belonging to the police force whom (he) shall think remiss or negligent in the discharge of his duty or otherwise unfit for the same." [1] Apart from the question of pensions and financial support, where permissive legislation would obviously be necessary, no attempt has been made in the eighty-eight years of London's police force to determine by statute the limitations of the executive in the administration of his department. In England, as well as in France and Switzerland, emphasis is centered upon the character and experience of the police commissioner. It is assumed that a trained administrator will be found and there is no disposition to hamper such an incumbent with restrictions or to erect barriers against the possible abuse of his powers. The development of the organization and its adjustment to shifting necessities are his responsibility. Answerable to his superiors and to the public for the success and propriety of his methods, he shapes his administrative tools to the work to be accomplished, unimpeded by the arbitrary rules of an uninformed legislative body.

This point of view is gaining some ground in American cities. The present law governing the police force of Boston, for example, while irritatingly detailed in certain sections, represents a substantial improvement over the laws which it superseded. According to its provisions

[1] *Ibid.* The act was originally framed with two commissioners as executives. In 1856 these powers were vested in a single commissioner.

the police commissioner has authority " to appoint, establish, and organize the police of the city, and to make all needful rules and regulations for its efficiency. . . . He may employ such clerks, stenographers, and other employees as he may deem necessary for the proper performance of the duties of his office." [1] So, too, in certain states where the doctrine of home rule has been accepted in some form or other — notably in Ohio — the temptation to establish by law the administrative machinery of the police department has been discouraged, and charters have been framed, as in Cleveland and Toledo, conferring wide discretion upon the police executives in the management of their forces. Home rule, however, is not in itself a remedy for the evil of inelastic administrative processes decreed by law. A charter framed by a community under grant of full powers of local self-government may be just as effective in tying the hands of a police administrator as a charter framed by a legislature. The same thing is true of ordinances passed by local assemblies. Detailed prescriptions as to methods and practices will create rigidity in any departmental machinery, and block intelligent efforts to make it produce the best results, no matter whether the prescriptions are framed at the city hall or in the state capitol. The sole advantage of home rule in this regard lies in the fact that the responsibility for bad machinery rests with the people affected by its operation, and a remedy is consequently more easily obtained. An executive whose effectiveness is circumscribed by unnecessary limitations, or thwarted by foolish mandatory decrees, can free himself by an appeal

[1] Acts of Mass., 1906, Chap. 291, Secs. 8–10.

to his community more readily than he can by appealing to the representatives of the entire state.

Unnecessary Functions.

The irrational development of American police organization is not ascribable alone to legislative interference with the details of administration. Another causal factor, perhaps equally important, is found in the willingness of charter-makers to complicate the police machinery by the addition of extraneous and unrelated functions. Instead of building an organization around the single duty of maintaining law and order — a duty in itself onerous enough — in many states the attempt is made to employ the machinery for all sorts of governmental purposes. This indiscriminate use of the police department is not characteristic of America alone. It is even more pronounced in continental Europe, particularly in Germany and Austria. In these countries, however, it has developed not through any haphazard distribution of functions, but rather from the peculiar continental conception of police power as comprehending all activities of government which have not been directly transferred to other branches of the administration.[1] This conception, with its historical basis in the necessities of autocratic government, never gained a foot-hold in Great Britain, with the result that English police machinery is singularly free from complicating factors.[2] Indeed such a conception would find little place in any liberal government. In America the tendency to load the police force with irrele-

[1] See *European Police Systems*, pp. 18–24.
[2] *Ibid.*, pp. 140–148.

vant functions is largely a matter of careless and untidy governmental housekeeping. The department has been made a sort of catch-all for such miscellaneous activities as cannot easily be accommodated elsewhere. Thus, the police in many American cities have had given them the judicial responsibility of issuing licenses for saloons, restaurants, taverns, ice-cream parlors, masque balls, markets, and lodging houses. So, too, they license hawkers, peddlers, junk gatherers, employment house " runners," newsboys, boot-blacks, dog-breeders, auctioneers, and other special professions. In New York city the police department is charged with the duty of inspecting steam-boilers and fixing the maximum pressure allowed for each; it also licenses and passes upon the qualifications of steam engineers.[1] In Chicago the department has charge of dog-catching and the pound [2] and the censorship of moving pictures; [3] in Baltimore it takes the yearly census of school children; [4] in Washington, D. C., it has charge of the inspection of pharmacies; [5] in Milwaukee it collects arrears in personal taxes; [6] in Detroit a member of the force performs the duties of sealer of weights and measures, and the commissioner appoints the city scavengers; [7] in Boston the commissioner establishes rates of interest for pawnbrokers,[8] and investigates the qualifications of jurors; [9] in Philadelphia the fire marshal's office

1 New York City Charter, Chap. 8, Secs. 342–345.
2 Chicago Code of Ordinances, 1911, Chap. 20, Sec. 771.
3 Chicago Code of Ordinances, 1911, Chap. 46.
4 Laws of Md., 1914, Chap. 90.
5 34 U. S. Statutes at Large, p. 182.
6 Wisconsin Statutes, Sec. 925–148.
7 Detroit Charter, Sec. 665.
8 Revised Laws of Mass., Chap. 102, Sec. 41.
9 Mass. Stats., 1907, Chap. 348.

is under the superintendent of police, who is thus responsible for the inspection and storage of combustibles and the condition of fire escapes and exits.[1]   For years in New York the cleaning of the streets was under the supervision of the police department.

In consequence of this confusion with irrelevant activities, the primary function of the police has often been left to drift along with little guidance or oversight by the administrators.   In their endeavors to accommodate themselves to such judicial functions as issuing licenses, or to such spectacular functions as managing elections, the commissioners and directors have neglected their weightier responsibilities.

This confusing use of the police machinery, particularly for excise licenses and election purposes, has often led to sinister results.   The wide powers thus conferred upon the police force have made it the prize of every municipal contest.   A department for the maintenance of order would in itself be a tempting bait to politicians; but when the control of licenses and of the election machinery is added, the department becomes practically indispensable to the success of a political party.   To this unwise and unsound partnership between the police force and unrelated functions of government much of the corruption and demoralization in American municipalities can be traced.   In New York, for example, a law passed in 1872 [2] and maintained for 29 years [3] gave the police commissioners full charge of the election machinery.

[1] Laws of Penn., 1911, p. 705.
[2] Laws of N. Y., 1872, Chap. 675.
[3] Repealed by Laws of N. Y., 1901, Chap. 95.   For an interesting review of the development of the electoral machinery in New

Every important step in the conduct of elections, both prior to and after the polling of the vote, was under their supervision and largely under their control. They appointed the inspectors of election and the poll clerks; they passed upon the certificates of nomination of candidates; they received and were charged with the custody of election returns. At the same time their subordinates, the members of the uniformed force, were assigned to maintain order at the polling places. The practical operation of this partnership under a board of police commissioners dominated by Tammany influence is described in the following excerpt from the report of the Lexow investigating commission of 1894:

> " It may be stated as characteristic of the conditions shown to exist by a cloud of witnesses that the police conducted themselves at the several polling places upon the principle that they were there not as guardians of the public peace to enforce law and order, but for the purpose of acting as agents of Tammany Hall in securing to the candidates of that organization, by means fair or foul, the largest possible majorities." [1]

Conditions of the same kind if not of the same degree

York, see William M. Ivin's *On the Electoral System of the State of New York* — a paper read before the New York State Bar Association, January, 1906, and published in pamphlet form.

[1] From the majority report, pp. 15–16. In spite of this condition, the separation of the police department and the bureau of elections was not recommended in the majority report, the members of the commission clinging to the idea of a bi-partisan board as an effective remedy. Such a separation, however, was urged in the minority report, which at the same time argued for a single-headed police department rather than a bi-partisan board. With a bureau of elections independent of the police force, one of the chief arguments commonly used for a bi-partisan board falls to the ground.

existed in other cities where the election machinery was part of the police organization — notably in Buffalo. Disorder, fraud, and continual suspicion followed the wake of this unhappy partnership. As a result, the partnership has almost universally been dissolved, and the police force has been freed of a demoralizing incumbrance.

Equally unhappy was the association of the police with the issuance of liquor licenses. The almost uniform result was misunderstanding, suspicion, and the neglect by the police commissioners of the real function of their departments. The question continually before the public was not: " Is this department efficient in maintaining order and preventing crime?" but, " Should a saloon license have been given to this or that neighborhood?" In consequence the real function of the police, overlooked by the public, was neglected by the commissioners. Police machinery cannot be complicated without losing in effectiveness.

Inadequate Leadership.

Far more than to any other factor the irrational development of American police organization is due to inadequate leadership. To the lack of trained and intelligent administrators, obtaining and holding office on favorable conditions, much of the confusion and maladjustment of our police machinery is ascribable. The crude political conceptions which have allowed such specialized community functions as police and health to be managed by a periodically shifting body of unskilled, unfit, unprofessional executives, have wrought almost irremediable injury not only to our forms of organization but to the whole public life of America. In so far as the police department is concerned, mechanical causes such as we have considered have undoubtedly contributed to this evil result; but the fundamental factor, underlying all others, is one of personnel. This question is so vital to an understanding of the American police problem that the two succeeding chapters have been devoted to its consideration.

CHAPTER VI

THE COMMISSIONER OR DIRECTOR

The task of police administration.— Police administrators promoted from the ranks.— Chicago.— Civilian police administrators.— Their handicaps.— Examples.— Police administration and politics.— Limited tenure of office.— Europe and America in this respect.— Residence requirements for commissioners.— European and American examples.— The dilemma and the approach to its solution.

WE have already observed the trend toward single-headed management in the police department. The irresponsible multiple-headed executive is giving way before the demand for definitized leadership, and the civilian commissioner or director is taking the place of the board. This change has been brought about in most cases without disturbing the position of the chief or superintendent who is still the agent through whom the department is administered. Only in New York, where the commissioner and his deputies are directly in charge of the force, has the office of chief been abolished. In many of the smaller cities, as we have already noted, particularly in those in which the board form of control never obtained a permanent foothold, there is no civilian commissioner as an intermediary between the chief and the mayor, and the chief, as head of the force, is the responsible leader. Chicago alone of the larger cities still clings to the small city type of administration. Indeed Chicago holds the distinction of being the largest city in the world in which the head of the police department has generally been promoted from the ranks.

This point suggests some interesting questions which may well be considered at the beginning of our discussion. What would justify a city in employing a civilian commissioner? Why should not the Chicago arrangement be more generally accepted? Assuming that an officer promoted from the ranks can manage successfully the police affairs of a small city, at what point in the city's growth is it desirable to introduce a different type of administrator?

The Task of Police Administration.

One is helped to answer these puzzling questions by a consideration of the task of police administration in a large city. It is far more than a matter of supervising the actual work of men in uniform. It involves qualities of leadership which come only from broad administrative training and experience. The New York Department costs $18,000,000 a year; the Chicago department, $7,000,000; the Philadelphia department, $4,500,-000. Of the 63 cities of the United States with a population of 100,000 or over, twelve have an annual police cost exceeding $1,000,000, and in twenty-five the annual cost is over $400,000. The head of a police department is thus the business manager of a huge concern. He must map out its policies, define its methods, and hold himself responsible for program and performance. He must be able to organize the complex functions of his department into some kind of coherent whole. To insure success, he must be as eager to keep abreast with his profession and as alert to see the possibilities of improvement in his force, as if municipal management were a competitive business. Vision and imagination are as essential to him as they are to any administrator. Furthermore, he must possess the unimpaired confidence of his hundreds or thousands of men, and be able to meet with firmness and decision the perplexing situations which constantly arise in the police affairs of every large city. In brief, he must be accustomed to *leading*.

Moreover, the task of police administration involves the handling of complex and intricate community problems, for which a background of social ideals and experience is essential. The head of a police department is called upon to consider sympathetically, and if possible to reconcile, the widely divergent points of view of all classes. He must be able to meet on their own planes rich and poor, citizen and alien, learned and unlearned. Constantly before him must be the conception of his department as an agency for the *prevention* of crime, and the consequent relation of his work to all activities, social, economic, and educational, operating to that end. He must approach the problem of racial mixture in his city with a keen appreciation of the contrasting standards of order and conduct which arise from diverse racial habits and traditions. Tact, intuition, and a quick intelligence are indispensable factors in his equipment. He must be able to gauge the drift in public temper, and distinguish between substantial and fictitious public opinion. He must be ready to adjust his organization and its methods of operation to changes in public ideas without compromising himself or lessening the influence of his department. Because his is public business rather than private business, he must know how to popularize it and how to rally public support behind his leadership in times of crisis.

Police Administrators Promoted from the Ranks.

One perhaps would be something of a superman who could fulfill satisfactorily all the requirements just mentioned. They represent, however, standards to be considered in the choice of a police administrator. In large cities like New York and Chicago, and in many cities of lesser size, the task is so great and its responsibilities so heavy that the best man obtainable is none too good, and in an endeavor to discover him no search can be too thorough. That such a leader can be found in the ranks of a police force is in the highest degree improbable. The officer who has walked his " beat " as a patrolman, investigated crime as a detective, and managed the technical routine of station house activity as lieutenant or captain, is not fitted by this experience to administer the complex affairs of a large police department. The chances are rather that he is unfitted for the task. Lacking in administrative experience, with scant appreciation of the larger possibilities of his position, often, indeed, without imagination or resourcefulness, he has little chance of success, and it would be unwise and cruel to saddle him with the responsibility. If police management were merely a matter of assignments, promotions, and discipline, if it had to do only with the ordering of a well-defined routine, any capable man who himself had been through the mill might be well adapted to handle it. But as we have seen,

The Commissioner or Director

the task, particularly in large cities, is so much broader than routine and involves activities of such vital consequence, that only a high order of creative intelligence can cope with it.

The idea that effective heads of large police departments cannot often be found in the ranks is frowned upon in some quarters as being somehow or other " undemocratic," and the argument is occasionally advanced that this principle clashes with the belief which we Americans hold inviolate : that humble and modest beginnings can be no barrier to ultimate success and reward. This point of view completely misses the issue. Of course humble beginnings do not disqualify a man for service; neither do they qualify him. They simply have no bearing, one way or the other. We are concerned with facts and conditions and not with theories or labels. It is not a matter of democracy or lack of democracy, of caste, or birth, or position, or anything else. *It is solely a matter of finding the best possible brains to handle a most difficult public task.*

To the failure to grasp the significance of this point is largely attributable the long demoralized condition of the Chicago department — in size the second police force in the United States. In this city the head of the force has generally been promoted from the ranks, under an arrangement by which he can return to duty in his old position when his services as superintendent are no longer required. In 25 years, eleven different men, only two of whom were chosen from outside the department, have occupied the post of superintendent. Most of the men thus promoted retired after a disastrous and often inglorious experience, for the reason that from the very nature of their training they could not measure up to the task. No opportunity to develop qualities of leadership had ever been afforded them. They could not reorganize the department, for they knew nothing about organization. They could not think in terms of progress or possibilities. With two or three exceptions, they were dull and ineffective. With little administrative experience to guide them in their new tasks, with no background of general information, they carried out what they conceived to be the duties of their position: meeting visitors, handling perfunctory routine, signing their names to official documents, and joining in an occasional spectacular hunt for a murderer or thief. In this last activity they bore out the popular theory — often expressed in Chicago and elsewhere — that the head of the police force, whatever other virtues he possesses, must be a "good, practical thief-catcher." Thief-catching is a highly technical and very important phase of police work, and skilled men should be engaged in it. But the training that creates proficiency in this line is not the training to produce an intelligent administrator. Little connection exists between the two activities. So far from fitting them for their new work, the previous experience of the Chicago superintendents of police was a positive handicap. They could not get away from the point of view which they had acquired during their years on the force. They were still police sergeants at heart, concerned with small precinct details, or district detectives absorbed in the game of catching thieves.

The Commissioner or Director

That a high type of intelligence is necessary in police administration has long been recognized in Europe. Only in the smaller cities is it possible for an officer in the ranks to become head of the force. In London, Paris, Marseilles, Geneva, Vienna, Rome, and in scores of cities of lesser importance, the head of the department has never in history been promoted from the ranks.[1] To be sure, in some cities, particularly on the continent, this is in part ascribable to prevailing class distinctions and social cleavages, as a result of which but few in any walk of life can rise from humble to high position. But fundamentally the arrangement is based upon the conception of the police commissioner as a highly trained administrator. A man of limited education and scant opportunity for development is not likely to be equipped to handle large questions in a large way, or deal administratively with the intricate business of a complex department.

Our consideration, of course, has nothing to do with chiefs of police promoted from the ranks, who serve under civilian commissioners. In such a relationship the chief is the head of the technical service and is not called upon to assume broad administrative responsibilities. A training in the ranks may exactly fit him for his work; indeed, it would be difficult for him to obtain elsewhere the necessary specialized experience. Thus in Boston the uniformed superintendent of police, with his intimate knowledge of the details of police activity, serves as an aide to the commissioner, and the arrangement is satisfactory

[1] See *European Police Systems*, Chap. IV.

because the chief has no duties beyond the limit of his ability or experience. Similarly in Philadelphia the superintendent of police is the adviser of the director of public safety, and in New York the chief inspector occupies the same position in his relation to the commissioner. The administrative machinery breaks down when, as in Chicago, the superintendent with his technical education is given a responsibility for which he has never been trained.

It is obviously unfair and indeed inaccurate to assume that a man who has come through the ranks is thereby unfitted to serve as the head of a police department. In small cities, where the responsibilities of administration are not heavy and do not call for special gifts, some officer in the force can probably be found who, under right conditions, can manage the department satisfactorily. Even in respect to large cities there is no unvarying principle that can be dogmatically asserted. A police department may contain an officer of broad vision and real administrative ability, well fitted to assume the leadership of a sizeable department. The writer has in mind several such executives, competent to manage large affairs, who worked their way up from the rank of patrolmen. They represent, however, the exception; they are men who would doubtless have succeeded in any profession and in spite of any handicap. Generally speaking, in most cities exceeding 100,000 in population it would probably be difficult to find in the ranks of the police force an officer of such education and promise that the administration of the entire department could wisely be committed to his hands.

The Commissioner or Director

Civilian Police Administrators.

It is obvious, therefore, that our police administrators must in many cities be recruited from outside the force. In arriving at this conclusion we are bound to consider grave difficulties whose importance is not to be underestimated. First of all we are confronted with the lack of any class of trained governmental executives such as one finds on the continent in Europe and to a certain extent in England. In Great Britain the Royal Irish Constabulary or the imperial administrative service furnish the principal cities with their police heads. In London, for example, the commissioner who resigned in 1918[1] had spent his life in police work. Entering the Indian civil service as an assistant magistrate, he became successively inspector general of police in Bengal and commissioner for the entire southern district of India. During the South African War he organized the civil police of Johannesburg and Pretoria, and later came to London as assistant police commissioner. In 1903, after thirty years devoted exclusively to the profession of policing, he was chosen to be head of London's force. He was a thoroughly trained man; no problem arising in connection with his department was beyond his grasp.[2]

In America, on the other hand, there is no profession or career of public administration to attract the talent of our schools and universities. No opportunity is afforded to develop through a course of years any particular ability to manage a specialized function of government, such as a police department or a department of health. Indeed,

[1] Sir Edward Henry.
[2] See *European Police Systems*, Chap. IV.

our political customs and habits of thought run counter to such an arrangement. American democracy has been colored by a distrust of special qualifications in public office; it has always regarded the expert in public life with suspicion and disfavor. Not only does the permanent tenure of office which his employment implies conflict with current ideas of popular control, but his very position in the community clashes with the conception of equality which would give every man a substantial opportunity to take part in the administration of public affairs. As President Lowell points out,[1] men desire not only to be well governed but to feel that they are governing themselves, and the readiest way of achieving this end is to throw the offices open to all aspirants. Rotation in office has been, and to a certain extent still is, a corollary of democracy, and its peculiarly wide acceptance in America has effectively retarded the science of public administration and prevented the development of a profession of trained government executives.

Moreover, in many parts of the country little appreciation exists of the need of specially trained men at the head of particular departments of city or state administration. We seem to assume that an appointment by a governor or mayor confers, without apprenticeship, an immediate capacity to manage public finances, direct schools, or run a police force. The practices of early rural communities, where the common experience of the average man enabled him to deal intelligently with the plain questions that came before the public officer, are often applied as standards to modern government, with

[1] *Public Opinion and Popular Government*, New York, 1913, p. 271.

the result that in this one field alone we ignore the specialization of occupations which the complexity of modern society and the growth of accurate knowledge have made necessary. City administration today is complicated by a variety of public services, many of them technical in nature, dependent upon the results of recent study and research in their particular fields. A high bacterial count in the city's water supply — to use the words of a former director of public works in Philadelphia — presents a problem incapable of solution by the political office-holder, even though he can carry every precinct in his ward. Such problems as the treatment of crime, the relation of a community to pauperism, the handling of mendicants, the responsibility of the criminal in the light of modern psychiatry, are matters with which even the intelligent citizen has little acquaintance. They can be mastered only by special study or long experience, and they can be dealt with efficiently only by those who have mastered them.[1] It is idle, therefore, to assume that a successful engineer or lawyer is preeminently fitted to manage a police department or a department of correction. In the pursuit of his ordinary vocation he has probably had no opportunity to familiarize himself with even the rudiments of his new profession, and only by hard, conscientious study, through an uninterrupted tenure of office, can he bring himself abreast of his work.

A city, therefore, honestly seeking an efficient police administrator, has a narrow field of choice. New York City in nineteen years has experimented with army officers, lawyers, newspaper men, and professional poli-

---

[1] *Ibid.* See Chap. XVIII on "Experts in Municipal Government."

ticians. Of twelve commissioners only six had had any previous experience with police work, and even this experience was of a limited nature. In two cases the commissioners, prior to appointment, had never even been inside a police station. In four cases they were without administrative training of any sort. In more than half the cases, they took up the task of managing the second largest police force in the world without the slightest comprehension of its meaning, its technique, or its vast responsibilities.

Similarly the directors of public safety in Philadelphia in the last 30 odd years have been for the most part untrained and without experience, coming from occupations which in no way fitted them for their new tasks. One was a candy manufacturer, one an insurance broker, one a banker, one a solicitor for an electric light company, and five were lawyers. Detroit in nineteen years has had in the police commissionership two bankers, one of whom was indicted and convicted while in office, a furniture dealer, a judge of the police court, a lawyer, a manufacturer, an automobile sales agent (the last named having been the campaign manager of the mayor who appointed him), a manufacturer, and a physician. Pittsburgh in twenty years has had in the directorship of public safety a clerk, a traction company official, a weather-bureau observer, a real estate man, a small hotel proprietor, a newspaper man, a hardware manufacturer, and a lawyer. Cleveland in recent years has had as directors of public safety a clergyman, a representative of a roofing business, two attorneys and a jeweler. In Chicago, as we have seen, the superintendent of police is customarily promoted from the ranks. The eight exceptions to this rule, occurring in 49 years, have comprised a stock-yard commissioner, a whiskey distiller, a brewer, a professional politician, a prison warden, a hay and feed merchant, two post office officials, one of whom was also an officer in the National Guard. In Salt Lake City, where the head of the force[1] is always a civilian, six more recent incumbents have been respectively a plumber, a merchant, an insurance broker, a stage coach operator, a livery keeper, and a traveling man for a tea and coffee house. At the time of my visit the head of the force was by vocation a fire insurance adjuster. Similarly Los Angeles has had newspaper men, a railroad man, an insurance broker, and a man engaged in the transfer and express business. The head of the force in San Francisco a few years ago was a laundryman.[2]

Investigation in other cities shows similar conditions. In the absence of trained men, appointing authorities are forced to make shift with the material they can get, with results often unfortunate, not infrequently disastrous. Such results must inevitably be expected when untrained, inexperienced men are placed in a position where training and experience — or at least the opportunity to develop them — are essential. In many cases, indeed, the question is not whether the new man will fail, but how quick and complete his failure will be. Occasionally, of course, in spite of a lack of special training, the results are highly

[1] His title is chief.
[2] New Orleans at one time attempted to shut the door on some professions. According to a statute passed in 1904 "no attorney at law or person engaged in the liquor business" was eligible as police commissioner. (Laws of La., 1904, No. 32.)

creditable. Mr. Pullman's administration in Washington, D. C., for example, was marked with ability and progressiveness of an unusual kind. A clean cut young newspaper correspondent, he brought to his task a vigor and a personality that reshaped the Washington force into an effective instrument. Similarly, Commissioner O'Meara of Boston, coming from a long experience in newspaper management which involved wide executive responsibilities, gave his city one of the cleanest police administrations in the United States. In the same breath it must be admitted that his success was in no small measure attributable to his uninterrupted tenure of service. In the twelve years of his commissionership he had the unique opportunity of making himself, by dint of long and patient study, an efficient police executive. In New York the work of Commissioner Woods was little short of brilliant and its effect has been felt throughout the country. In his case, however, success was certainly attributable, in some part at least, not only to his previous experience as deputy commissioner, which gave him a broad grasp of the problem, but to the complete lack of interference from the city hall. If some of his predecessors had been afforded the same independence, it is possible that long before the department might have enjoyed the distinction it reached under Commissioner Woods.

Such instances are exceptional. They stand out in sharp relief against the poor quality of leadership which one finds in most police organizations. The absence of administrative experience and special training and the lack of facilities for their development have made the task of building up our police departments an exceedingly difficult one.

Police Administration and Politics.

The situation is complicated by another factor of more ominous significance. Police administration in the United States is a matter of politics. It is organized on the basis not of individual fitness, but of political faith. It is part of the sordid system of jobs and spoils which so notoriously distinguishes much of our local government. It depends upon periodic elections, decided in most cases upon issues with which it is not even remotely associated. Although an expert service, whose efficiency is predicated on special ability and continuity of management, it is tossed about from one party to another as the prize of success at the polls. A Republican victory in Philadelphia means a Republican director of public safety, just as a Tammany victory in New York means a Tammany commissioner of police. Indeed in many parts of the country there is as yet no conception that politics and administration are separable. Such a view is thought to be somehow undemocratic. The policy-determining function of government, controlled in a democracy by popular will, is confused with the technical business procedure by which the policies are put into effect; and because the opinions of one set of officials are subject to popular review, it is held that, indirectly at least, the other set must pass the same test. In consequence, the administrative officers of specialized departments are selected primarily on the basis of party allegiance and political creed, and only secondarily because of particular training and ability.

With a few exceptions, therefore, political considerations constitute the dominant factor in the management of the police forces of the United States. It is unnecessary to dwell upon the demoralization which this situation produces or to attempt to catalogue in different cities its forms and ramifications. Essentially it is the same everywhere: the head of the department appointed because he is a Democrat or a Republican or " a personal friend of the mayor "; transfers and details made at the behest of some district boss or overlord; the force administered with an eye to the next election, and its work dictated by the political necessities of the moment. This is the dreary picture that one sees in all parts of the country and under all types of police management. Of the sixty-three cities in the United States exceeding 100,000 population, one can count on the fingers of both hands the number in which the police departments are administered on a genuinely non-political basis; and even in these cases there is no guarantee of permanence in the situation. In many places the presence of politics in the administrative service is admitted frankly and accepted with resignation. " You cannot divorce politics and the police," I was told in Kansas City, " at least not until the millennium."

This condition is all the more distressing when one examines the operations of European police departments. In London, Paris, Rome, Berlin, Vienna — indeed in all the larger cities — politics has nothing to do with the administration of the police force, directly or indirectly.[1]

[1] See *European Police Systems*, Chap. II.

The Commissioner or Director

The political opinions of the head of the department and his assistants are as irrelevant and immaterial as their opinions on art or literature. The outcome of a popular election has little or no relation to police administration. In other words, the policy and discipline of the force cannot be upset as an incidental consequence of the determination of political issues, with the result that the force is never the spoils of a political party nor the tool of a particular politician. The police departments of cities like Glasgow, Geneva, Liverpool, and Marseilles show no trace of the sordid politics which at the time of my visit frankly dominated the departments of Atlanta, Pittsburgh, Indianapolis, and Omaha. European superiority in this regard is not, as might easily be believed, the direct consequence of autocratic principles, for these conditions exist in such thoroughgoing democracies as England and Switzerland. It results from the fact that the technical administration of specialized departments is sharply distinguished from questions of public policy giving rise to legitimate political issues. When a man is wanted to head the London Metropolitan police force the sole test is the test of fitness, and the one aim of the appointing authorities is to obtain for the position the best mind that training and experience can produce. When such a man is found the authorities cling to him as any business concern would cling to an indispensable employee. Similarly in Manchester or Birmingham or in Leipzig or Stuttgart the personnel of the municipal council or of the *Gemeinderat* may shift a dozen times on ever changing issues, without in any way affecting the head of the police department. He represents the expert administrative arm of government, and, while subject to the control and supervision of some council or superior body, he is not concerned with the character of its membership or with the political issues which divide it. His position is that of a highly trained administrative manager serving under a board of directors: the personnel of the board may change and its policies may be altered; but the manager remains because the business cannot afford to let him go.

Under all types of government this cardinal principle of efficient administration remains the same. The policy-determining functions may be in the hands of a few as in Germany, or may be vested with the people as in England. Whatever the method by which public courses of action are decided, expert administrative service is the best tool for maintaining an efficient government, and in Europe it is employed alike by democracy and autocracy.

Limited Tenure of Office.

The intrusion of politics in American police administration brings with it an evil to which passing reference has already been made. It renders brief and uncertain the tenure of office of the commissioner. Indeed the transient character of its leadership is perhaps the most amazing feature of the American municipal department. The business managers of specialized city functions come and go in quick succession, their official life dependent upon political exigencies or personal whims. In some cases they follow one another with such bewildering rapidity that even departmental subordinates find it difficult to recall the names of the men under whom they have served in a dozen years.

The Commissioner or Director

In consequence there is little opportunity to train heads of departments to even a moderate understanding of their tasks and responsibilities. Without previous experience and with no preparation of any kind, a citizen takes up the administration of a large police force or a bureau of health; before he has had time to discover what his position really involves or to delve deeply into the intricacies of his organization, his official career is at an end, and another man, equally untried and inexperienced, begins at the point where his many predecessors began. Or again, a man serves long enough as head of a department to make himself fairly effective as its administrator, but through some political shift, generally irrelevant to any matter related to his work, his career is cut off, and his experience and training, gained at public cost, are lost to the community. Thereupon, experiment is made with another untried man, who, perhaps finally trained to the point of usefulness, is dismissed like his predecessor to make way for another beginner. In this way the dreary succession goes on, year after year, with little thought of health administration or police administration as a distinct career or profession, entirely removed from the political arena, and with just as little thought of the loss in consequence to public health and security.

The police department is peculiarly the victim of this principle of transient management. " Most of the commissioners are birds of passage," said Commissioner Woods of New York, in testifying before an investigating committee. " The force gets a glimpse of them flying over, but hardly has time to determine their species." [1]

[1] Curran Aldermanic Committee Report, 1912, p. 3127.

This statement is readily borne out by the facts. Whereas London has had seven police commissioners in 91 years, New York has had twelve in nineteen years. The average term of London's police commissioner is nearly fifteen years,[1] although Sir Richard Mayne, the first commissioner, served 39 years and his successor seventeen years, while the last incumbent, Sir Edward Henry, served a little over fifteen years.[2] The average term of New York's police commissioner is one year, seven months; the longest that any one succeeded in serving being three years, nine months. Three of New York's twelve commissioners served less than six months each; one incumbent served only 23 days. A change in the commissionership in New York has always involved a change in the deputy commissioners, with the result that where London has had fourteen deputy commissioners in sixty-four years,[3] New York City has had 43 in nineteen years.[4]

Comparisons of this kind could be indefinitely extended. It is not at all unusual, for example, to find in Great Britain or on the continent heads of police departments who have served from fifteen to twenty-five years or longer. The chief constable of Glasgow, Scotland, has held his position for eighteen years; the chief constables of Birmingham and Manchester have served sixteen and

---

[1] The present commissioner started his term in 1918.

[2] See *European Police Systems,* Chap. IV.

[3] The position of deputy or assistant commissioner was not established in London until 1856, when there were two assistant commissioners; in 1890 provision was made for three assistant commissioners and in 1910 the number was increased to four.

[4] There were four deputies from 1901 to 1915 when the number was increased to five.

nineteen years respectively. The police president of Hamburg, Germany, held his office for more than seventeen years; Vienna's police president, for more than ten years. The police president of Berlin had served eight years, when the exigencies of the war transferred him to another post. Copenhagen's commissioner recently rounded out 28 years of service. Indeed a short term of office for European police commissioners is the exception rather than the rule. It is assumed that they will hold office as long as they can render efficient service, or at least until their conduct proves unsatisfactory to their superiors.[1]

Radically different is the situation of America. Philadelphia has had thirteen directors of public safety in 33 years, an average of two years and a half for each incumbent; Cincinnati, four directors in seven years; Cleveland, five in twelve years. Twenty-five superintendents of police have served Chicago in 49 years, an average term of less than two years; in the last twenty years there have been nine superintendents, every incoming administration making at least one change. Detroit has had nine police commissioners in nineteen years. Many of the commission governments, recently inaugurated, are in a fair way to break all records in the number of their police administrators.

When one turns to the boards of police commissioners the succession becomes more rapid and the figures mount appreciably. In St. Louis 48 different commissioners have managed the police force in the last 31 years. In other words, the task of administering this technical

[1] See *European Police Systems,* Chap. IV.

branch of the city government has been committed to 48 men, inexperienced in police work, many of whom served but a year or two. Newark had 36 police commissioners in 32 years; San Francisco 41 in twenty years; Baltimore 50 in 60 years. In the forty-four years from 1857 to 1901 when New York's police force was under the control of a board, 52 different men were charged with the responsibility of management. During the last twenty years of this period 25 commissioners were in office.

The transient character of American police administration is not attributable alone to the sordid play of politics. Long tenures of office are repugnant to our political traditions. The fears and prejudices engendered in the early beginnings of our democracy remain a determining influence in our approach to questions of government organization. We have inherited a dread of " a class privileged to rule," and rotation rather than permanence in office has been our shield against the intrusion of " autocracy." Indeed the antipathy, fostered by our frontier conditions of life, to anything deemed aristocratic has given a strongly marked tone to our conception of popular government. Our attitude toward our representatives in office is one of continual suspicion. Constant fear of removal, and limited terms have been the weapons by which we have endeavored to keep them in touch with public opinion. As President Lowell aptly says, the American citizen is far less attracted by the idea of experienced public servants who retain their positions so long as they are faithful and efficient, than he is repelled by the dread of bureaucracy.[1]

[1] *Loc. cit.*, p. 106.

The Commissioner or Director

This point of view is shown in all our legislation, national, state and municipal, relating to public officers. Their terms of service are, with few exceptions, strictly limited and defined, as if in no other fashion could they be made amenable to public opinion, or responsive to popular control. To this practice the police administrator is no exception. In all our cities the law specifically implies that he is a temporary officer. His term ranges from two years in municipalities like Albany and Syracuse to five years in New York and Boston. Of the larger cities of the United States, twelve have two year terms for their police administrators; seven have three year terms; sixteen have four year terms; and three have five year terms.[1] In some cities, notably those in Ohio, the police executive serves " at the pleasure of the mayor," [2] apparently on the assumption that his position is semi-political in character and that every mayor should have the right to appoint " his own man." The same point of view is implied in the statutes governing the cities of Pennsylvania, where the tenure of the director of public safety is made coincident with the term " for which the appointing mayor is elected." [3] Some cities have attempted to avoid the implication of such an arrangement by giving the police administrator a longer term than that of the officer who appoints him. Thus the police commissioner of Boston has a five year term, while the governor of Massachusetts serves for two years. Similarly,

[1] These figures include boards of commissioners as well as single-headed management.

[2] See Cleveland City Charter, Sec. 80, and Columbus Charter, Sec. 60.

[3] See Philadelphia Charter, 1919, Art. V, Sec. I, and Pittsburgh Charter, Art. XII.

the term of the mayor of New York is four years, while his police commissioner serves five years. Again in Detroit, until recently, the mayor was elected for two years and the police commissioner appointed for four. However, in the absence of any restrictions on the appointing officer in removing an incumbent, this expedient has no practical value whatsoever. It is merely a bit of legislative jugglery. Every incoming mayor of New York has always appointed his own police commissioner, just as every incoming governor of Massachusetts, could, if he chose, appoint a new head of the police force in Boston.[1] The same result is reached in Chicago, which is the only large city whose charter contains no specific provision regarding the tenure of the police head. For all practical purposes it is coincident with that of the mayor.

This custom of pacing off in advance the term of a police administrator and writing it into the law is in direct contrast to the arrangement in European cities. There the police commissionership is always indefinite in tenure. In not a single English or continental city of size or importance is the head of the police force appointed for a fixed period.[2] In fact, the idea of establishing by some arbitrary rule the time when the administration of a police commissioner shall come to an end seems never to have occurred to European authorities. As we have seen,

[1] The governor has the right to remove the police commissioner with the advice and consent of the council, " for such cause as he shall deem sufficient. Such cause shall be stated in his order of removal." Acts of Mass., 1906, Chap. 291, Sec. 7. In New York City the police commissioner is removable by the mayor whenever " the public interests shall so require." New York City Charter, Chap. VIII, Sec. 270.
[2] See *European Police Systems,* Chap. IV.

they appoint their commissioners as a board of directors selects a general manager or other official, not for a definitely established term, but on the basis of satisfactory work. Their task is to find men capable of serving indefinitely — men who have the ability and the willingness to devote a life-time to the administrative problem. When such a man is found there is no disposition to experiment with anybody else. No one would care to assume responsibility for jeopardizing an organization in which, as in all forms of business enterprise, continuity of administration is the best guarantee of effectiveness.

This arangement contains nothing inharmonious with democratic principles. As a matter of fact, it has nothing to do with the *form* of government. It is a method of business management, a principle of administration, serviceable in democracies like Switzerland and bureaucracies like Germany. In Switzerland and England the police officials are invariably under popular control. Their policies are shaped and supported by public opinion, and their official acts express the will of the communities they serve. A serious misstep on their part would find short shrift at the hands of the watch committees or other superior bodies that supervise them. But their official heads are not periodically cut off just for the sake of cutting them off, or for fear that otherwise the police might get out of touch with popular thought.

We here in America have been slow to see that popular government can maintain trained administrators in public office without having its wishes strangled or thwarted. The distrust of permanent experts has no real basis if they can be kept in contact with public opinion through the control of representatives of the people. The experience of England and Switzerland is proof of the fact that this is not impossible, nor indeed difficult.[1]

Residence Requirements for Commissioners.

The difficulty of maintaining efficient police organizations in America is enhanced by another factor which finds its basis partly in politics and partly in the narrow provincialism with which each city regards its own public servants. Instead of selecting department heads on the sole basis of fitness, regardless of their residence at the time of appointment, great stress is laid, both in law and in custom, upon the principle of " local men for local positions." Our cities seem instinctively to resent " government by outsiders." It is taken as a reflection upon the community, a slur upon local talent. In the few cases where it has been tried it has met with considerable popular disapproval. The New York board of aldermen has frequently expressed itself in no uncertain tones on the policy of introducing " outside help," even when the " help " consisted of a well-known expert in school organization. In a recent municipal election in Philadelphia the fact that the outgoing administration had brought from other cities three or four men of technical skill to assist in the management of local affairs was one of the heated points of argument. " Philadelphia jobs for Philadelphians " became the slogan of the day and parades marched with signs and banners bearing the words : " The departure of imported office holders."

The conception of public office as a " job "— a reward

[1] See Lowell, *loc. cit.*, Chap. XIX.

for the faithful — no doubt underlies much of this widely prevalent feeling, although in many cities it is buttressed by local pride — a belief that from the community itself can be recruited all the expert service necessary for its management. The principle of a community governing itself is stretched to include the idea that the tools employed by the community in the process shall be of home manufacture. So real is this prejudice against "outside" assistance and so deeply is it imbedded in the political traditions of the country that in most cases it has the sanction of law, and appointing officers are obliged to choose as departmental administrators men who have resided in the city for a prescribed period. Thus in Boston the law provides that the police commissioner shall have resided in the city "for at least two years immediately preceding the date of his appointment."[1] In St. Louis the residential requirement is four years.[2] In Baltimore the police board consists of three persons "who shall have been registered voters in the City of Baltimore for three consecutive years next preceding the day of their appointment."[3] The San Francisco charter provides that "no person shall be appointed (police) commissioner who shall not have been an elector of the city and county at least five years next preceding his appointment."[4] "Qualified elector of the city" is the phrase used in many charters in limiting to home talent the choice of business managers of specialized departments.

In this practice we are again confronted by a striking

[1] Acts of Mass., 1906, Chap. 291, Sec. 7.
[2] Laws of Mo., 1899, Art. I, Sec. 466.
[3] City Charter (Rev. Ed., 1915), Sec. 740.
[4] City Charter, Chap. II, Sec. 1.

contrast between Europe and America. A European city, whether in England, Switzerland, or Germany, is concerned primarily in having its municipal business well administered and well maintained. Such functions as police, health, and fire control are regarded as technical divisions of government, for the management of which highly trained men are essential. The task of the appointing officer is to get the *best* men, and it is a matter of no concern whether at the time of appointment they happen to be living in one city or another. A residential qualification in such cases is as irrelevant as it would be if applied to the managing director of a railroad or the head of a medical school or experimental laboratory. Indeed in European cities there has been no thought of applying such a test for the reason that no one would care to limit so narrowly the field of choice. With the talent of Great Britain to draw from, for example, why should Liverpool or Birmingham insist that its chief constable be recruited from its own population? Or what would be gained if Stuttgart was barred from inviting an experienced deputy commissioner from Munich to join its staff as commissioner, and had, instead, to employ some inferior man from its own citizenship?

This is the conception that governs the public service of European municipalities. In consequence, men are called from one city to another, and the line of promotion is often from a lesser community to a greater. The police commissioner of the City of London [1] was twenty

[1] The police of the City of London are distinct from the police of the London Metropolitan district. See *European Police Systems*, p. 39, note 2.

years head constable in Liverpool; Liverpool had enticed him from Leeds, where he had occupied the same position. The chief constable of Manchester held the same post in Oldham and Canterbury for terms of seven and five years respectively before he was called to his present office. When the authorities of Preston wanted a chief constable they advertised in the newspapers, and of the seventy candidates who applied they selected a man who at that time was superintendent of police in the town of Devizes. Later this same man was called to Liverpool as assistant head constable. Indeed in England and in Scotland, except in cases of promotion, it is seldom that a police administrator is a resident of the city which chooses him.[1]

The same situation is largely true of the continent. The commissioner of police of Rome [2] held similar positions in Ancona and Naples, and was promoted from one city to another. The police commissioner of Amsterdam served in the same capacity in Rotterdam. The assistant to the police president of Dresden was taken from the police department of Munich. Among the smaller German cities the local councils are continually introducing into the public service departmental administrators whose work in other communities has attracted attention.

In brief, the system of employment of public officers abroad is much more elastic than in America; no narrow parochialism bars the search for talent wherever it can be obtained; the entire nation contributes to the effective administration of the city.

[1] *Ibid.,* Chap. IV.
[2] His title is *Questore di Roma.*

American Police Systems

The Dilemma and the Approach to Its Solution.

The facts thus far considered present a perplexing dilemma. Effective administrators of large police departments are not easily found in the ranks; indeed, it is not to be supposed that they could be found in the ranks, and this solution of the difficulty contains but little promise. On the other hand, the lack of trained government executives and the barrier which politics and American traditions have erected against their development make problematical any attempt to officer a police force from outside sources. What, then, is the solution for a city with a difficult police situation to handle?

That there is no simple or single solution — certainly that there is no immediate solution — must at once be admitted. Political customs cannot be changed over night nor can the fears and superstitions, inherited from frontier conditions of life, be sloughed off at will. The solution of the difficulty, therefore, will be a matter of development. If a solution is reached it will be through application to the problem of government administration of the same common sense principles upon which success in private business depends. A manufacturer who committed his plant to a periodically shifting line of untrained managers could not hope long to keep his business out of bankruptcy. He aims, therefore, to obtain the best ability adapted to his work that can be anywhere secured, and success in handling the plant is the only condition of continued employment. Adapted to police organization this principle would involve the selection of a commissioner on the sole basis of fitness regardless of residence or political belief, and his continuance in office so long as his work is effective, no matter what changes occur in the politics of the city hall. It is possible that public administration as a science will at some period be so far developed in America that a training school for police administrators will be a practicable project. In such a school would be developed the men who, after long apprenticeship in smaller cities or in the lesser positions of larger cities, might wisely be promoted to posts of heavy responsibility. Such a school, indeed, could be utilized to include not merely the police department but the whole technical administrative service of the country, so that trained and experienced executives could be readily available to all branches of local government. This plan, however, is for the time being too visionary for consideration. In the present state of American politics it has no immediate practical value.

In the last analysis, of course, the problem will be solved, if solved at all, not by way of any specially devised machinery or legislative short-cut, but by popular education. It is idle to think of experts superimposed upon a listless or unsympathetic community. In America, initiative and motive power in any program of governmental reform must come from an intelligent electorate; and this way lies the only avenue of approach. The increasing demand for efficiency in government, and the growing appreciation that the hindrances to its realization are found not so much in democracy itself as in some of the peculiar methods by which we have attempted to put democracy into effect, promises to create a public opinion perhaps strong enough and intelligent enough to place the administrative service of all specialized departments of government on a permanent, expert basis. In this, as in other perplexing problems of social organization, no progress can be made without steadfast popular support.

CHAPTER VII

THE CHIEF OF POLICE

Inaccurate analogies.— The chief and his relations to the director.
— The impermanent tenure of the chief.— Illustrations.— Impermanent tenure due to politics.— Examples.— The chief and civil service.— Difficulties of civil service.— Personnel in the position of
chief.— Politics and the chief.

THE point is sometimes advanced that the commissioner
or director of a highly specialized municipal department,
like health or the police, is properly a layman, representing the public opinion of the community and answerable
for general results. It is urged that such men, chosen
from time to time, can establish with the technical heads
of their departments, like the chief of police or the chief
health specialist, the same relation as exists between a
board of directors of a railroad and its executive officer.
The board makes no pretense to technical knowledge to
manage the railroad; it merely represents the business
public. Its function is not to run the railroad, but to see
that the railroad is properly run. The executive officer,
on the other hand, is a professional expert, thoroughly
skilled in the science of railroad administration and responsible under the policies of the directors for its successful operation. Another analogy often employed to
define this conception of the police commissioner is the
use of laymen as heads of such divisions of government
as our War and Navy Departments.

American Police Systems

Unfortunately, these analogies cannot be maintained in relation to the management of a police department. As we have already seen in the preceding chapter, the commissioner is far more than a general business administrator. His acquaintance with police work must be intimate and detailed if he is to have any effect upon its efficiency. For in the police field there are no easy standards of work-accomplishment such as one finds in other businesses, both public and private. Faults in operation and failures in achievement are readily covered up. A police administrator who is insufficiently acquainted with methods and processes has no way of gauging the adequacy of results. Everything is relative and there are no arbitrary measurements of success or failure that inexperienced directors can apply. For example, arrests may decrease over a period of time; this may be the result of police effectiveness in preventing the commission of crime or it may be due to ineffectiveness in apprehending criminals. Only a skilled administrator can make the proper interpretation and apply the necessary remedy. Again, the increase of crime complaints in a given period may or may not have relation to the size of the force. It is a problem for the determination of an experienced director. Similarly, an increase of felonies and misdemeanors may be attributable to laxity in the uniformed force, to a poorly managed detective bureau, or to inadequate constructive treatment of the causes of crime. It may be due to none of these factors, but to peculiar economic or social conditions. Only training and skill in the head of the department can diagnose the situation, and the responsibility cannot be delegated to a subordinate officer.

The Chief of Police

I have emphasized this point because in many quarters the chief of police is loosely thought of as the real " expert," responsible to a transitory layman director, and on this theory the department has been built up. From the attempt to maintain this relationship confusion and bad administration have resulted.

The Chief and his Relations to the Director.

The failures attending the proper adjustment of the relation between commissioner and chief arise in large measure, as we have seen, from the inherent difficulty of dividing the functions of police administration between two different administrators. The position of commissioner or director was originally superimposed upon the older position of chief without any clear differentiation as to powers and authority, and for years the lawmakers and the officials themselves have laboriously endeavored to find some rational line of demarcation.[1] Such an attempt, however, clashes with the principle of responsible administration. Moreover, no line can be drawn which will practically meet the demands of varying occasions

[1] Occasionally, in an attempt to protect the prerogatives of the chief, his powers are elaborately set forth in the charter and hedged about with intricate legal defenses. In some of the Ohio cities, for example, he is given full right to make details and transfers and to suspend his subordinates pending final disciplinary action by his superior. Moreover, he is protected against arbitrary removal at the hands of the director of public safety by a provision which places the power in this matter in the civil service commission. But even these restrictions do not insure a well-balanced relationship between the director and the chief, nor do they necessarily confer upon the latter any appreciable amount of administrative responsibility. The civil service commission, like the director, is appointed by the mayor; but even in the absence of any coercive influence such as this arrangement might imply, the wishes of the chief's superior officer in matters of detail customarily prevail.

and temperaments. Even more clearly impossible is it to establish such a line generally for all departments. The size and character of the community must determine whether both an administrative expert and an executive officer are needed. Assuming that some degree of permanency is assured for the commissioner, a small city may well dispense with the position of chief, or at least the two positions can be merged. In a larger city, where perhaps a number of bureaus are grouped under a single administrator, it may be equally advisable to retain the post. In any event, the matter should rest with the responsible head of the department — the commissioner — free to select such executive agents as he needs or none at all if no necessity arises. If a chief executive officer of some sort is thought essential, the duties of the position as well as its scope should rest with the commissioner. There would thus be avoided the elaborate legal distinctions in function between the two officials which hamper rather than aid the relationship, and render the whole organization rigid and inflexible. This is the plan in operation in Boston, where, under the present administration, the relations between the civilian commissioner and the uniformed superintendent are well adjusted. The commissioner is under no legal obligation, however, to appoint any superintendent; he could, if he chose, administer the force without one. Practically the same principle has for nineteen years been in operation in New York City; since the position of chief was abolished the successive commissioners have assigned executive duties sometimes to the chief inspector, sometimes to other uniformed officials.

The Chief of Police

This suggestion is of course predicated upon the belief that ultimate efficiency can be secured only if one man is held completely responsible for the operation of his department. The line of progress in police organization points toward a trained commissioner, holding office for an unlimited term, rather than toward a plan which attempts definitely to separate, between two officers, administrative and executive powers. The chief of police should bear to the commissioner or director the same relationship which any of the vice presidents of a railroad bear to the president. That is, he should be entrusted with such responsibilities as will relieve the commissioner of the burden of administrative detail, and promote a smooth working organization. The commissioner, however, should at all times be empowered to rearrange his duties, to overrule his decisions, to correct his judgments, and if necessary to abolish his position altogether.

As to what sort of work a chief might be entrusted to perform, no definite rule can be laid down. Assignments, details, transfers, the arrangement of shifts and hours would, under ordinary circumstances, form part of his duties. So, too, he could digest for the commissioner the daily reports of crime and the records of unusual occurrences, presenting his expert opinion and recommendations gained from a careful study of the subjects. Because his connection with the daily operations of the force is intimate and continuous he might well be given a reasonably free hand in disposing of minor disciplinary cases. In all these matters, however, he should be merely the agent or representative of the commissioner, exercising only such powers as the latter may delegate to him.

American Police Systems

The Impermanent Tenure of the Chief.

If any single factor were fatal to the position of the chief of police as an expert, in the relationship in which we drew the analogy at the beginning of the chapter, it would lie in his impermanent tenure of office. The success of a non-professional, transitory head, such as the British cabinet minister, is predicated on the existence under him of a permanent administrative manager, and the analogy between the chief of police and the under-secretary of a British department breaks down in the face of the constant shift and change that characterize this branch of police service in the United States.

The limited tenure of the chief of police is a matter of both law and custom. In many cities he is appointed under the charter for a prescribed term. Thus in San Francisco he serves four years, in Los Angeles four years, in San Antonio two years, in St. Paul two years, and in Memphis one year. In many more cities it is an accepted custom for an incoming board or administration to appoint its own chief of police, regardless of the fact that the chief's term of office is not legally limited. Occasionally a single administration will make two and sometimes three appointments to the position. Consequently police management is marked almost as much by a shifting succession of chiefs as by an ever changing line of commissioners. San Francisco in the eleven years between 1900 and 1911 had eight chiefs; Pittsburgh in the five years between 1901 and 1906 had six; in the last 43 years Los Angeles has had 25 chiefs, making an average term of less than two years. Minneapolis in 32 years has had thirteen; Seattle in nineteen years has had ten; Des Moines in the sixteen-year period between 1901 and 1917 had eleven. Denver furnishes a typical illustration of the point, with fifteen chiefs in 38 years, an average of two years and a quarter for each man; of the fifteen incumbents, two were removed on charges of dishonesty, one for improper conduct in connection with the search of a woman prisoner, one for drunkenness in a disorderly house, and the others for political reasons, generally in connection with changes in the municipal administration. The present chief of police in Denver held the same office on three prior occasions, each time being thrown out by an unfavorable turn of the political wheel.

A survey of other cities shows the same situation, although in some the rate of change is not as rapid as in Pittsburgh or San Francisco. Philadelphia has had six chiefs in 33 years, an average of over five years apiece.[1] Five chiefs have held office in Cincinnati since 1887, an average term of over six years. Cleveland has had six in 23 years, an average term of four years. Louisville since 1870 has had thirteen chiefs, or an average incumbency of approximately four years. Since 1885 Baltimore has had five chiefs,[2] St. Louis and Detroit, seven, and Newark, seven.[3] In some few departments, gener-

[1] The title is *superintendent* in Philadelphia.
[2] This includes one chief who served at two different periods. The title in Baltimore is *marshal*.
[3] From 1844, when the position of chief was first established, to 1901, when it was abolished, New York City had twelve chiefs of police, an average term of four years, six months. Atlanta in 47 years has had ten chiefs, one of whom served sixteen years, making an average for the others of less than four years apiece. New Orleans in 68 years, excluding three years of military occupancy, has had 25, an average term of two years, nine months.

ally in the smaller cities, one finds chiefs of police holding over creditably long terms. The chief of police of Grand Rapids, recently retired, served 21 years; in Manchester (N. H.) the chief has served 28 years. Milwaukee's chief of police, with 31 years of continuous service to his credit, probably holds the record in the United States at the present time. These cases, however, are exceptional; one must search the records to find them, and they stand out in sharp relief against the common practice of our municipalities.

Impermanent Tenure Due to Politics.

The impermanent character of the chief's tenure is ascribable, as has been indicated, largely to politics. A Democratic administration wants a Democratic chief, just as a Republican administration insists upon a chief from its own party. It is one of the accepted rules of the game, and the idea of the chief as an expert in a specialized department is subordinated to the conception, difficult to overcome, that the spoils belong to the victors, and that the police department must be kept in line for the next political battle. Consequently the chief is the victim of recurring political changes — appointed to his position, losing it, often reappointed and losing it again, as the political wheel registers success or failure for the party with which he is affiliated.

This point is amply borne out by a study of the changes occurring in the position of chief in a city like St. Paul. John Clark, a Republican, was appointed chief in 1883, retired in 1892, reappointed in 1894, retired in 1896. John J. O'Connor, a Democrat, appointed chief of police in 1900, resigned in 1912 when the Republicans came into power, but was reappointed in 1914 when his party was again victorious. In the interval between the Clark regime and the O'Connor regime a varied succession of Republicans and Democrats held the post. Similarly in Minneapolis in 32 years the succession of chiefs has been as follows: two Democrats, two Republicans, two Democrats, one Republican, two Democrats, one professedly non-partisan, one Socialist and one Independent Republican. Needless to say, the mayors responsible for these appointments followed in the same political succession. According to a practice which we shall discuss in a later chapter, each change in the head of the department from one party to another was accompanied by wholesale removals in the rank and file.

The chief of police of a city in Pennsylvania writes me as follows: "I was first appointed chief of police in this city in 1893, and served in that capacity for two years. . . . A political change occurred and I worked as superintendent for a private detective agency for six years. I was then reappointed chief of police, serving for six years, when I was again thrown out by a turn of the political wheel. I was again appointed in 1912 and have been on the job since." The experience of this official has been duplicated in scores of instances.

It is not at all unusual for a chief of police at the expiration of his service to be returned to the ranks as captain, or in some other subordinate capacity where, with some hope, perhaps, he awaits the return of more auspicious days. This custom, as we have seen, is practised in Chicago; at the time that this is written there are two captains in the ranks, who formerly administered the entire force. At the time of my visit to Indianapolis two officials in the ranks, one in charge of the detective bureau and the other a desk sergeant, had once held the position of chief. In St. Paul the chief under a Republican regime was made a captain when the Democrats came into power. In Atlanta a former chief was allowed to continue on the force as a patrolman.

In Toledo in 1914 the mayor appointed as chief of police a traffic officer who had actively espoused his election. Later, as a result of disagreements the mayor brought charges against him before the civil service commission, forcing his reduction to the rank of patrolman. In the following municipal campaign the officer himself ran for mayor, seeking vindication from the public, as he expressed it, for the unfair treatment which he had received. Defeated at the election, he was reinstated in the department as a plainclothesman. "We are so riddled with politics," an officer of the Toledo force told me, "that nobody knows who is going to be chief tomorrow."

In Birmingham (Ala.) it was the custom a number of years ago, to have the chief run for appointment at the Democratic primary elections, the members of the board of police commissioners pledging themselves to appoint the man thus selected. The term was for two years, and rival candidates for the position took the stump in an endeavor to win the citizens to an appreciation of their respective abilities. Naturally the prize went to the man who had a special gift for catching the fancy of a crowd, or whose promises and favors seemed the more substan-

The Chief of Police

tial.[1] In twelve years five different chiefs held the post.

These examples represent, of course, somewhat unusual cases. Nevertheless they are typical, if not of the actual circumstances, at least of the spirit of many American cities in subordinating conceptions of expert service to the exigencies of politics.

The Chief and Civil Service.

In some cities definite steps have been taken to counter-act the transient character of the chief's position by placing it under civil service regulations. This is true, for example, of the cities of Ohio,[2] of some of the cities of New Jersey,[3] and many of the municipalities of Massachusetts.[4] The Ohio law, which was pased in 1915, provides that charges against the chief of police must be heard by the municipal civil service commission. Under the New Jersey statute removal of chiefs of police is lodged in the hands of the appointing authorities, but the state civil service commission reviews the action and has the right, after calling witnesses and considering all the evidence, finally to determine the case.[5] In the Massachusetts cities which have adopted the act, removals are

---

[1] This system was abolished in 1911.

[2] Ohio Laws of 1915 —" An act to amend sections 486-1 to 486-31 inclusive and to repeal section 4505 of the General Code relating to the civil service of the State of Ohio, the several counties, cities, and city school districts thereof." pp. 400-419.

[3] Newark, Trenton, Jersey City, Paterson, East Orange, South Orange, and Elizabeth. In these communities the state civil service law (Laws of N. J., 1908, Chap. 156) was adopted by referendum.

[4] Cambridge, Fall River, Lynn, New Bedford, Newton, Pittsfield, Springfield, Worcester, and twelve others. The civil service law which these cities accepted is Chapter 468 of the Acts of 1911.

[5] In addition a review by the courts could probably be obtained.

made by the appointing boards or officers after the presentation of written charges and a hearing; and opportunity is afforded for a full review by the courts.[1]

In most of the cities where the chief of police is protected by civil service, the law is too recent a development to make possible more than a tentative appraisal. That it will discourage constant changes in the position and lengthen the term of office of the average incumbent is not to be doubted. In so far as this is accomplished the law will represent a worthy and substantial advance over old conditions. It is hardly probable that the cities of Ohio, for example, will ever again see the long succession of police chiefs that for many years past has filed in and out of the doors of their police departments.

On the other hand it is improbable that the law, certainly as it is now framed, will prove an unmixed blessing. The trite remark that civil service is the lesser of two evils will doubtless find reinforcement in this new application. In just the proportion that removal is made legally formidable is the difficulty increased of getting rid of unfit men when public interest demands it. Civil service has too often proved a bulwark for incompetence and neglect, to justify over sanguine hopes in its extension to this new administrative field. Too often, too, it has served as a respectable cloak for political juggling, defeating its own purpose, and bringing the whole cause of reform into disrepute. No head of a police department in Great Britain — indeed no member of a police force — is protected by civil service, and yet removals for political or personal reasons are practically unheard

[1] Acts of Mass., 1911, Chap. 624.

of. Custom and public opinion unite to maintain the administration of this department on a high plane. We in America, on the other hand, attempt to substitute law for public opinion, and too often become the victims of its rigidity and inelasticity. At the same time, in choosing between two difficulties such as confront us, it is the course of wisdom to select the less formidable. An investigating committee in New York, in reporting a plan to increase the term of office of the police commissioner, aptly expressed the idea as follows:

" The purpose of our recommendation is to give fixity of tenure to the commissioner. We believe that this can be accomplished only by making his removal really difficult. The disadvantage of being unable easily to get rid of an inefficient commissioner is evident, but we cannot devise a satisfactory plan to be operated by human beings (the only raw material available) that will give fixity of tenure to a good commissioner, and still make it easy to remove a bad one. Of the two horns of this dilemma, we prefer fixity of tenure." [1]

A difficulty peculiar to such civil service laws as those we have noticed above lies in the unnecessarily complex machinery by which removals are secured. In an endeavor to give ample protection to the chief, the laws have surrounded the position with a defense too intricate and elaborate to insure the best results. In the New Jersey cities, as we have noticed, discretion in the last analy-

[1] Report of the Citizens' Committee appointed at the Cooper Union Mass Meeting, August 14, 1912.

sis is vested with the state civil service commission, a body bearing no responsibility to the local government, and probably unfamiliar with the facts and circumstances leading to the removal. In consequence, authority in police management is scattered, and the department, as well as the community it serves, suffers from the lack of sharply defined responsibility. This condition is true of the Ohio cities where the director of public safety, answerable for the conduct of police business, has no voice whatever in the removal of the chief; instead, the power is vested with the civil service commission, a body without responsibility for police management, and with no vision of the whole police problem of which the removal of the chief is but a single phase.

There is danger that in protecting the chief from capricious removal the fundamental principle of responsible leadership will be compromised. In most cases ample security would be afforded if the officer or board, with power to remove, were required to file written charges, and with due notice give a public hearing at which the defendant would have full opportunity to present his case. A review by the courts could be allowed to determine, not the adequacy of the charges, but merely the regularity of the proceeding. To go further is to rob the community of any right to hold one man responsible for what happens in the police department. Public opinion rather than law must increasingly become the chief corrective of our institutional ills if any substantial improvement is to be looked for.

One more difficulty in connection with the civil service laws above cited remains to be noticed. In Ohio, New

Jersey, and Massachusetts, the statutes provide that the chief shall be promoted from the next lowest rank,[1] a limitation which may seriously cripple the leadership of the department. It is by no means certain that the best material for the position of chief can invariably be found in the next lowest rank. Indeed, it is possible that men of far better calibre for the post can be obtained either from another rank or from another force or from private life. To narrow the field of choice for an administrative position such as this, in which personality and special ability count for so much, is to deny the department the benefit of the best intelligence obtainable. For a number of years in one of the large cities of Massachusetts, for example, permanent appointment to the position of chief was long deferred because of the lack of promising material in the rank of captain. Four of the captains were far too old for the post, while the remaining two had political affiliations such as to make the appointment of either of them a questionable expedient. Similarly in a New Jersey city at the time of my visit, the retirement of the chief would have opened the position to two officers, one of whom had no administrative capacity what-

---

[1] Ohio civil service rules, January 27, 1916, Rule VIII; Acts of Mass., 1911, Chap. 408; New Jersey Laws of 1908, Chap. 156 (accepted by East Orange, Elizabeth, Jersey City, Newark, Paterson, and South Orange). This restriction is somewhat modified in that persons from any grade may take examination for promotion to the position of chief if there are not the required number of eligibles in the next lower grade. Despite the apparent elasticity of these provisions, the fact remains that in Ohio (except where the state civil service law is superseded by such home rule charters as contain specific provision for civil service, as in the case of Toledo) and in the twenty cities of Massachusetts which have accepted the law of 1911, it is mandatory that all possible candidates within the force be exhausted before recourse may be had to an original examination for the position of chief.

ever, while the integrity of the other was not above suspicion.

Obviously it is unfair to a department to limit the appointment of chief to such undesirable candidates, nor is
a restriction of this kind essential to the principle of civil
service.

Personnel in the Position of Chief.

It cannot be said that the average chief of police represents a conspicuous order of ability. In fact only occasionally do the incumbents of this rank seem to interpret
police work in any other terms than those of handcuffs
and the night stick. Frequently possessing genuine ability in such matters as handling traffic or managing crowds,
they are often unable to understand involved problems
of organization or to conceive of police work in its
broader relationships. The common practices of the business manager in securing administrative control of his
plant are frankly beyond their comprehension. Even
when their offices are equipped with such mechanical aids
as daily reports or statistics of work, these appliances
are not used as instruments of management, because such
use is not understood. Most of the chiefs have had no
opportunity to develop administrative ability. They have
served for years as patrolmen, sergeants, and captains,
and their experience thus acquired has little relationship
to the task of management; it does not necessarily equip
them to obtain maximum results from their subordinates
or make them alert to the possibilities of improvement in
their organizations.

To this situation may perhaps in part be ascribed the

The Chief of Police

tendency of commissioners and directors to infringe upon the proper functions of the chief. They see in him an official, inadequately trained for his tasks, struggling with more or less intelligence and zeal with what is at best a difficult problem. Their assumption of his duties, with the confusing consequences which we have already noted, is doubtless prompted in many cases by a genuine desire to have the police department well run, and by a belief that this result cannot be secured with so poor an instrument.

In many cities, too, the chief has the appearance of being more interested in politics than in the administration of his force. He realizes that the length of his service depends upon his ability to maintain political affiliations powerful enough to keep him in office, and his energies are bent in that direction. In consequence his real work is neglected, partly because it is not continuously on his mind, and partly because its active prosecution might antagonize the forces upon which he relies for support. His administration is therefore devoted to the maintenance of the *status quo* of his department, and change and innovation are discouraged.

To imply that these characterizations are true of all chiefs of police would, of course, be grossly unjust. One finds some officers of this rank splendidly equipped for their work: keen, progressive, eager for new ideas. In Berkeley, California, for instance, the chief is capable to an unusual degree and his influence is felt throughout the West.[1] Chief Quigley of Rochester, N. Y., may be mentioned in the same breath. One finds many more

[1] August Vollmer.

chiefs honestly striving with poor equipment and against hostile influence to build up an effective department. On the whole, however, the impression gained from a composite picture of chiefs of police would be one of limited resourcefulness and lethargy.

The police department of one of the largest industrial cities of the South was, at the time of my visit, demoralized and chaotic. Uniforms were patched and shabby; policemen patrolled with coats unbuttoned, and often with toothpicks or cigars in their mouths. There was no criminal identification system in the detective bureau, and no records of any kind were maintained for control or statistical purposes. Serious crimes were of frequent occurrence, but except as some one in the department remembered them there was no way by which the chief or any of his assistants could tell who was handling the cases or what had been done. "The less you say about our police department the better," I was told by the secretary of the local chamber of commerce. Who was the chief responsible for these conditions? He was a dull, ignorant, untrained man with no idea of administration, indeed with no conception of what his position meant. Much of his time he spent sitting on a box in an alley back of police headquarters, whittling on a stick and swapping stories with his lieutenants.

Again emphasis must be laid on the fact that this picture is by no means true of our chiefs of police as a whole, nor indeed, in its entirety of many of them. It serves to show, however, why the average level of ability in this position is no higher than my previous characterization would indicate.

The Chief of Police

Nevertheless in passing judgment such as this, it is well to remember that the average chief of police is more sinned against than sinning. He is the victim of a political system for which he is in no way responsible, often owing his appointment and continuance in office to the sinister forces that control many of our municipalities. With a public opinion on the one hand none too well formed or articulate, and on the other hand the constant pressure of powerful party influences, it is small wonder that many of the chiefs are mediocre in calibre, ambition-less and unimaginative in their work. Rather the wonder is that some of them, without hope of appreciation, are effective and undiscouraged. "If the politicians would keep their hands off I could build up one of the finest departments in the country." This remark, made by the police chief of a large city in Ohio, is typical of what many of them say in confidential moments. In the words of the chief in a western city: "Give us five years without politics and we will revolutionize police organization in the United States."

At bottom the police problem is a problem in public education. American municipalities are not impotent. They are in a position to obtain what they want. That so many of them are content with the rule of the politician and its train of ugly consequences, that highly specialized social functions like policing are thrown into the political arena and battled for as a matter of course, is indicative of low community standards and a public will weak and undeveloped. Because it demands so much from so many, democracy is the most difficult form of government to work. Its sole hope of success lies in the slow process of popular education — intensive, unremitting, undiscouraged.

CHAPTER VIII

THE RANK AND FILE

In the task which confronts the police — i.e., maintaining the security of persons and property and safeguarding public morals — the uniformed or patrol force is the first line of defense. Its responsibility is the enforcement of laws and ordinances and the protection of the public against physical hazard. It preserves order on the streets and in public places, makes arrests for violation of law, regulates traffic, rescues lives endangered, and renders first aid and assistance to persons who may be injured or ill. In addition it is in respect to such matters the eyes and ears of the community. It discovers and reports unsanitary conditions, fire hazards, defective pavements, dangerous buildings and other situations to which official attention should be given.

Multifarious as are its duties, the uniformed force

The Rank and File

alone cannot handle the whole task of the police. It is not possible to have uniformed men in a community in numbers sufficient to guarantee the enforcement of all laws and ordinances or the arrest of all criminals. Moreover many violations of law occur in places where the policeman cannot readily go. It is necessary, therefore, to have a second line of defense — a corps of trained investigators or detectives — operating in citizens' dress, so as to work unobserved. These officials are called upon to apprehend lawbreakers whose activities the uniformed force has failed to suppress. Inspector Cornelius Cahalane of the New York force who has contributed in no small measure to a better understanding of police work expresses the relationship in the following succinct statement: " The uniformed force is the infield and the outfield on the home diamond. The detective force gets whatever the crooks bat over the fence." [1]

A third line of defense in the police department is the crime prevention service, consisting of miscellaneous squads and units, engaged in discovering conditions that produce crime and in suppressing offenses against public morals. Perhaps a better figure would be to liken this branch of the police to the intelligence service of an army. It gathers information regarding conditions to be attacked by the police department, which would otherwise remain undiscovered. Its work is always positive and aggressive.

While it is possible to differentiate thus broadly between these three main branches of police organization, it must be recognized that their functions are not mutually

[1] Personally communicated.

exclusive. As opportunity arises, each section performs work that receives the special attention of other sections. One of the purposes of the patrol work by the uniformed force is the prevention of crime, and similarly the crime prevention section is frequently engaged in the detection of criminals. But in one form or another, the task of every police force involves these three approaches.

In maintaining these three approaches, the question of tools is paramount. With what kind of men are we to work? How are we to get them? How shall they be trained? How shall we use them to accomplish the ends of police duty? After all, the heart of the police problem is one of personnel, and it is to the many questions involved in personnel management that the next three chapters are devoted.

Civil Service and the Police.

A rough classification of police departments in the United States could be made by dividing them into two groups: those that operate under civil service rules, and those that do not. Most of the large forces in the eastern states and in the far west are now under some form of civil service. In the south and middle west, however, and in some parts of the northwest, it is possible to find many police departments to which these principles have never been applied. Some of these departments are large; many of them are small. Of the 63 cities in the United States having a population of 100,000 or over, ten have no civil service system whatever. These cities include Birmingham, (Ala.), Indianapolis, Kansas City, Louisville, San Antonio and Salt Lake

City.[1] In a number of other cities, such as Omaha, civil service regulations have only partially been adopted, generally as regards dismissals rather than appointments. St. Paul and Minneapolis have joined the civil service group within the last few years. New York City adopted the civil service plan in 1883, and Chicago followed in 1895.

On the basis of this classification the generalization easily follows that those forces in which a civil service system is maintained are better administered and better managed than those in which no such system has been adopted. The reason for this is at once apparent. Whatever evil results it may have — and we shall discuss some of them later — civil service tends to exclude the political factors which are peculiarly characteristic of American local government. Without civil service, appointments to the police department are generally a matter of political faith, involving allegiance to the local " boss " and fidelity to the party machine. Consequently, in such departments, the " boss " rather than the commissioner has the loyalty of the force, for commissioners are temporary creatures, birds of passage, subject to sudden political decapitation and retirement to private life, while the " boss," representing the permanency of the

[1] The other four cities are Bridgeport, Camden, Hartford and Reading. In addition to these ten cities, there are three cities in which civil service is maintained in a modified sort of way, administered exclusively by police authorities: St. Louis, Milwaukee and Providence. In Baltimore civil service is administered by a board of police examiners apart from the authority of the board of police commissioners. In Washington, D. C., civil service is administered by the city commissioners sitting as a board. Of the 47 cities in which civil service is established, it is controlled by a municipal civil service commission in 35, and by a state civil service commission in twelve.

party machine, is always in a position to provide " jobs."

In such departments the upset of a party machine at the polls means thorough changes in the personnel of the police force. " It is to be a sweeping housecleaning of everyone who ever smiled at a Republican commissioner," said the Kansas City *Star*,[1] referring to contemplated changes in the force of Kansas City when the new Major board was appointed in 1913. The prophecy was true. Within a few weeks eighty Republican patrolmen and sergeants, in addition to the chief of police, had been dropped and Democrats took their places. With this beginning, the board proceeded leisurely through bureau after bureau, dismissing the politically obnoxious. Out of two hundred Republicans, only thirty were left. Captains and lieutenants were reduced to patrolmen, and the vacancies thus made were filled by " good Major men." By such proscriptive methods a " Democratic force " was created out of what had been a " Republican force." [2] At the time of my visit to Kansas City it was estimated that the Republicans constituted but five per cent of the entire department. " And you bet they are not shouting their affiliations from the housetops," I was told.

Similarly in Indianapolis, without the restraining influence of a civil service system, the force is thoroughly political. Indeed it is made so by law. " The force

---

[1] August 5, 1913. "We are going to exact the grandfather clause. Any man who can't show that his family has voted straight for three generations need n't try to borrow one of our blue uniforms." This was the way a Democratic worker expressed his view of the situation. See *Star* for November 14, 1912.

[2] The story of this reorganization of the force can be found in the columns of the Kansas City *Star* from June to September, 1913.

shall be as nearly as possible equally divided politically "
— this wording of the statute furnishes the guiding principle of administration.[1] Half the force are Republicans and the other half Democrats, and this division
runs through all ranks — captains, lieutenants, sergeants
and patrolmen. If a vacancy occurs in any rank, due
to the death, resignation or dismissal of a Democrat,
another Democrat is put in his place. The same is true
of Republicans. Moreover an incoming administration
generally makes sweeping changes in all the higher ranks.
Captains and lieutenants are reduced to patrolmen, and
their places filled by those who, for personal or political
reasons, are more acceptable to the appointing power.
Not infrequently men are introduced into the higher
ranks without passing through the lower grades. I
talked with a captain of police in Indianapolis who entered the service as a sergeant, skipping the grade of
patrolman, and was then promoted to captain, skipping
the grade of lieutenant. Another officer whom I met
was brought into the department as a lieutenant, never
having been in police service before. As long as the
even balance is kept between Democrats and Republicans, there is nothing to prevent juggling with the personnel.

In Louisville largely similar conditions exist, although
not prescribed by law. In 1907 a Republican mayor, un-
expectedly acceding to the office, " tore the whole force
to pieces, putting in Republicans wherever he could." [2]
All the captains were reduced to patrolmen, and Republi-

[1] *Cities and Towns Act.* Laws of Ind., 1905, Sec. 159.
[2] Personally communicated.

cans took their places, many of them new men without previous police experience, appointed in a single day up through all the ranks. When the Democrats succeeded in the following election, the Republican policemen were similarly served. Again in 1917 a Republican victory at the polls was followed by the dismissal of more than 300 policemen out of a force of 429. Not a single officer above the rank of sergeant survived.

In Salt Lake City changes in police personnel as the result of the accession of a new city commissioner frequently run as high as 85%. "For the good of the service" is the brief formula used in effecting dismissals. In Birmingham, Alabama, there are no requirements for admission to the force, physical, mental, or otherwise — not even a standard of height. "Some places need small men, some places don't," the chief of police told me. Conditions of this kind typify the management of the police where a civil service system is lacking, and it is no exaggeration to say that civil service stands between the police and utter demoralization in the cities of the United States.

It is at this point that we are confronted with an amazing contrast between the police departments of Europe and America. There are no civil service arrangements in European police forces. Discretion as regards appointments and dismissals is invariably lodged in the commissioner or prefect, or whatever title the responsible head of the force may bear. The entire system rests upon his judgment. He " hires and fires " on the basis of standards which he himself creates. It is assumed that politics and favoritism will play no part in the result

The Rank and File

because it is taken for granted that the commissioner will have a greater interest than any one else in securing and maintaining the best possible personnel. And this assumption is well based. Politics has nothing whatever to do with the selection or dismissal of policemen in European cities. The political opinions of members of the force cut no figure whatever. The conception of policing as an essential and highly technical public task to be handled only by trained and experienced men makes any other point of view unthinkable to the European, and no formal legal barriers are necessary to protect the police department from the spoilsman.[1]

With us, a far lower standard prevails. Ideals of public service such as obtain in the cities of England and France seem to be utterly lacking, and we are forced to resort to law to secure a measure of control which in a healthier political atmosphere would be furnished by public opinion and buttressed by sound tradition.

Civil Service in Operation.

Civil service rules and practices bulk so large in the selection, promotion and dismissal of police department personnel, that more than passing attention must be given to them. In most cities, indeed, where civil service has gained a foothold, it has literally taken over almost the entire problem of personnel management, in so far as it does not relate to the disposition of the forces, reducing it to a rigid and more or less perfunctory routine,

[1] For full discussion of European methods in selecting policemen and making promotions see *European Police Systems*, Chapters VI and VII.

in which the police administrator himself has little part
to play. The following paragraphs briefly describe
its operation in its three principal relations to the police
department: appointments, promotions and discipline.

(a) *Appointments.*

In most cities where civil service is in operation the
entire task of advertising for recruits and of examining
and selecting the applicants is lodged in an independent
civil service commission. This commission establishes
physical and mental standards for entrance to the classified service, of which the police service is but a part,
and determines the eligibility of all applicants by means
of competitive or qualifying examinations. On the basis
of these examinations lists of eligibles are prepared, from
which the responsible police authority is obliged to make
a choice, generally in the order in which the names appear on the lists.

The standards of eligibility and methods of procedure,
as well as the schemes for marking and rating, vary in
minor details from city to city, but the general practices
are similar. The entrance examination is usually in two
parts: one, the physical and medical, and the other the
mental, which may be either oral or written or both.
Provision is generally made, also, for a character investigation, sometimes conducted by agents of the civil service
commission and sometimes by police officers working
under the direction of the commission. Although this
phase of the examination is of the utmost importance,
in too many American cities it is slighted, if not actually
abused, and amounts to little more than a perfunctory

checking of the references submitted by the applicant in his application blank.[1] In most civil service schemes the appointees serve a probationary period ranging from three months to a year, during which they may be dropped by authority of the police head without the usual procedure of a trial. In many of these cities, however, police authorities are lax in making any effort to measure the work of the probationers. So long as they do not commit any overt breach of rules there is little likelihood of failure to obtain permanent appointment.

A notable contrast between American and European practice is found in the requirement, uniformly in vogue in the cities of the United States, of a residence qualification in the selection of policemen. That is, an applicant for appointment as patrolman must have been a resident of the city in which service is sought for a specified period immediately preceding the date of his application. In San Francisco and Oakland, California, five years is the residence requirement; in St. Louis four years; in Buffalo, Rochester, Newark, New Orleans and Washington, D. C. two years; in Cleveland, Boston and Pittsburg, six months, although in the last two cities a year's residence in the state is required. In St. Louis, New Orleans and a few other cities the further requirement is made that applicants must be qualified voters. In Europe, on the other hand, notably in Great Britain, every endeavor is made to secure policemen from outside the community in which they are to serve. Of the Lon-

[1] For a discussion of the technique of conducting civil service examinations for police service, see Fuld's *Police Administration*, New York, 1910.

don policemen only a small proportion come from London, and the same condition is true in the provincial cities of England and Wales. These communities do not care to have on their forces policemen with local ties and connections. One-fourth of the municipalities in England refuse to accept men on their constabularies who for any length of time have lived in their cities, and the rural districts are searched to provide available material. " Straight from the plow " is the motto of the recruiting agents who are constantly traveling from place to place in the country districts of Great Britain looking for available constables.[1]

In America, there is no policy in regard to what occupations shall be preferred or what experience is necessary as a training for policemen. Civil service standardizes everything. Whoever presents himself and meets the published requirements is welcome to compete in examination. An analysis of the previous occupations of 219 policemen appointed to the New York department in 1916, made from the records of the police training school for recruits, showed the largest number to have been clerks, of whom there were 39; general workers and laborers came next with 28; drivers and chauffeurs numbered 27; plumbers, gas and steam fitters 21; motormen and conductors 12.[2] A similar analysis made in 1912 by the Bureau of Municipal Research showed that out of 42 recruits who had held one position for five years or more previous to entering the police department, twelve

[1] For detailed analysis of methods of recruiting in England, see *European Police Systems*, Chapter VI.
[2] Personal investigation.

had been drivers, six clerks, three butchers, three plumbers, the remaining eighteen falling in classifications of less than three each.[1]   These figures represent fairly well the sources of recruits in other American cities.

(b) *Promotions.*

Promotions to all ranks of the uniformed force except the rank of chief [2] are made through the instrumentality of civil service examinations in Chicago, Cleveland, Baltimore, San Francisco, Cincinnati, Los Angeles and other cities. In Newark and Jersey City the civil service system for promotions includes the rank of chief of police. In New York promotions are made by civil service examination to the ranks of sergeant, lieutenant and captain, while the ranks of inspector of police and chief inspector are not included in the classified service. Similarly in St. Louis, Boston, Milwaukee and Pittsburgh the civil service is used for promotion to the ranks of sergeant and lieutenant only.   In Detroit and New Orleans the civil service system has nothing to do with promotions.[3]

Civil service laws in all cities provide of course that promotion shall be effected through successive ranks and generally the examinations are open only to those who

[1] These figures are to be found in the *Report of the Special Committee* (Curran) *of the New York Board of Aldermen* to investigate the Police Department, 1912.

[2] The title is *superintendent* in Chicago and *marshal of police* in Baltimore.

[3] In Detroit examinations for promotion to the various ranks in the uniformed force are conducted by a board of promotions, composed of the superintendent, assistant superintendent and chief inspector. On the basis of these examinations the board makes recommendations to the police commissioner.

have served in the next lower grade for a specified period of time. The time which a patrolman must serve before he is eligible to compete in an examination for promotion to a sergeantcy varies from five years in New York City to six months in Philadelphia, Boston, Buffalo and Minneapolis.[1] Before a sergeant is eligible for promotion to the rank of lieutenant he must have served as a sergeant for a period of from six months to three years.[2]

The mental examination, usually written, is the chief factor in determining a candidate's standing on the list of eligibles for promotion. In most cities seniority in service is also given a specific weight in the examination. Physical tests are rated on a competitive basis in Chicago, St. Louis, Los Angeles and Seattle, but in most cities they are employed merely to establish a qualifying standard of health and soundness in physical condition. Another factor commonly employed in promotions is the efficiency or *merit* test as it is generally called. This is supposedly based on an efficiency record system which under most civil service regulations is kept for each member of the police force. These records are usually negative in that they show only demerits for infractions of rules or neglect of duty. In no city in the United States is there a real efficiency record system which gives systematic credit for the accomplishment of good every-day police work. Wherever a thorough going efficiency rec-

[1] The period is four years in Chicago and Los Angeles; three years in St. Louis, Cleveland and Cincinnati; two years in Milwaukee; one year in Newark, Seattle and Jersey City.

[2] The period is three years in Milwaukee; two years in New York, Cleveland, Los Angeles and Cincinnati; one year in Chicago, St. Louis, Newark, Seattle and Jersey City; six months in Philadelphia, Boston, Buffalo and Minneapolis.

ord system has been attempted, to record currently the positive factors of a man's work, it has fallen into disuse or has been carelessly kept after an initial trial.[1]

After the examinations are completed and the men are listed in the order in which they have passed, the appointing authority in the police department is generally given the opportunity of selecting for each promotion one out of every three names presented to him from the head of the list. This is true in New York, Chicago, Cleveland, Pittsburgh, Buffalo, San Francisco, Los Angeles, Newark, Seattle and Jersey City. In Philadelphia the appointing authority may select one out of four eligibles. Selections may be made from any place on the list of eligibles in St. Louis, Boston and Milwaukee. In Baltimore, Cincinnati and Minneapolis, it is the practice to fill vacancies only from the names that appear at the head of the list of eligibles.

(c) *Discipline.*

Civil service laws and regulations have gone to extreme lengths in the United States in safeguarding policemen against unjust disciplinary action. In some cities the civil service commission itself assumes sole re-

---

[1] The most noteworthy attempt to establish an efficiency record system was in New York under the regime of Commissioner Woods. The scheme was dropped by his successor. The writer has seen in some police departments a so-called efficiency record system in which the same rating, i. e. *excellent,* was given to every member of the force from the chief of police down to the newest patrolman. The objections which one encounters to rating efficiency by a system of markings are, first, that under such a system there is not an equal opportunity between men on busy and those on quiet posts to make arrests and perform acts of meritorious service, and second, that favoritism may influence a commanding officer in grading his subordinates in the matter of general qualifications.

sponsibility for discipline; in others, the commission has the right to review the action of the police administrative authority, and may order reinstatement in case of dismissals, or lesser penalties than those imposed.[1]   In most police departments when disciplinary action is taken, charges must be preferred in writing and the case submitted for trial.   The trial may be conducted along the lines of a criminal proceeding as in New York with due regard for legal rules of evidence and all the technicalities of regular court procedure, or it may be a more or less formal method observed by an administrative officer in enforcing discipline.   The various practices that are employed differ from city to city, and there is no standardized arrangement.

The trial system of New York City is the most elaborate and the most completely judicial in character of any city in the United States.   Minor derelictions may be disposed of by inspectors of police without submitting the cases to formal trial, but charges involving more serious offences must be preferred in writing by a commanding officer and are tried before the police commissioner or one of his deputies.   The accused member is permitted to be represented by counsel, and may take an appeal to the courts through certiorari or mandamus proceedings against the decision of the police commissioner.[2]

[1] Extensive powers of review over the disciplinary actions of the police administrative authorities are granted the civil service commissions in the large cities of Ohio and New Jersey, and in Chicago, Pittsburgh, Philadelphia, San Francisco, Seattle, Portland (Ore.) and others.   Under commission government in Omaha and Memphis a member of the police force who has been removed from office may appeal to the whole city commission.

[2] The judicial appeal is employed in varying degrees of frequency in the cities of New York and Massachusetts, with the exception of

The Rank and File

In Chicago minor charges are handled by the superintendent of police but serious offences involving dismissal are tried by the civil service commission. Judgment is rendered by the commission and the superintendent is obliged to enforce it. In Philadelphia under the new charter similar conditions obtain. The civil service commission is given full authority to " hear, investigate and determine " all charges against policemen which, if substantiated, would constitute cause for discharge from the service. " The finding and decision of the commission . . . shall be certified to the appointing authority and shall be forthwith enforced by such authority." Even suspension from duty by superior police officers is subject to the review of the commission, which in case of disapproval has the power " to restore pay to the employee so suspended." [1]

In Cleveland disciplinary action involving removals by the director of public safety is subject to review by the municipal civil service commission which may " affirm, disaffirm, or modify the judgment of the director of public safety and its judgment in the matter shall be final." [2] In some southern cities, notably Augusta, Athens, and Macon, Ga., civil service ideas are carried to such an extreme that the commission, is the sole administrative head of the police department as regards all matters of discipline, while the chief of police is little more than a

Boston; in Philadelphia, St. Louis, Chicago, St. Paul and Milwaukee. In some jurisdictions the courts have held that their review is limited to questions of law, while in others, notably in New York, the courts consider questions of fact as well as of law, and pass upon the adequacy both of the charges and the procedure.

[1] Charter adopted June, 1919, Article XIX Sec. 18.
[2] Cleveland charter Sec. 110.

dummy, robbed of all power of initiative and leadership.

In Boston the law provides for a trial board composed of three captains. The personnel of the board may be changed at the will of the commissioner who may also set aside its findings and order a re-hearing before the same or another board. The action of the commissioner is absolutely final, and in this respect Boston affords the most complete centralization of responsibility for disciplinary action of any city in the United States.

The Limitations of Civil Service.

In its application to a police department civil service has serious limitations. In the endeavor to guard against abuse of authority, it frequently is carried to such extremes that rigidity takes the place of flexibility in administration, and initiative in effecting essential changes in personnel is crippled and destroyed. Too often, as we have already seen in connection with the chiefs of police, civil service is a bulwark for neglect and incompetence, and one of the prime causes of departmental disorganization. Too often does the attempt to protect the force against the capricious play of politics compromise the principle of responsible leadership, so that in trying to nullify the effects of incompetence and favoritism, we nullify capacity and intelligence too.

The extensive powers of civil service commissions which we have cited above constitute in themselves ample evidence of this situation. The arrangements in Chicago and Philadelphia, for example, by which the members of the force are answerable to an independent body having no responsibility for their work and no direct concern

The Rank and File

for the morale of the department, result inevitably in divided leadership and demoralization. Similar consequences can be expected when the disciplinary acts of a police executive can be overturned on appeal to a civil service commission or other higher authority. The uncertainty of punishment, the incidental delay, and the loss of respect for the nominal police head on the part of his subordinates — such factors as these go far to outweigh the value of the protection against the play of politics which such a system affords.

As a result of this divided responsibility between police executives and civil service commissions, there are in most large departments many men whose continuance in office is a menace to the force and to the community, but who cannot be dismissed because the *proof* of incompetence or dishonesty does not satisfy the requirements of the civil service law. In city after city commissioners and chiefs will freely admit that certain of their officers or men are " crooked." " But what can we do?" they say, " we can't prove it." One has only to sit with police trial boards or tribunals in cities like Philadelphia, Chicago or New York to realize that the forces contain not a few unfit, shiftless and dishonest employees, who would be summarily dismissed by an energetic administrator endowed with adequate authority. Certainly no business man would attempt to conduct a private business with such a personnel. He would be foredoomed to failure from the start.

Consequently police administrators are forced to resort to such pitiful makeshifts as " transfers " in order to circumvent the recognized dishonesty or incompetence of their subordinates. A man is shifted to a precinct or post where he will have the smallest possible scope for mischief. Instead of devoting their energies to the positive task of building up their forces with the best personnel obtainable, our police heads devote themselves to the negative duty of guarding their departments from ship-wreck at the hands of subordinates through whom they are forced to carry on their work. Commissioner Woods of New York, as well as many of his predecessors, was constantly obliged to shift from one post to another men whose utter uselessness and at times dishonesty were known to the whole force. In Philadelphia a former director of public safety told me that although during his incumbency he knew that most of his detectives were " crooked," he was able to get rid of but one — and that was a man caught red-handed while stealing five dollars from a fellow detective who lay asleep in the dormitory.

Often such situations as these are due not only to an inability to secure the necessary legal proof of delinquency, but to the conflict which constantly arises between police executives and the higher appellate authorities. The records of police departments are full of cases where the officials have sought in vain to punish delinquent members against determined opposition from above. The following disciplinary record of a member of the force in Pittsburg speaks for itself.

" Drunkenness, fined $5. Under influence of liquor while on duty, second offense, discharged — subsequently reinstated. Under the influence of liquor on duty, third offense, fined $10. Neglect of duty, fourth offense, under the influence of liquor, discharged — subsequently reinstated. Drunk on duty, fifth offense, discharged — subsequently reinstated. Visiting saloon in uniform, sixth offense, discharged — subsequently reinstated. Drunkenness, seventh offense, fined $25. Eighth offense, fined $25 and transferred. Ninth offense, suspended for three months. Intoxication, tenth offense, suspended for thirty days. Drunkenness, eleventh offense, no record of punishment." [1]

A record such as this can be duplicated in many cities throughout the country. In Chicago indeed, where the civil service commission has the power to reinstate, without the approval of the superintendent, men previously dismissed from service, conditions bordering on chaos have not infrequently resulted. Often this power is viciously abused and men are put back on the force after being dismissed for offenses which would have landed them in the penitentiary, had they been tried in a criminal court. [2] Thus two officers who accepted a bribe to drop a case against a chauffeur were dismissed in February, 1914, and reinstated in May, 1914. Another officer who, on evidence furnished by the police themselves, was discharged for accepting a bribe from a prostitute, was reinstated a year later by a civil service commission newly appointed. Still another officer, discharged for operating a taxicab business which incidentally catered to

[1] This record is among those given in "The City of Pittsburgh, Penn: Report on a Survey of the Department of Public Safety made by the New York Bureau of Municipal Research." (1913)
[2] For full discussion of this point see *Report of the City Council Committee on Crime*, Chicago, March 1915, p. 174 ff.

houses of prostitution, was reinstated by the commission and was a sergeant of police at the time of my visit. It must be recognized that bias and favoritism may influence a politically appointed civil service commission quite as much as it may influence the head of a police department. Certainly under such a system as Chicago possesses, the allocation of definite responsibility and the opportunity for positive leadership are alike impossible.

Judicial appeals against the disciplinary actions of police executives have led to situations almost equally demoralizing. In the fourteen years from 1899 to 1913, 683 proceedings were brought in the courts of New York against the police commissioners of New York City to compel the reinstatement of men dismissed for cause. Reversal or modification of the commissioner's determination resulted in 46 cases. Of the 46 cases, 26 were decided against the department because in the judgment of the court the commissioner had decided contrary to the weight of evidence; nineteen were decided against the department because of what were called serious defects in procedure; one case was decided against the department on both grounds.[1]

Two recent cases of the dismissal of captains of police in New York illustrate the point. After trial before the police commissioner, one captain was found guilty of accepting a bribe for the protection of a person charged with the illegal sale of liquor. The charge was sustained

[1] See *Report of New York Aldermanic Committee on Police Investigation*, 1912. Similarly, during the three years from 1914 to 1916 inclusive, 134 members were dismissed from the New York department. Of this number, 49 obtained writs of certiorai, and eight of these were reinstated. (From the records of the department.)

on the testimony of a patrolman who had been involved in the case. In the court's review, the question turned upon the veracity of the officer dismissed as against that of his accuser, and it was held that the evidence brought forward by this single accuser was insufficient to justify the finding of guilt.[1] Similarly in another case, dismissal was ordered on the ground that the officer had been guilty of making an improper entry in the station house blotter, and that a belated explanation of the circumstance amounted to false testimony. The court gave weight to the belated explanation, and holding that it was reasonable to believe that the officer had made an honest mistake, ordered his reinstatement.[2]

The unrestricted right of appeal to the courts from the decision of a police administrator is a menace to the proper exercise of discipline. The police executive cannot manage his department according to his knowledge and experience. He is forced into a position which would ruin the management of any private business, and which no European police administrator would tolerate for a moment.

But the shortcomings of civil service regulations in the police department are not confined to questions of discipline. In the matter of promotions their defects are almost equally obvious. " Civil service examinations," said Arthur Woods of New York, " even when conducted with intelligence and integrity, are not successful in putting at the top of the list the men who have done the best work. Promotion, therefore, which is so desirable to a policeman, is looked upon as something unconnected with

[1] 169 App. Div. 146.　　　　[2] 171 App. Div. 684.

his success in performing his duty day by day."[1]   One gathers this idea in every city where civil service is closely interwoven in the police department.   The civil service standard gives the impression of being an *outside* standard, ill-adapted to the needs or merits of the police force. It ranks symmetry above real efficiency.   It exercises its judgments from long range, and such external factors as seniority and the ability to answer written questions fluently must necessarily play a determining part.

Stephen O'Meara, who for many years served creditably as police commissioner of Boston, defined the situation as follows: " No written examination can possibly disclose the qualities and habits which are of vital importance in a police officer of rank and can be known only to his superiors.   Among them are judgment, coolness, moral as well as physical courage, executive ability, capacity for the command of men, sobriety and other moral qualities, standing among his associates and in the community, powers of initiative, temper, integrity, energy, courtesy."[2]   Theodore Roosevelt in his Autobiog-

---

[1] *Proceedings of the Academy of Political Science,* April, 1915.

[2] From a private memorandum which he gave me. In a letter to the Civil Service Commission dated February 12, 1913, he made the following interesting statement: " Length of service as a patrolman beyond a reasonable minimum should have no influence in promoting before a fit man, as sergeant, a man who is less fit.   When two men appear to be equally qualified the senior should have the preference again up to a reasonable age maximum, beyond which age becomes a disqualification.   But neither this minimum of service nor maximum of age can be made an official fixture without risking the loss from time to time of individual sergeants of especial merit.

" For promotion from sergeant to lieutenant or lieutenant to captain all rules as to length of service in the force or in the old grade fail.   An exceptionally able sergeant may well be made a lieutenant after a comparatively short service as sergeant, even if for no other reason than the necessity for bringing forward men who may later be made captains while still in their prime. . . . In

raphy expressed himself in similar vein. " I absolutely
split off from the bulk of my professional Civil Service
Reform friends when they advocated written competitive
examinations for promotion.   In the police department I
found these examinations a serious handicap in the way
of getting the best men promoted, and never in any office
did I find that the written competitive promotion examination did any good.   The reason for a written competitive entrance examination is that it is impossible for the
head of the office, or the candidate's prospective immediate
superior, himself to know the average candidate or to
test his ability.   But when once in office the best way to
test any man's ability is by long experience in seeing him
actually at work.   His promotion should depend upon the
judgment formed of him by his superiors." [1]

A Rational Civil Service.

Civil service ideas have been pushed much too far.
They have undermined the whole principle of responsible
leadership.   They have tied up great police forces like
Chicago's and Philadelphia's almost beyond hope of reorganization.   Indeed in these two cities and in not a few
others there is little chance of sound conditions or effective work in the police department until some strong
executive, freed from civil service entanglements, is allowed to sweep out the undesirable personnel.   It sometimes seems doubtful whether these departments can be

the promotion of a lieutenant to be a captain in command of a
division with from 60 to 120 men under him and serving the varied
interests of communities with populations running as high as 100,000,
length of service in the case of officers who are conspicuously fit
should have no weight whatever.". . .

[1] *Autobiography,* p. 161.

completely resuscitated if they are not started afresh.
The extremely able performance of the new police force in
Boston is a promise of what could be obtained in Pittsburgh and Chicago if the present civil service regulations
could be at least temporarily loosened and faith imposed
in an honest executive.

A far better balance between civil service protection
and effective leadership can be achieved than has been
reached up to the present. In our endeavors to eliminate
the spoils system we have swung too far toward rigidity,
and a rational approach is needed to a compromise which
will protect the police force from the politician without
robbing the police executive of initiative and leadership.
Is such a compromise possible?

In the first place, it is doubtful whether any change is
desirable in the present civil service practice as far as
appointments to the force are concerned. Civil service
provisions have done a great deal to raise the standards of
eligibility and eliminate the unfit. Moreover they relieve
the police administrator of a vast burden of detail. His
whole concern is to secure raw material of a kind that
can be turned into honest and intelligent policemen, and
any plan or machinery which will produce this material
upon demand adds to the effectiveness of his administration. Arthur Woods of New York, who cannot be
charged with being over-friendly to civil service, defines
its application to the problem of police appointments as
follows: " It is undoubtedly about as good a method as
any other for picking out qualified candidates, for the
men come from all walks of life, and seemingly from
every profession, trade, and job there is. No compara-

tive record could be obtained, nor could the judgment of employers fairly be used to distinguish between one man and another, since there might be a thousand different employers for a thousand applicants, and as many varying standards as employers." [1]

If, therefore, civil service could be looked upon as machinery for furnishing raw material, and if the police executive had the unchallenged right to reject, after probation, any candidates who proved unsatisfactory, there would be little in this phase of activity which could interfere with the principle of responsible leadership. It might be added, in this connection, that the civil service commission should be free to select the best material available wherever it could be found, regardless of residence or any other factor.

The question of promotion, however, furnishes a far different problem, and it is doubtful whether civil service has any proper relation to it except to assist the police administrator, perhaps, in passing upon the qualifications of those whose work and record seem to guarantee their fitness for higher positions. Certainly the civil service cannot of itself determine these qualifications. No written examinations, set by an external body, can possibly distinguish between faithfulness and unfaithfulness, between honesty and dishonesty, or between workers and shirkers.

The Boston plan of non-competitive examination for promotion, which was in effect for nearly 26 years prior to 1919, seems to be best adapted to the difficulty. Under this system the police commissioner of Boston determined

---

[1] *Policeman and Public,* New Haven, 1919, p. 107.

for himself which of his men were deserving of promotion. The names of these men were sent to the civil service commission which thereupon gave them a qualifying, non-competitive examination to test their general capacity. In other words, the official responsible for the administration of the police department nominated men of long service in whose character and efficiency he had complete confidence, and the civil service commission subjected them to further tests, educational or practical, written or oral, as they chose. The candidates who satisfied the civil service commission were eligible for promotion, but the police commissioner was free to make his own choices from the list. Those candidates who did not satisfy the civil service commission could not be promoted.[1]

---

[1] Commissioner O'Meara in a memorandum dated May 19, 1913, described the detail of the arrangement: "Under the present system the first step when a new list of sergeants is needed is to note the divisions which have been longest without a promotion to sergeant, for although the smaller and less active divisions cannot expect to receive as many promotions as those larger and busier, all divisions should be kept in mind.

"The commissioner then decides upon the divisions where promotions should be made. The captains of these divisions are instructed to write with their own hands, neither informing nor consulting any other person, and to forward under seal to the Commissioner the names of the patrolmen under them whom they regard on the whole as most deserving and most likely to succeed as sergeants — each captain to send twice as many names as it was intended should go upon the list.

"The Commissioner then examines his own memoranda of names — men whose work had attracted attention or much favorable expression. After weeks of inquiry, examination of records, without interference from any source, the Commissioner decides upon the men whom he will nominate to the civil service commission for examination." At the time of my examination of the Boston police force the opinion both within and without the department seemed to be that promotions were absolutely divorced from politics or considerations of favoritism.

The Rank and File

This scheme of making promotions succeeded the old competitive system which in the seven or eight years of its operation had proved disadvantageous to the whole department. " It worked disastrously," the chief inspector told me. In 1913 the civil service commission proposed the re-establishment of the competitive system for promotion in order to bring the practice of the entire state to a standardized form. The police commissioner successfully opposed the move, and in a series of frank letters to the civil service commission he developed the principle of his position. " Nothing that your commission could do," he said, " would work greater injury than the suggested change from the method of promotion which has produced such good results for so many years. Indeed the proposal involves by far the greatest danger that has threatened this department from any source in my seven years of service as commissioner.[1] . . . The police of every large city in the United States, except Boston, are suffering a public disgrace which would have been spared them if the official personality of their officers of rank had been the first consideration of those who appointed them." [2]

The non-competitive system of promotions is the method in vogue in London. There the civil service commission enters the situation only upon the invitation of

[1] Letters of Commissioner O'Meara to the state civil service commission dated February 12, 1913, May 19, 1913, and May 27, 1913.

[2] Under Commissioner Curtis, in 1919, the plan of competitive examinations conducted by the civil service commission was re-established for promotion to the ranks of sergeant and lieutenant of the uniformed force. The non-competitive plan still applies to the rank of captain and to the ranks of detective sergeant and inspector in the detective service.

the police commissioner to assist the department in weeding out men whose lack of education makes them unfit for promotion, and the examination which it gives is merely to test the general educational capacity of the applicant. A second examination in the elements of police duty, both oral and written, is given by a board of police officials, and those who emerge from these two tests are eligible to promotion, although the commissioner, of course, makes his own choices from the list.[1]

Some such system as this is necessary if our police departments are to be saved from lifelessness and dry rot. With promotions the result of real excellence in police work under the watchful eye of superiors, much of the present inertia would disappear.

The question of discipline is the final factor in regard to which current civil service procedure needs radical modification. There is no chance for progressive improvement in a police department if the hands of the responsible executive are tied in his dealings with his men. Here again we must turn to Boston for an example of a rational system. As we have seen, complaints against members of the force are heard by a special trial board of three captains appointed by the police commissioner.[2] The commissioner, however, is always

---

[1] For a fuller discussion of the system of promotions in London see *European Police Systems,* Chapter VII. Some years ago in Boston a somewhat similar arrangement was in force and a private competitive examination was given by the police commissioner to those applicants who had passed the non-competitive examination of the civil service commission. Past record and general ability counted as points.

[2] As a matter of custom only captains who have never had the deliquent member under their commands at any time are chosen to sit as members of the trial board.

supreme. He can at any time change the personnel of the trial board, order a new trial, or set aside the recommendations of the board in regard to the punishment to be imposed. His word is final and from it there is no appeal to a higher civil authority.[1] On no other basis can responsibility be definitized and a police force be rid of useless or dishonest employees. To divide responsibility with a civil service commission, a mayor, a court, or any other authority, is to sow the seed of demoralization and to make real success impossible for any administrator, no matter how able.

I am conscious that these views will meet with opposition from those who dread the incursion of the spoils system into our police departments and are honestly frightened at the vicious forces in our municipal governments which civil service barriers have served, partially at least, to keep in check. It must be admitted that this alarm and anxiety are not without basis. One has only to look at Kansas City or Indianapolis to see how the unrestrained play of these forces contributes to the demoralization of a police department. But we shall never solve the police problem in America until we give honest and effective leadership an opportunity to show what it can do. Sometime or other we have got to make a beginning of trusting our public officials. Checks and balances to curb and minimize possible abuses of power have gotten us nowhere. Complex systems to prevent

[1] In the history of the department there has been but one appeal to the court from decisions of the police commissioner This appeal failed and the court stated that it would not review questions of fact in cases of this kind, but only the regularity of the procedure. (Welch *vs.* O'Meara, 195 Mass., 541.)

bias and unfairness have brought nothing but confusion. It is time to take off a few of the yokes that have made public administration an impossible task, and put a new emphasis on positive qualities. The problem before us is not how to build up a structure that will circumvent the dishonest and incompetent official, but having found a competent and honest official, to surround him with the conditions in which he can make himself effective.

The Police School.

Entering upon new tasks for the first time, police recruits are raw material to be molded and shaped into efficient police officers. How is this to be accomplished? Two answers to this question are given by American municipalities: one group of cities, constituting, it must be confessed, a small proportion of the total, holds that there is need for thorough-going instruction by classes with a prescribed curriculum of studies relating to police methods and procedure. In this group are such cities as New York, Chicago, Philadelphia, Detroit, Cleveland, St. Louis, Cincinnati, Newark, Louisville and Berkeley, California. Another group of cities, by far the larger number, holds to the view of the old time police official, that text-books, classes of instruction and written tests are of little worth in training a recruit for his task. In these cities, therefore, men are turned out on the streets in uniform with no previous preparation, beyond perhaps a little preliminary practice in patrol in company with an older officer. Occasionally this so-called instruction goes hand in hand with physical drill.

Of the police training schools there are of course many

types, ranging from the well-organized institution operating on a full time basis to the part-time " school " which actually amounts to little more than a periodic assembly of policemen to hear a lecture on some phase of police work.   In many cities, particularly those under 100,000 population, the school has only a temporary existence, as substantial periods of time elapse during which no new appointments to the force are made.   Probably the most ambitious police school at the present time is in Berkeley, California.   Here the class, which meets one hour a day, takes three years to complete the courses included in the curriculum.[1]   The New York school involves two months of full time instruction; in Chicago, Philadelphia, St. Louis, Detroit and Newark, the training period is four weeks; in Cleveland it is three.   In Cincinnati and Louisville only part of the day is devoted to school work, the remainder being spent in the performance of regular duty.

The New York police training school was the first to be established as an independent unit of the police department.   In point of size, scope, method and equipment it easily takes first rank among the police schools of the United States, and it has served as a model to similar in-

[1] The courses given for the first year are: physics, chemistry, biology, physiology and anatomy; criminology; anthropology and heredity; toxicology. For the second year courses are given in criminal psychology; psychiatry; theoretical and applied criminology; police organization and administration; police practice and procedure. The third year's courses include microbiology and parisitology; micro-analysis; public health; first aid; elementary and criminal law. For a fuller description of the Berkeley school see article by August Vollmer and Albert Schneider in *The Journal of the American Institute of Criminal Law and Criminology*, Vol. VII, No. 6.

stitutions established in other municipalities. For that reason it is permissible to follow its operation in some detail.

Because of the varied use of the term " school " it is difficult to determine when the New York institution was first inaugurated. If a single instructor, a number of students and a certain amount of time devoted to instruction constitute a school, then the New York department has been equipped with a school for half a century. In earlier times, however, the instruction 'was of the most elementary kind. Police recruits were taught for a period of thirty days by a sergeant specially detailed for that purpose, and in addition the students were sent out on patrol during certain hours of the day or night. No particular attention was paid to this preparatory work; it was thought sufficient to acquaint the recruit with the rules and regulations of the department and to give him a rudimentary knowledge of the laws and ordinances of the city. Formations, drills and exercises also formed a part of this early training.

The development of these educational activities in New York has been irregular and uncertain, dependent upon the interest and enthusiasm of the changing police commissioners. At times the teaching corps has been enlarged and the instruction broadened, only to be reduced by succeeding commissioners. The elementary preparatory instruction in laws, ordinances and rules has for most part remained fairly constant, and has never been discarded altogether, although considerable fluctuation has occurred in the amount and variety of physical drill.

A general reconstruction of the school occurred in 1914

at the beginning of the administration of Commissioner Woods. The title was changed from " School of Recruits " to " The Police Training School," indicating that thereafter it would not only offer instruction for the new recruit, but would include specialized courses for older members of the service, with the idea particularly of assisting them in preparation for promotional examination. The scope of the school was broadened in every way, necessitating the lengthening of the term for recruits from six weeks to three months.[1]   New courses were added to the curriculum, with the consequent enlargement of the teaching staff, and a unit organization was established for the supervision and control of the school's operation.

As far as the school for recruits is concerned, the methods instituted by Commissioner Woods remain practically unaltered.   The school day begins at 9:00 A. M. and ends at 5 : 00 P. M. for the first five days of the week, and from 9 : 00 to 12 : 00 on Saturdays.   The day is divided into periods according to the following schedule : the first period from 9 : 00 to 9 : 30, is spent at the regular detective bureau " lineup " of criminals arrested on the preceding day and night for serious crimes; 9 : 30 to 11 : 00, classroom instruction; 11 : 00 to 12 : 00, drills and physical instruction; 12 : 00 to 1 : 00, luncheon hour; 1 : 00 to 3 : 00, classroom instruction; 3 : 00 to 4 : 00, physical; 4 : 00 to 5 : 00, classroom.   The curriculum of classroom instruction includes 22 subjects taken up in the following order: deportment, patrol, observation, crime classifica-

---

[1] In 1917 owing to the war emergency this period was reduced to two months and the time required for the training of recruits has not since been altered.

tion, arrests, traffic, animals, fires and accidents, ordinances and sanitary code, disorderly conduct, felonies and misdemeanors, assaults and weapons, homicide, larceny and robbery, burglary, children, court procedure, public morals, report making, election law, malicious michief, Sabbath law.

Each recruit is supplied with the rules and regulations of the department and a copy of a text-book.[1] In the course of several years of experience the instructors have evolved a practical sort of pedagogy by which they combine the lecture method with actual experiments in the classroom. Questions involving legal rights and limitations as well as police technique are illustrated by hypothetical cases which are worked out by the instructors in the class, a recruit generally acting as a policeman while the instructor poses as a criminal or citizen with whom the policeman has to deal. Every conceivable circumstance involving police action is illustrated and discussed, and the recruit is enabled to visualize the actual practical situations with which he will be called upon to deal. Extensive use is made of charts and blackboard illustrations, and every effort is made to rivet the attention of the student by vivid example and dramatic incident.

This daily course of instruction is supplemented by a schedule of special talks and lectures given by other members of the department of various ranks and grades, chosen because of some achievement or proficiency in a particular line of work. Thus lectures are given on the care and purchase of uniforms, on discipline, first aid

[1] The text-book used is *Police Practice and Procedure* by Inspector Cornelius Cahalane of the New York Department.

to the injured, finger prints, " trailing," handling of beg-
gars, statistical purposes and uses of police reports and
the preparation of cases for the magistrates' courts. In
addition to the daily class work, a certain amount of
home work is assigned for each night, to be submitted in
writing on the following day. This work is reviewed
by the instructors and briefly discussed at the lecture
period. Bi-weekly written tests are held and the papers
in these examinations are graded and made a matter of
record.

The field work, embracing practical demonstrations of
methods of patrol, observation and reporting, is a very
important part of the recruit's training. Each recruit is
assigned to " student patrol " from six P. M. to ten P. M.
every Saturday, Sunday and holiday throughout the two
months' period. He reports to a different precinct on
each assignment, and thus visits during his training course
about eighteen or twenty precincts. The patrol is done
in the company of an experienced patrolman who is regularly attached to the precinct. At the end of such a
student tour of patrol, the recruit is required to prepare
a written report setting forth the details of what he has
seen and learned.

Two hours each day are devoted to physical instruction and drills and they serve as a pleasant break in the
monotony of classroom work. The methods of training
in use in West Point have been introduced in the police
school with excellent results. The men are daily put
through regulation calisthenic exercises and are taught to
keep their bodies in the best possible condition. Self-
defense is taught in its several branches, including the

Japanese system of jiu jitsu. Exercises are given in ladder-scaling, and in carrying persons in rescue work. Every policeman must be able to swim and be able to use the approved methods of life-saving. Swimming is taught in the municipal pools, and in the harbor during the warm season. At the end of the two months' course, the class must be able to execute drills and formations perfectly, and each member must be capable of taking command in the direction of drill work.

Prior to 1917, during Commissioner Woods' administration, the scope of the school, as we have seen, was broadened to include training for superior officers. Indeed, Commissioner Woods' idea was to make the police department a university in which all ranks would constantly be " freshening up "— to use his expression — in police technique. With that end in view, inspectors and captains were given courses of lectures by criminologists, jurists, identification experts, and other specialists in fields relating to police work. So-called " review courses," extending over a period of two weeks, were compulsory for lieutenants, sergeants, " near "-lieutenants and " near "-sergeants — the latter being members of grades that had passed promotional examinations and were on the lists for appointment. The purpose of these courses was to keep the officers from becoming " rusty," lest the recruits, fresh from school, be better versed in special subjects than their superiors. Lectures were also given in these courses on such special phases of police activity as discipline, the preparation of records and the giving of bail. In all this work the men gave full time to their studies, as experience showed that best results were obtained when policemen undergoing these review tests were excused from all other duty.

In addition, classes were organized to train regular patrolmen who were applicants for special policy duty. Thus a class was conducted for members desiring to enter the motorcycle squad, and the time was spent between mechanical shop work and road work. Another class was given two weeks' training for mounted traffic duty, while still another was instructed for the same period for foot traffic duty. The men were rated according to proficiency shown in the school and assignment to these special details was made on the basis of a list prepared by the school officers.[1]

We have considered at some length the details of the New York school curriculum because it represents the best training system in police work which any American city of size has produced. Surely the experience not only of New York but of other large cities like London and Paris amply demonstrates the fact that a properly equipped and administered school is perhaps the most indispensable single feature of the police force of a modern community.[2] For it must be repeated that the primary problem in police administration is the problem of personnel. The establishment of reporting systems and the building up of organization schemes can not wisely be disregarded or slighted, for they are important and have a definite place in regulating the daily work of the force. But they are aids and means, not ends. The

[1] All these advanced and special schools were dropped by Commissioner Woods' successor.
[2] For a full description of European police schools see *European Police Systems*, Chapter VI.

heart of police work is the contact of the individual policeman with the citizen. There are very few times when the department as a whole or even any large part of it proceeds directly to do police work. Nearly all police activity is initiated in the field away from headquarters and station houses. The action that is first taken by the policeman of lower rank, operating independently, must, in each case, remain the foundation of the department's action. In the final analysis, police business is but the aggregate of personal enterprise, and the quality of a department's work depends on the observation, knowledge, discretion, courage and judgment of the men, acting as individuals, who compose the various units or branches of the organization. The operation of mere organization machinery may achieve a high degree of perfection, but if the members of the force, acting in their individual capacities, go about their tasks without intelligence, tact or public spirit, the " system " counts for little and the whole administration is a failure. Only as the training of the policeman is deliberate and thorough, with emphasis upon the social implications and human aspects of his task, can real success in police work be achieved.

Patrol Service.

The policeman's work is built largely around the patrol system. Indeed the patrol post has become through years of custom the basic unit of police organization, and no discussion of police work would be complete which did not make especial mention of it.

No one can examine the methods of patrol employed throughout the country without being struck by the amount of waste which they involve, due largely to the rigid adherence of police authorities to old conventional ideas. In many cities, as we have already pointed out,[1] the same methods of patrol that were in use 30 or 40 years ago have been continued to the present time.[2] It is not at all uncommon to find the boundaries of posts remaining unaltered for years, notwithstanding the fact that the whole character of the district has changed — often with business, warehouse and factory buildings completely taking the place of former residences. Moreover there are many districts in which the night problem, from a police point of view, is entirely different from the day problem, yet the posts in such districts are often policed in exactly the same way during all hours of the day and night.

There are several respects in which the whole police problem has been so altered as to lessen the need of foot-patrol or at least to reduce its effectiveness. Public disorder, such as street fighting, disturbance by intoxicated persons and general rowdiness, while not unknown, does not occur with the same frequency as in earlier days, and even when occurring it is restricted to comparatively small areas where the population is congested. Moreover the extensive use of automobiles has rendered foot-patrol a handicapped method of defense, if it has not actually made it obsolete in many situations. If the criminal is equipped with an automobile a patrolman on

[1] See *ante,* Chap. V.
[2] One exception can be noted. Formerly it was the practice to send patrolmen out in pairs. This practice has been almost universally abandoned and a patrolman is now given a post or beat for which he alone is responsible during his tour of duty.

foot has little chance to catch him. Formerly when a patrolman encountered a stranger prowling about by day or night, he watched his actions and followed him if necessary, and if the suspected person was equipped with horse and buggy it was easy to obtain an identifying description. Now that the automobile has made travel by night much more common, identification is difficult and the occupants of vehicles cannot easily be observed.

Another factor which is rapidly undermining the usefulness of foot-patrol is the increasing area of residential districts in large cities. The old type of patrol cannot adequately meet this situation except at a cost which would be prohibitive. To be effective, the foot-patrolman must have a post small enough to enable him to cover it quickly and continuously. In the absence of enough patrolmen to man this kind of post, policemen in outlying districts are given beats frequently more than a half mile in length and width. The results are largely negative, as the chance of being at the right place at the right time is the element which determines a patrolman's effectiveness on a large post. Even if cost were not a factor necessary to be considered and patrolmen could be employed to any number, this type of patrol is ill adapted to new conditions. In the outlying residential districts, made up of detached houses, very little crime or disorder is committed by persons residing there. Most of the crimes take the form of attacks against property, such as robbery, burglary and larceny, and are perpetrated by non-residents who plan their crimes in advance and await their opportunity to act. It is obvious that the uniformed patrolman on

The Rank and File

beat is not fitted to cope with this type of crime. He is simply a signal and a warning, and the criminal waits until the patrolman has passed out of sight and hearing before beginning operations.

Police technique in the average city has not kept pace with modern developments, and hundreds of thousands of dollars are annually paid out for services which are largely wasted. Only as mechanical equipment is introduced in outlying districts as a substitute for the old foot patrol system can the police department keep abreast of its work. It is encouraging, therefore, to note the use in a few cities of motor vehicles for patrol work, and of other devices such as patrol booths and flashlight signal systems. Creditable beginnings in the use of these mechanical aids have been made notably in Detroit, Los Angeles, Kansas City, New York and Berkeley, California. New York has had a thorough test of the booth system and has proved its adaptability to the protection of large residential districts. A single booth was established as an experiment by the Detroit department in 1918; its value was so clearly demonstrated that thirteen additional booths were erected shortly thereafter.[1] The patrol booth is in effect a miniature police station. Its chief advantage lies in the fact that a policeman in a given territory is made immediately available to citizens and headquarters alike. A proper operation of the booth system requires that not less than two men, equipped with motorcycle or automobile, be attached to a booth at the same time. One

[1] For an account of the Detroit patrol booth system, see the Annual Report of the Detroit Police Department, 1918.

man remains at the booth while the other circulates through the district, returning periodically to the booth. In case the booth man is absent on an emergency call, the other remains at the booth until his return. By this arrangement a district is given the benefit of patrol — in point of fact the motorcycle or automobile man gives better patrol service than the foot-patrolman — and at the same time a policeman can be had at once in case of need. Citizens have a far greater feeling of security in knowing that they can get a policeman immediately than in knowing that a foot-patrolman is somewhere in the district and that there is a chance that he is near enough to hear a call for help.

The use of automobiles for patrolling the streets is also gaining in favor and will doubtless soon supersede the present foot-patrol method as far as the outlying sections of our cities are concerned. Kansas City, Mo., and Berkeley, Cal., were the first cities to give the automobile a thorough-going trial. Because of a reduction in the number of policemen in the Kansas City department it became necessary to use automobiles so as to enable the small force to cover the whole city. The innovation proved profitable from the beginning.

In Berkeley every patrolman in the department is equipped with a small Ford car. Chief Vollmer in speaking of the value of automobiles in patrol service made the following report: " Patrolmen thus equipped (with automobiles) travel over one thousand miles of streets per month; respond promptly to emergency calls; are in good physical condition when they arrive at the site of trouble; are protected during inclement weather, and able to per-

The Rank and File

form their duties in a more satisfactory manner." [1]   The
excellent results that have been achieved by the Berkeley
department through the close supervision of the training
and work of individual policemen and through the use
of motor equipment in patrol are reflected in the statistics
of operations covering the seven-year period from 1908
to 1915 inclusive.   In this period the population increased
from 37,000 to 64,000.   The total membership of the
force was increased in this time by but five men.   Reports and complaints of crime or other conditions requiring the attention of the police increased only 14% as
against a 73% increase in population.   The value of
property reported stolen was $20,789.47 in 1908 and $14,-
892.91 in 1915, a decrease of 28%. [2]   These figures indicate the value of corrective and preventive work done by
the department in increasing the effectiveness of each
member of the organization through improved methods of
operation.

In April, of 1918 the Detroit department placed over
150 Ford automobiles on the streets to patrol beats formerly covered by foot-patrolmen.   Each machine carries
two policemen, one in plain clothes and one in uniform.
During the first month of the operation of these machines,
felony complaints were reduced from 654 reported in the
previous month to 528; in the second month there was a
further decrease of 65 felony complaints over the previous month.   " The innovation of the automobile as a
preventive (of crime) has proven a great success," said

[1] From the Annual Report of the Chief of Police, Berkeley, Cal.,
1915.
[2] *Ibid.*

311

an official of the Detroit department, " for two men can now do the work that formerly took four or five, and are able to do any kind of work with more success in residential districts than officers on foot." [1]

Similarly other cities, such as St. Louis, Seattle, Los Angeles and Louisville, are making small beginnings in the use of automobiles for patrolling beats. The hesitation of many departments in taking up the automobile for patrol purposes is due to the expense involved in the initial outlay and maintenance charges. On the other hand, if two men equipped with an automobile can do the work of five, or perhaps eight men on foot, a reduction in the patrol force is possible, and the saving in salaries may more than offset the cost of providing the necessary motor equipment.

The modern development of patrol service is in the direction of limiting foot-patrol to congested districts where large numbers of people are passing in the streets, where accidents are likely to occur and where public disturbances may develop with little warning. Uniformed men patrolling in non-congested districts and in business districts which are closed during the hours of the night may be supplanted for the most part by junior detectives, plain clothes operatives, and men equipped with automobiles. By the adoption of the booth system and the installation of signal devices, the certainty of police assistance will furnish a greater degree of security than can be had by relying on the accidental presence of a patrolman circulating on foot over a large post.

[1] Inspector Kinney in the Annual Report of the Detroit Police Department, 1918.

The Rank and File

The Rigidity of the Police Department.

There is a widely prevailing disposition on the part of police officials to view the force as a mechanism created to operate automatically. More thought is given to the perfection of the organization as a machine of smoothly working parts and to the employment of systematic reporting schemes than to the primary problem of adjusting individual persons to their tasks. This emphasis upon the mechanical side of organization is accentuated by hard and fast rules and regulations which prescribe, often in great detail, the duties of each member of the department according to his rank and assignment. The idea is to put each member of the force in a place provided by a " paper " scheme of organization, and then to find means of checking his routine work through supervising officers. Sergeants of police give immediate direction to patrolmen and in turn report to lieutenants or captains; these report to officers of higher rank, and so matters come ultimately to the chief officer. The aim of this hierarchial arrangement seems to be to provide a set of superior officers who will see to it that members of the next lower rank are performing their duties as required by regulations.

This mechanical system is deemed a safeguard against the too frequent changes in the office of the administrative head of the department. " Commissioners may come and commissioners may go but the ' system ' goes on forever." [1] This expression is often heard in explanation of the unchanging character of police organization and

[1] The term *system* is not here used in any sinister sense.

313

of police procedure based on precedent. The implication is that the department performs the great bulk of its routine work automatically and that the machine can and does operate without the aid of administrative supervision.

It would be foolish, of course, to underestimate the value of orderly machinery. But it can be over-emphasized to the point of rigidity, so that the organization ceases to be a vital, living thing and becomes merely a mechanical device. As far as the police department is concerned, it is undoubtedly true that this over-emphasis is the result of the old analogy between an army and a police force and the attempt to put this analogy into active operation. But the analogy is largely fallacious. An army does its work through groups of its units — divisions, brigades, regiments and companies — in all of which the private is little more than a cog. Initiative and imagination not only have no place in his career, but, for the sake of discipline, their exhibition is discouraged. The work of a police force, however, depends, as we have seen, upon the capacity of the individual policeman. On his beat or at his post he must do his duty alone, usually dealing with emergencies by his own unaided action. However difficult or novel the circumstances which confront him, he must decide instantly on his own responsibility whether or not they call for his interference. Only occasionally is there an opportunity for concerted action in connection with his brother officers. For the most part he must depend upon his own resourcefulness and originality, characteristics which in army training remain largely undeveloped.

The Rank and File

Consequently, the same insistence upon system and procedure which makes an army successful often becomes the cause of defeat in a police force. The organization stands between the police and their objective. The objective is not clearly conceived and the machinery becomes an end in itself. Thus police needs are generally estimated in terms of quotas of men prescribed for the various divisions of the department, and policemen are thought of as being more or less standardized units to fill precinct, district or squad quotas. One set of ten men, accordingly, is supposed to be the equivalent of any other set of ten men for ordinary police work. It is the number of standardized units that is chiefly reckoned with, and not the special abilities of individual officers in their contact with crime conditions or the difficulties and perplexities of citizens on the street.

Perhaps the chief objection to this over-emphasis on the mechanical side of organization lies in the resulting inability of police departments to mobilize their forces speedily and effectively. They are unable to make sudden shifts of personnel in attacking pressing problems or to modify the methods of their procedure as necessity may dictate. This immobility is due partly to a fear of disrupting the orderly processes of the machine and partly to a lack of appreciation of the value of having a *flexible* force.

Mobilization of police forces is of two kinds: one consists in assembling units of men at designated places at a given time, and the other consists in concentrating the work of several different units of the organization on a single problem irrespective of normal function.

315

American Police Systems

The value of the physical mobilization of men is universally recognized, although the provisions for effecting it vary considerably from city to city. In some communities squads of men are kept in station houses on reserve duty. They are subject to call and immediate assignment, and by the use of automobiles where districts are large, they can be despatched without delay to a scene of disorder or accident. In other cities no regular reserve system exists, but in cases of emergency men are summoned from patrol posts or from special office assignments. The tendency at present is to reduce the number of reserve men who remain idle except during emergency service, and to rely more and more on gong or bell signals in day time and flashlights at night for summoning men who are on patrol. In the largest cities, however, the congestion of population and the possibility of disturbance make it necessary to maintain some kind of a reserve force at a few, at least, of the station houses.

The other type of mobilization to which we referred actually amounts to a temporary readjustment of the department's program by giving special attention to conditions calling for immediate correction. It is in this respect that the weakness of police departments in general is to be observed. Hard and fast organization lines prevent any considerable concentration of the energies of various divisions on a common problem. Police forces cannot readily be shifted from point to point, or rapidly mobilized to meet some new development of crime, vice, or delinquincy; nor can the whole department be bent to aid in the correction of an abnormal situation. To be sure efforts are often made to meet bad conditions by de-

316

tailing members of the force as special investigators apart from their regular routine. For example, when burglaries or robberies are committed with unusual frequency in a certain residential district, detectives are often sent to operate there on general assignment. Similarly, whenever complaints of prostitution or gambling begin to multiply, the common practice is to detail, temporarily, an extra number of men from the uniformed force to do duty in plain clothes under the special direction of an officer in charge of the suppression of vice.

This practice is a step in the right direction but it is only a step. It could be extended throughout the whole organization. Any unusual crime conditions could be treated in the same way. Juvenile delinquencies, gambling, swindling schemes of various sorts, mendicancy, vagrancy, rowdyism, violations of sanitary regulations, violations of motor vehicle laws — all of these as they developed could be met with especial vigor by the concentrated effort of all divisions or by temporary enlargement of the special divisions.

In Berkeley, Cal., where more than usual intelligence is given to police problems, it is customary to set the whole machinery of the department to work in *cleaning up* special crime conditions as they become evident. If vagrancy or minor trespassing is the immediate problem, uniformed patrolmen, detectives, plain clothes men and superior officers devote especial attention to stamping it out. As quickly as conditions have been remedied the men return to their customary duties, and no organization changes are required.

In most cities, however, a temporary aggravation of

some phase of the police problem is held to require an increase in the number of men specializing in that phase of work. Thus if violations of motor vehicle laws become unusually numerous and cannot be handled by the traffic squad, no other branch of the service is called temporarily to the assignment. Either more members are added to the permanent traffic squad or else the offenses continue to be inadequately handled.

The chief fault in the present situation is that the police department is not readily sensitive to changes in its problem. It is only when extreme conditions of crime or delinquency appear and after much damage has been done that the police organization is in any way altered to meet the situation. Even then the department as a whole is not immediately responsive to the circumstances nor are its parts concentrated to correct the abnormal situation. The final test of the effectiveness of a police organization is first, its success in acquiring accurate and complete information as to crime conditions in the community, and second, its ability, through the generalship of its officers, to proceed against such conditions with the least delay and with all available forces. The problem of increasing or developing either permanently or temporarily the special branches best fitted for handling emergency situations is one that requires constant study and experiment.

Police Unions.

The strike of the Boston police and similar difficulties in London, Liverpool and other English cities, have resulted in a widely accepted belief that in the public interest the right to strike cannot be granted to police bodies, nor can they be allowed to affiliate with other labor unions. The policeman, like the soldier, occupies a unique position in the community. He represents the state in its power to compel obedience. As an agent of the government he exercises its ultimate force. In this capacity he is responsible solely to the legal representatives of the community, and control cannot be permitted to drift into the hands of any other men. If the armed agency of the state for compelling obedience assumes to determine for itself the conditions under which it will obey the state, then the principle of ordered majority rule is destroyed, and in its place is militarism.

The same objections hold in regard to the affiliation of the police with organized labor. The police force is a public instrument. Its allegiance is to the state. It is not the tool of any class or subdivision of the community. If the right to exercise the ultimate force of the state is surrendered to any special interest, if the police department loses its neutrally minded character and becomes representative of a particular fraction of the community, the state as a public instrument ceases to exist. Indeed such a course would immediately provoke a reaction. Other classes in the community, having lost confidence in the police, would proceed to organize militia, constabularies and vigilance committees of their own, and the result would be chaos. The subordination of armed force to the legal state, and the principle that the legal state represents the common interest, without regard to class, lie at the basis of social progress.

If this point of view is accepted, if in the public interest the right to strike and to affiliate with organized labor is denied the police, the legal representatives of the community are under peculiar obligations not only to deal sympathetically and generously with the genuine grievances of the police, but by continual study and observation to forestall such grievances before they can gain a foothold. This is a point which seems to have escaped the attention of many commentators. Five years before the London police strike of 1918, it was palpable to an outsider that the " Bobby " could not live decently on such wages as he was then receiving.[1] And yet in the ensuing period, through an era of rising prices, his endeavors — tactless and ill-conceived, perhaps — to have his grievances considered by his superiors, met with scant courtesy and meagre result.[2] Similarly in many American cities — and among them is Boston — it has been apparent for years that the police were underpaid. They have appealed to their superiors, they have appeared before finance committees and councils, they have taken their claims to the public through the press — too often with no result, sometimes, indeed, meeting with nothing but brusqueness and abuse. There are large cities in the United States today whose policemen are paid less than one hundred dollars a month, from which they must purchase their uniforms and equipment. There are many other cities where the police work seven days a week or where their hours of employment are inexcusably long. There are cities where the conditions surrounding the life of the men in station houses are a disgrace to the

[1] See *European Police Systems*, pp. 242–244.
[2] For discussion, see interesting series of articles (anonymous) appearing in the London *Times,* April 1st, 2nd and 3rd, 1919.

community that tolerates them. If the police may not strike to improve their situation, and if they may not affiliate with organized labor, then the community that employs them owes them a responsibility which up to the present time, certainly, it has not fulfilled. It cannot strip them of the weapons of defense which other workers have, and at the same time ignore their just claims because they are pressed merely by argument.[1]

---

[1] Very interesting legislation has recently been passed by the British Parliament as a result of the police strikes in England in the summer of 1919. A Police Federation was created, consisting of all members of the police forces, both county and municipal, in England and Wales. The members of each separate police force are constituted into three Branch Boards, one for constables, one for sergeants and one for inspectors. Branch Boards may submit their grievances or other representations to the chief of police, and also to the Secretary of State for Home Affairs, who is charged with the responsibility for police arrangements in England and Wales. The members of each Board annually elect a delegate or delegates to a Central Conference, made up of representatives elected by the members of the Branch Boards of corresponding rank of all police forces of England and Wales. Thus there are three Central Conferences — one for constables, one for sergeants and one for inspectors, and their annual meetings are held in November. The members of each Conference elect a Central Committee of six members, and the three Central Committees, or any two of them, may by agreement, sit together at a Joint Committee. The Central Committee, either separately or as a Joint Committee, may submit representations in writing to the Secretary of State, and in matters of importance the Secretary of State will give any Committee or a deputation from the Committee a personal hearing. All regulations as regards the government, mutual aid, pay, allowances, pensions, clothing, expenses, and conditions of service of the members of the police forces of England and Wales are submitted for the consideration of the Joint Committee before promulgation, and the Secretary of State is bound to consider any representations made by this Committee before putting the regulations into effect. (For a fuller description of the operation of this legislation, see 9 & 10 Geo. 5, Chap. 46, and the schedule attached thereto.)

American Police Systems

The Police and Industrial Disturbance.

We have said that the police force is a public instrument for the protection of life and property and the preservation of order, that its allegiance is to all the people, and that it is not the tool of any class or subdivision of the community. Upon this principle we base the objection to the affiliation of the police with organized labor. No one can intensively study the work of the police in American cities, however, without realizing that this same principle is frequently violated in respect to other class interests than those of labor unionism. The police are often used on behalf of employers as against employees in circumstances which do not justify their interference at all. This has been especially true in the handling of strikes. Lawful picketing has been broken up, the peaceful meetings of strikers have been brutally dispersed, their publicity has been suppressed, and infractions of ordinances which would have gone unnoticed had the violators been engaged in another cause, have been ruthlessly punished. Sometimes, too, arrests have been made on charges whose baselessness the police confidentially admit. " We lock them up for disorderly conduct," a chief of police told me when I asked him about his policy in regard to strikes and strikers. " Obstructing the streets " is another elastic charge often used on such occasions. Sometimes the arbitrary conduct of the police passes belief. Newspapers favoring the strikers' cause have been confiscated and printing establishments closed on the supposition that they would " incite to riot." Meetings of workingmen have been prohibited or broken up on the theory that the men were *planning* a strike, and specific individuals have been denied the right to speak for the reason that they were " labor organizers." " I have this strike broken and I mean to keep it broken," a director of public safety told me, as if breaking strikes were one of the regular functions of the police. I asked the chief of police of a large industrial city on what legal ground he denied the privilege of assembly to the striking operators of an extensive plant. " We assume that their meeting-halls are disorderly houses," he replied. " Detrimental to the public welfare " is the easy generalization with which the rights of citizens are often over-ridden by the police, apparently on the theory that the interests of employers are necessarily identical with public interests. The industrial cities of northern New Jersey, of Pennsylvania, and of Illinois, furnish ample substantiation of this indictment.

The situation in this respect is apt to be at its worst when the mayor or commissioner of public safety is himself an officer of a large industrial plant, or when the chief of police comes under the influence of a commercial association, some of whose members, perhaps, are parties to the conflict. Under such circumstances, strikers have frequently been hounded and punished, often with physical violence, in contravention of all law and tradition and the principles of a free government.

In 1917 Commissioner Woods of New York issued an order to his force in connection with the handling of strikes which has attracted wide attention and may well serve as a model. It reads in part as follows:

" The duties of the Police Department in connection with strikes and industrial disturbances are, in the last analysis, as on all other occasions, to protect Life and Property, and to maintain the Public Peace.

" Unless otherwise advised by the Courts or Commanding Officers, it is to be assumed that the purposes of a peaceful strike are legal.

" Since such affairs are often accompanied by much bitterness and hard feeling on both sides, it is imperative that the Law be administered with the utmost impartiality.

" In so far as this Department is concerned, one or more employees may refuse to work, and one or more employers may refuse to hire any particular person, or persons, for such reasons as may seem to them best, or for no reason at all. The employees who have gone on strike may gather in front of one or any number of places where they were formerly employed and address, within certain limits, such arguments as they may desire to their fellow workmen who are still employed, urging them to go on strike. Similar arguments may be addressed to those who they may have reason to believe are considering taking their former positions of employment either permanently or temporarily as strike-breakers. The strikers or their sympathizers may, also, advise prospective customers of the fact that they are on strike and the nature of their grievances — be they real or supposed. The words used, in all such cases, however, must not be of such a nature as to incite to violence or offend public decency.

" While both sides to such a controversy have the right of assembly, no violence or even physical contact between opposing factions shall be permitted.

" The right of the strikers to conduct peaceful picketing has been upheld by the Courts, but the numbers so employed must not be so great as to interfere with the free passage of vehicles or pedestrians, nor by their very number to constitute an intimidation. The number of pickets that may be lawfully permitted depends upon the circumstances of the case, such as the width of the street and the sidewalk, the number of employees who are working, the number and size of the exits to the building, the size of the building, and the number of neutral persons using the sidewalk or thoroughfare in question.

" Members of the police Department have no proper official interest in the merits of the controversy, and their action is not to be affected thereby." [1]

It must be repeated that the police owe their allegiance to all the people and not to any class or subdivision of the community. To use them in behalf of any special interest, whether that interest be a labor union, a street-railroad company, or an industrial plant, is to destroy the principle of ordered majority rule upon which democracies depend.[2]

[1] Circular Order No. 19, June 9, 1917.
[2] For further discussion see Woods' *Policeman and Public,* p. 67 ff., and *Police Functions in Labor Disputes,* an address by Arthur Woods before the City Club of New York, printed in the New York *Evening Post,* Nov. 18, 1916.

CHAPTER IX

THE DETECTIVE FORCE

WE have now to consider the detective bureau — a branch of the police service as essential to the preservation of public security as the uniformed division itself. Operating for the most part after crimes have been committed, its duty is to apprehend those offenders who have escaped arrest at the hands of the uniformed force. To that end it requires a degree of talent and specialization in its personnel distinct from the qualifications of the uniformed men. How this personnel is commanded, chosen and trained, and how its work is controlled and guided are matters discussed in this chapter.

The Chief of the Detective Force.

Heads of detective bureaus are chosen in most cases from among the officers of the uniformed forces. In some cities the selection is made by the administrative

326

head of the department; in a few, by the chief of police subject to confirmation by his superior. Almost invariably, therefore, the appointment is merely an assignment and is subject to change at the discretion of the head of the department.

In a few cities, the head of the detective bureau is occasionally appointed from civil life without previous service in the police department. While on its face this arrangement might seem to provide some advantage in the latitude which it gives in selection, in actual practice, due obviously to politics and favoritism, it has yielded poor results. In East St. Louis a few years ago a man who had been running a hat-cleaning establishment was selected to head the detective force. Recently in Pittsburgh a politician without previous experience in police work was chosen as chief of the bureau of detectives. On the whole better results are observable when the chief of detectives is recruited from the ranks of the detective bureau.

The same evils as regards rapid shifts in personnel which we discussed in connection with the chiefs of police are to be found in relation to the heads of detective bureaus. Due to changes in political control, the heads of detective forces often follow one another in rapid succession. In San Francisco, in the last fourteen years, there have been eight different officers commanding the detective force. In Chicago, at the time of my visit, there had been four heads of the detective bureau in as many years. Obviously no consistent development of detective bureaus can be maintained under such circumstances. Only as a responsible official is given time to shape and mature his policies and work over a term of years can substantial results be looked for.

Selection of Personnel.

Members of the detective bureau may be chosen from the uniformed force or from outside the police department altogether. The former course is the rule in most cities of the United States. In only a very few cities, notably Kansas City, Louisville, Pittsburgh, Memphis and Birmingham, are detectives ever chosen from civil life without previous service as uniformed patrolmen. Pittsburgh is the only large civil service city in which detectives may be recruited directly from civil pursuits.

Where detectives are chosen from the personnel of the police force the selection may be made either by civil service examination or by direct assignment at the hands of the administrative head of the department. The former practice is followed in Chicago, Philadelphia, St. Louis,[1] Los Angeles, St. Paul, Dayton, Portland, (Ore.), and a few other cities. The latter method of choosing detectives — whereby the administrative head of the police designates certain members of the uniformed force to serve in this grade — is followed in New York, Cleveland, Detroit, Boston, Washington, San Francisco, New Orleans and many other cities.

The same advantages and disadvantages of civil service as a means of selection and promotion which we noted in connection with the uniformed force are observable in

---

[1] In St. Louis the examination for detective — title is detective sergeant — is the same as the examination to the grade of uniformed sergeant of police.

relation to the detective force. Indeed, the short-comings of civil service are, if possible, even more pronounced in its application to the detective bureau than to the uniformed rank. For no written examination can fairly test the peculiar qualifications of a successful detective, such as ability to remember faces, developed habits of observation, aptness in securing evidence from witnesses, and above all, a facility in obtaining the pertinent and essential facts of a given situation. In those cities in which civil service requirements are not in force, many of the most successful detectives, who achieve the best results in identifying and arresting pickpockets, confidence men and other specialists in crime, are without any ability to pass a written examination. The services of these men would be lost to a city in which promotion to the grade of detective was determined by civil service examination.

The result of the attempt to apply civil service tests is seen in such cities as Philadelphia and Chicago, where men are selected as detectives often without any of the special qualifications required for the task. In both these cities the heads of the detective bureau, at the time of my visit, were emphatic in denouncing the quality of the personnel through whom they were forced to carry on their work. " Men are appointed detectives who might make good clerks or school teachers," said the head of the detective bureau of Philadelphia, " but they do not know how to catch crooks."

An even greater difficulty is presented by reason of the fact that under civil service regulations a man who obtains the permanent rank of detective is practically " fixed " for the rest of his career, regardless of the results which he may achieve in the prosecution of his work. He is " frozen into his job "— to use the police expression. He may be totally without positive qualifications; he may not possess the enthusiasm for the task so essential in a good detective; he may be clearly outranked in ability by a score of men in the department who are not on the detective force; nevertheless, his position as detective is fixed for the present and future because of his success in answering a series of written questions years before. Only as dishonesty is conclusively proved against him is there any practical prospect of removing him. A former chief of the Chicago department told me that when he assumed his duties in that position he knew that the detective bureau was honey-combed with inefficiency and corruption, but that during his career as chief he did not remove or demote a single detective because he was unable to obtain the necessary proof. " The old gang was still in the saddle when I left," he said.

On the other hand, it cannot be denied that the lack of civil service standards in the selection of detectives often opens up the entire force to politics of a mean and petty sort. Inasmuch as assignment to detective work carries with it a certain measure of personal freedom as well as the prestige which goes with a higher quality of work and additional compensation, it is much sought after. In San Francisco, at the time of my visit, the entire detective bureau was shot through with politics, and assignments to this grade were the inevitable result of " pull " and favoritism. While the rest of the force in this city had been partly freed from politics, these sinister influences had not yet been driven from the detective bureau. Similarly

The Detective Force

in Atlanta appointments to the detective bureau have all too often been the result of political affiliations recognized by the board of police commissioners. In Pittsburg, where detectives may be chosen from civil life, the results are far from satisfactory. "They are not detectives, they are politicians," a high ranking officer of the uniformed force told the investigator.

On the whole, however, in spite of the unhealthy conditions which often surround the appointment of detectives in departments where no civil service standards are applied in their selection, it cannot be denied that better results are obtained when the administrative head of the force is free to appoint the best men or to demote those incumbents in the detective rank who have not measured up to their tasks. Certainly, in large cities like New York, Boston, Cleveland and Detroit this method has brought a measurable degree of satisfaction. It centers upon the head of the force a responsibility which cannot be evaded. It provides a constant stimulus to the members of the detective force; and while men are undoubtedly often demoted for no worthy motive, the fear that such demotion may follow poor work tends to keep the entire bureau constantly on the alert.

Training of Detectives.

No standardized method obtains in American cities for training detectives. In many departments the men are assigned to their new duties as if no training or special aptitude were necessary at all. In some cities, however, notably Boston, Seattle, Newark and Detroit, an effort is made to establish a period of apprenticeship in which men are assigned to plainclothes duty for the investigation of vice and minor complaints either in their own precincts or as members of special squads operating from headquarters. In no cities, with the exception of Berkeley, (Cal.), are any efforts made to provide formal specialized instruction as a method of training the personnel of the detective force. The experiment begun under Commissioner Woods in New York, of courses of instructions for detectives, was never followed in other cities and has been abandoned even in New York. In a few cities detectives are sometimes included in the training courses given for the members of the uniformed force, but they receive no instruction peculiarly applicable to detective work.

This is in marked contrast with the system followed in Continental Europe, where detective schools and courses are often maintained as part of the machinery of the police department. In Vienna, for example, while the detective school is not allowed to interrupt the regular duties of the men, it involves two hours a day in lectures and recitations, and covers a period of six months. Similarly in Paris the detectives are obliged each year to attend a series of lectures in connection with their work. In England, on the other hand, the training of detectives takes the form of apprenticeship in plainclothes duty, handling such special problems as betting, street-begging and prostitution. Those who show aptitude and intelligence in this line of work are promoted to the detective force.

It is doubtful whether in American police departments at the present time any formal school instruction as a method of training detectives is practicable. Most detective forces are too small to justify elaborate arrangements, and such courses of instruction as are given in Vienna in physical science, photography, criminology and other subjects would have little applicability to the average American detective bureau in its present state of development. On the other hand, in large cities which contain colleges or universities it would easily be possible to arrange special courses for detectives and other police officers in subjects adapted to their day-to-day work. Such an arrangement has been effected between the Berkeley police department and the University of California, and has been proposed for the Chicago force in conjunction with Northwestern University.[1]

Organization of the Detective Bureau.

There are two prevailing types of internal organization of detective bureaus in American cities : the centralized bureau, operated at headquarters, and the decentralized bureau working largely from precincts or other sub-units. Of these, the decentralized bureau is the more common type in the larger cities where the uniformed force is distributed geographically by precincts or districts. This plan of organization is in effect in such cities as Chicago, Detroit, Boston, Buffalo, San Francisco and others. In each of these cities, however, there is a small central division at headquarters, together with special groups, such as pickpocket, pawn-shop and automobile squads,

[1] During Commissioner Woods' régime in New York an interesting experiment was made of giving courses in criminal law at Columbia University to such members of the police department as applied.

which work from headquarters and operate over the whole city; but the bulk of general detective work is done by detectives attached to precincts generally under the command of uniformed officers, who also have charge of the operations of the uniformed forces in those precincts. The precinct detectives are assigned to work on specific complaints arising in their respective territories. In important cases the central division of the detective bureau is called upon to assist or perhaps to take complete charge of the investigation.

The completely centralized bureau is found in such cities as Birmingham, Indianapolis, Newark, Baltimore and Denver. In these cities all detectives are assigned to the headquarters' office and the control of their work is centered in the hands of one man who serves as a commanding officer. Under this plan the work of general criminal investigation and of special squads, is carried on from a single central office.

There has been much discussion regarding the relative merits of centralization and decentralization, and no general conclusion can be reached as to the superiority of either of these plans. Aside from considerations of actual detective operations, the geographical size of a city, the number of detectives employed, and the existing organization of the uniformed force are factors which materially influence the question. Those who favor the decentralized bureau point out that detectives should work in comparatively small districts, where they may become thoroughly familiar with neighborhood conditions and with the people residing there. It is claimed also that there are definite advantages to be derived from having the detectives stationed in precincts with uniformed men, for the reason that this close association makes possible a greater degree of cooperation between the two branches of the police service. Finally it is contended that quicker action can be given on complaints when the men are already distributed throughout the city ready to undertake work in the small areas to which they are assigned.

The advocates of centralization, on the other hand, contend that there is need for specialization in criminal investigations which cannot be effected when detectives are distributed throughout precinct units, and that better control of operations results when all the detectitves are included in one unit of organization and under the more immediate direction of the chief detective officer. It is claimed also that uniform standards of detective work can be applied throughout the whole city under the centralized bureau, whereas with decentralization there may be as many ways of conducting criminal investigations as there are precinct commanders.

The claims for both plans are largely met in the modified form of centralized bureau which was in effect in New York from 1914 to 1918 and is in effect at the present time in St. Louis. The detective bureau under such a plan consists of a detective headquarters' division and detective branch offices. In New York there were nine such detective offices, as compared with more than eighty precinct stations; in St. Louis there are six detective branches and thirteen police districts. This arrangement makes possible the concentration of a sufficient number of detectives at the central office to permit of specialization, and at the same time it places men in localities small enough to enable them to become acquainted with local conditions. Even though detectives are distributed over the city, they are subject to the direct control of the central office, and the head of the detective bureau can view in the large the crime problem of the entire city, and can make immediate disposition of his men to meet changing conditions.

Under both the centralized and decentralized system, small special squads are maintained at headquarters under the direct supervision of the commanding officer of the detective bureau. These squads devote their attention to the detection and apprehension of pickpockets, bad check passers, automobile thieves and other specialists in crime. In the New York detective bureau the following special squads are organized at headquarters: homicide, safe and loft, pickpocket, automobile theft, gangster, narcotic, bomb, truck and wagon, and industrial squad. In Detroit there are Italian, automobile recovery, homicide and pawnshop squads. Similar groupings are to be found in most of the large cities of the country.

Detective bureaus often suffer from too frequent alterations in the plan of organization. Each new head has his own ideas and changes are of frequent occurrence. Occasionally the centralized and decentralized plans are alternated to suit the notions of each successive incumbent without giving either plan a chance to prove itself. In New York, for example, during the fourteen-year period from 1906 to 1920, the detective bureau was reorganized four times. Prior to 1906 the bureau was centralized at police headquarters. In addition, detectives and plain-clothes men were operating in the precincts but were not under the control of the detective bureau organization. During General Bingham's incumbency as police commissioner the bureau was decentralized, being divided into sixteen districts to correspond with the inspection districts of the uniformed force organization. Each of the sixteen divisions was under the control of a detective division commander, and the uniformed officers in charge of inspection districts had nothing to do with detective work. In 1912 Commissioner Waldo abolished the system of detective divisions and re-established the precinct as the unit of detective work, under the control and immediate direction, however, of detective officers. The next change came under Commissioner Woods in 1914, when the bureau was reorganized with a headquarters' staff and with nine branch offices operating in geographical districts which did not coincide with any scheme of districting used by the uniformed force. The next reorganization came under Commissioner Enright in 1918 when the precinct was again made the unit of detective bureau organization.

St. Louis has also made rapid changes from one plan to another. Prior to 1912 plainclothes men or detectives were assigned to patrol districts under uniformed captains of police. In 1912 the city was divided into six detective districts, under the command of detective officers, and the captains of police no longer had precinct detectives. After approximately a year and a half of this regime the detective branch districts were abolished and the precinct plan re-established. In the early part of 1919 the system of detective branches was again adopted. Arbitrary changes of this kind, generally following upon shifts in political control, make constructive development of the detective bureau next to impossible.

Lack of Co-ordination in Detective Work.

In a number of cities some confusion exists in the matter of the relation of the detective bureau to the uniformed force in handling complaints of crime. This is true notably in Boston, San Francisco and Pittsburgh. In these cities no definite rules of procedure have been established to determine which branch of the service shall be responsible for taking charge of an investigation of particular complaints of crime. Sometimes both branches conduct an investigation of the same complaint. In Boston members of the uniformed force are permitted to complete an investigation begun by them even though the detective bureau may be better equipped to do the work. This practice has been allowed to continue apparently in deference to the professional pride of the uniformed men. A situation directly opposed to the Boston practice prevails in San Francisco, where members of the detective bureau are assigned to cases in which arrests of felony charges have been made by members of the uniformed force, the assumption being that a uniformed man is not as well fitted to present a felony case in court as is a detective. In Pittsburgh both the central office detectives and precinct plainclothes men do detective work, but the head of the detective force has no control over the work done by precinct men. Consequently, both plainclothes men from precincts and detectives from headquarters may work on the same case, and there is no rule to determine which group shall supersede the other if any conflict of authority arises.   A dual investigation sometimes, indeed, a competitive investigation is the result.   This confusion of authority and responsibility exists in a lesser degree in a large number of cities in which plainclothes men attached to precincts are assigned to investigate minor complaints of crime, especially where the borderline between minor and major complaints is not clearly drawn.   Under such arrangements friction and jealousy between the two major branches of service are bound to occur.

Obviously, the department's rules of procedure should establish a clear-cut division of authority and responsibility, and should indicate the method of cooperation between the two branches in the solution of crimes.   From the time the complaint is received until the case is presented in court no ambiguity should be allowed to exist as to the precise part which the representatives of either branch will play.

Lack of Business Methods in Detective Bureaus.

One of the outstanding facts disclosed by an investigation of detective bureaus in America is the amazing lack of ordinary business system in the prosecution of the work.   The head of a detective force deals with crimes which come to him generally in the shape of specific complaints.   It would seem, therefore, that some knowledge of the relation between complaints and arrests — that is, between crimes known to the police and crimes " cleaned up "— was absolutely indispensable to adequate supervision.   In only a few police departments, however, are records maintained upon which this knowledge can be based. Indeed in only a few cases in the course of the investigation were officers encountered who could understand why such knowledge was necessary. In most departments the records of complaints have no relation to the records of arrests, with the result that it is impossible for the head of the department to establish any standard for measuring the effectiveness of his effort.

In city after city the item of *arrests,* regardless of *complaints* or *crimes known to the police,* is the only information at hand. The annual reports of most chiefs of police in the United States solemnly set forth the number of arrests during the preceding year, as if this number, large or small as it may be, were something of a badge of distinction — a certificate that time had not been wasted. In Kansas City the chief of police boasted that in the current year his force had made 15,000 more arrests than during the previous year. It seems unnecessary to point out that the bare figure of arrests, even when classified according to crimes, is utterly meaningless. As we have already seen,[1] it may be interpreted in any one of half a dozen ways. A large figure may mean an excess in crime, or it may mean over-zeal on the part of the police force in making unnecessary arrests. Judging from the activities of the police in many American cities, this latter interpretation is too often true. Similarly, a small number of arrests may mean a low crime rate, or it may be interpreted in terms of negligent police work. To compare the number of arrests in 1919 with the number of arrests in 1920 has no significance whatever and is utterly

[1] See *ante,* p. 250.

misleading. It is only as arrests for crime in a given period are balanced against the crimes known to the police in that period that we have any basis for measuring the effectiveness of the force.

We have said that in most departments the records of complaints have no relation to the records of arrests. As a matter of fact in many police departments in the United States no records of complaints are kept at all, or if kept they are not compiled in such fashion as to serve the purposes of supervision and control. It is literally true that in many cities such as Philadelphia, Seattle, San Francisco, New Orleans, Atlanta and Kansas City, neither the chief of police nor the head of the detective bureau has any idea of the aggregate number of burglaries, robberies, larcenies, or any other crime, occurring within his territory from week to week or month to month. Nor are there any records in these departments upon the basis of which such information can be obtained without laborious research. In these cities, therefore, it is impossible for the head of the force to know whether crime is increasing or decreasing over a given period, or what success his department is achieving in solving particular classes of crime. In short he has no precise knowledge of the volume of the business he is handling or what results are being obtained.

Even in the few cities where an analysis of crime condition is currently made—notably in St. Louis, Chicago and Cleveland — it is seldom that the chief of police or the head of the detective bureau makes use of it in the day to day direction of his department. This is due in most cases to lack of administrative training. The use of such instruments of management as statistics of work, daily reports, and other mechanical aids is not understood, and perfunctory attention to routine takes the place of informed and skillful leadership.

Lack of Supervision in Detective Work.

The lack of ordinary business system in detective bureaus is further shown in the failure to control the work of the individual operatives. An officer of the New York department has described in the following words the condition that existed in his force, some years ago, before an adequate system of supervision was installed: "When a 'squeal' came in over the telephone the lieutenant at the desk wrote it down on a piece of paper and handed it to a detective. 'Here Bill,' he'd say, 'look that up.' Bill took the paper, put it in his pocket, and when the paper wore out the case was closed." [1]

This condition is still true in many police departments in the United States. Indeed, in not a few of them not even "a piece of paper" is used to assign a case, but the matter is given to the detective orally without any subsequent check or follow-up. Even in many large police departments there is no method of recording currently for purposes of supervision the cases that are being handled by each detective, nor is there any way by which the head of the detective force can keep track of cases pending. The determination of these essential facts, under generally existing arrangements, would involve laborious search through cumbersome documents and journals, even if they could be determined at all. I asked the head

[1] Quoted in Woods' *Crime Prevention*, p. 17.

of the Philadelphia bureau,[1] for example, how, in the absence of a "tickler" or other record system, he kept track of the particular cases which each detective was handling. He replied that if he wanted the information he could get it from the journals in which complaints of crime are entered in the order in which they are made. When it was pointed out that this would involve a great deal of work and long delay, he replied that he kept the cases in his head. The fact, that there are thousands of cases pending and that they often run over a period of years shows the absurdity of the answer.

Similarly in San Francisco, Seattle, Newark, Buffalo, New Orleans and a dozen other cities of size and importance the heads of the detective bureaus have no systematic method for keeping track of or following up the work of their men. Even where reports from the detectives are required they are too often perfunctory and meaningless. In Chicago, for example, at the time of my visit, cases were "closed" as far as the detective bureau was concerned, as soon as the detectives filed their first reports. These reports could allege in general terms that progress was being made or that no clues had been discovered. Regardless of what information they gave, they were filed away with the original complaints, and that was the end of the matter. Thereafter, if the detectives chose to report further, their records were simply added to the original file. "We reopen the case if the complainant hollers," I was frankly told by one of the officers. Altogether the system was as shiftless as could be devised, and the wonder was not that thousands of cases remained

[1] Since retired.

American Police Systems

unsolved, but that any criminals at all were ever arrested.

It is because of this complete lack of ordinary business system that complaints of crime can be "lost" or "canned"— to use the popular police word. In San Francisco, for example, in 1915, the records of the coroner's office showed that during the year there were 54 cases of murder, six cases of manslaughter and eleven cases of justifiable homicide. The records in the police department, however, showed but 39 cases of murder, four of manslaughter and seven of justifiable homicide. In other words, the police department had no record of twenty-one homicides occurring during the year. The fifteen cases of murder, of which the police had no record, were all found recorded in the detective bureau as felonious assaults.[1]

A similar study in New York, based on comparisons between the records of the police department, the coroner's offices and the district attorneys' offices, brought to light the fact that of the 323 murder and manslaughter cases reported during the year 1913, the police department had records of but 261; while in 1914, of 292 such cases the department had record of only 209. Of the 323 cases in 1913, twenty were carried in the records of the detective bureau under such classifications as "felonious assaults" and "under investigation," and 42 cases were not recorded at all. Of the 292 cases in 1914, 42 were carried as "felonious assaults" or "under investigation," and in 41 cases there was no record.[2]

[1] See *Survey Report of the Government of the City and County of San Francisco,* prepared by the Bureau of Municipal Research, New York, 1916, p. 214.
[2] See *A report of the study of Homicide Records in the New*

The Detective Force

In 1919 in Chicago, an investigation of the discrepancies between crimes reported to precinct stations and the total number of crimes reported to the central department by the police precincts disclosed the fact that many crimes of violence never got further than the blotters of the local police stations. It was found for instance, that the captain of a certain precinct had carelessly or intentionally failed to report to the central office 104 out of 141 crimes reported in that precinct for the month; that is, out of 141 crimes of violence known to the police, a record of only 37 found its way into the central office of the department. In another precinct the investigation disclosed that 40 crimes of violence occurring during a given period were not reported to the central office. When the captain of this precinct was asked for an explanation, he gave as his reason for not reporting these crimes the fact that the money stolen could not be identified and that the masked burglars could not be recognized. Appar-

York Police Department, 1913–1914, made by the Bureau of Municipal Research, March, 1915. This report contains the following additional paragraph on the homicides in 1914:

" Of the 292 cases occurring in the year 1914, the records of which were examined, there were 21 cases in which the manner of killing was not disclosed; 94 cases in which no reference to the possible motive for the crime was made; 37 cases in which the age of the persons arrested in connection with the murder was not recorded on the detective bureau's records; 150 cases in which the age or probable age of the persons murdered was not indicated; 38 cases in which the nationality or birthplace of the persons arrested in connection with murder cases did not appear; 165 cases in which the nationality of the persons murdered was not entered upon the records; 143 cases in which there was no description to indicate the place the crime occurred, such as in saloons, in homes, upon streets, etc.; 49 cases in which persons accused were discharged without any reference as to the possible cause for discharge, such as insufficient evidence, wrong persons arrested, etc., etc.; 27 cases in which the accused was discharged from custody, of which the records failed to show the authority discharging the prisoners."

345

ently, in his opinion, therefore, no crimes had been committed![1]

A better explanation of the Chicago situation would probably be found in the desire — shared by many precinct heads and even chiefs of police — to return as good a crime record as possible for their particular districts. A reduction of crime is readily accomplished by suppressing the record of complaints —" canning the squeals," to use the vivid phraseology of the police. That this practice is by no means confined to Chicago is evidenced not only by confidential admissions of police officers in various cities but by the startling reductions in crime statistics which often accompany the installation of a new police administration.[2] Obviously, nothing is gained by a good record system if dishonestly used.

Detective Record Systems.

It is of course impossible in a book of this kind to discuss in detail the various report and record systems necessary in a well-equipped detective bureau. In several cities, notably St. Louis, Detroit and New York, a number of admirable records are maintained which can be studied with profit, although they vary in thoroughness and practicability with changing administrations. Certainly no record system is complete which does not afford the head of the detective bureau constant control over the work of his men by giving him at a glance a list of the cases which each is handling. To the absence of this

[1] See the various reports of the Chicago Crime Commission, particularly the account of this Commission's work in the *Journal of Criminal Law and Criminology*, Vol. XI, No. 1.
[2] See *ante,* p. 15, note 2.

information and control may be ascribed much of the careless hit-or-miss work which characterizes many of our detective bureaus today. Nor can a record system be called successful which fails to show the cases pending at a given moment, classified according to crimes, so that the head of the bureau, as well as the chief of police, has constantly before him the statistical measure of his accomplishment or failure. Without this information there is no way of ascertaining the weak spots in the department's work; consequently the force cannot be shifted to meet new problems or mobilized to attack an overwhelming outbreak of crime in a particular precinct.

As far as crime records are concerned, it is a safe generalization that every scrap of information worthy of being recorded on a precinct police blotter is worthy of permanent classification at police headquarters, whether it be a complaint, an arrest, a fire, a lost child or a stray animal. Sooner or later all this information is useful to the police in the prosecution of their work. Upon its careful tabulation a great deal of their success depends. Classifications of missing persons, or stolen property, and of all sorts of crimes and criminals are increasingly indispensable to police forces as social relationships become more complex, and the problem of delinquency more difficult to handle. In the development of criminal files and indexes America has lagged far behind Europe. No city in the United States has the physical equipment in this respect possessed by Dresden, for example, or Vienna or Stuttgart. We have none of the carefully elaborated mechanical aids in the way of criminal registers which one finds in most of the important cities in Continental

American Police Systems

Europe. All of Europe's intricate appliances for the apprehension of criminals such as the use of chemical and physical analyses, the extensive application of photography, the infinite number of devices for establishing identification, are largely missing here. At least they are not continuously and systematically employed.[1] In most cities, indeed, they are not known, and a rule-of-thumb method takes the place of scientific attention to details.[2]

It may be that we cannot hope for any particular development in this field until our police departments are better stabilized and the principle of continuity of administration is firmly established. If that is the case we cannot now expect to obtain the same success in the detection of criminals with which the police forces of Europe are so often rewarded.

Criminal Identification.

The importance of an accurate method of identifying criminals which will defeat the invention of an alias, or any other disguise, is well understood. Two systems of identification have been widely accepted in Europe and the United States — the finger-print or dactyloscopic method and the measurement or Bertillon method. Around the merits of these two principles of identification a long and heated controversy has raged, with the result that in Europe the Bertillon system is fast being discarded in favor of finger-prints. Only in France today

[1] Berkeley, Cal., has made probably the greatest advance in this direction.
[2] For a discussion of European methods of crime detection, see *European Police Systems*, Chap. IX.

348

has the Bertillon method a foothold. American police departments have been slow to understand the significance of the controversy. Uncertain as to the validity of the arguments, and unwilling to lose the advantage of either method, most cities at the cost of convenience and at great expense have adopted both. To maintain two elaborate files, classified on a different basis, when one will adequately answer the purpose, is of course to load the department with a cumbersome routine which, particularly in a large city, with its many prisoners to examine, is practically impossible to carry out. The time is bound to come in America, therefore — and in some cities a beginning has already been made [1] — when one of these systems will have to be discarded. In point of simplicity and accuracy the finger-print method is so far superior to the Bertillon method that there is no question as to its fitness to survive.

These facts seem to be unknown in many of the smaller police departments in the United States. At the very time that European cities were discarding their Bertillon cabinets as superfluous, these departments were busy installing them. I visited a number of cities that were inaugurating Bertillon systems for the first time, under the impression that they represented the latest word in the identification of criminals. One cannot escape the impression in many cities, particularly in the south and middle west, that both finger-prints and Bertillon measurements are looked upon by police officials as something

[1] Not a few American cities are willing now to discard the Bertillon system except for the fear that it would cut them off from their exchanges with other cities that are reluctant to take the step.

of a charm or talisman rather than as scientific methods of identification. Certainly in more than one department that I visited, where not a single officer understood the principles of finger-print classification or knew how to hold a pair of calipers, the boast was made that the force had *two* identification systems! [1]

America has fallen behind, too, in its failure to develop an adequate national system of criminal identification. Some method is necessary, either of centralization or of distribution, by which the identification records of one city can be available for all. For under modern conditions of life the traveling criminal has come to constitute the chief factor in the police problem. The same man will commit burglaries in Detroit, Chicago and Cleveland; the same pickpocket will operate in San Francisco and Salt Lake City. For lack of certain finger-prints filed in St. Louis, Kansas City may allow a well-known counterfeiter to go free. No single department by itself can cope successfully with the traveling criminal. The problem calls for wide cooperation under national auspices. Already a beginning has been made in a number of states; in California, for example, chiefs of police, sheriffs and marshals must file with the Central State Bureau of Identification, copies of all finger-prints which they take.[2] Even more promising is the fact that fifteen western cities, including Seattle, Portland, Tacoma, Vancouver, San Francisco and Oakland, are systematically

---

[1] For a fuller discussion of the systems of identification see *The Passing of Bertillon System of Identification* by the writer in the *Journal of Criminal Law and Criminology*, Vol. VI, p. 363.

[2] *Statutes of Cal.*, 1917, Chap. 723. For a descrption of the California State Bureau of Criminal Identification see the *National Police Journal*, October, 1919.

exchanging finger-prints and photographs, and there are groups of cities all over the country where similar cooperative arrangements exist. The National Bureau of Criminal Identification, created in Washington by the International Association of Chiefs of Police is another step in the right direction; but it is largely a private enterprise, inadequately financed, and representing only a portion of the police departments of the country.[1] What is needed is an official bureau, amply supported financially and located perhaps in the Attorney General's office, to which, on standardized forms, would be sent all finger-prints taken by any city or county authority in the United States.

The United States is practically the last country to inaugurate a system of this kind. A national bureau of identification is maintained for Great Britain at Scotland Yard, London; for France, at the *Service de l'identité judiciaire* under the Ministry of the Interior in Paris; for Italy, at the Ministry of the Interior in Rome; for Belgium, at police headquarters in Brussels, and for Canada, in the office of the chief of the Canadian police in Ottawa. In all of these countries information as regards the identity of a particular criminal is immediately available, and the police departments are bound together in a common warfare against the profession of crime. A similar centralization of information is necessary in Washington or at least under national official auspices, if our police authorities are to keep abreast of their task.

[1] Another agency acting as a clearing house is the Federal prison at Leavenworth, Kansas. The scope of this agency is similarly limited.

Other National Indexes Needed.

A central bureau of identification, supported and controlled by the government, should provide for the identification not only of criminals but of property as well. Property stolen as well as property recovered should be indexed and classified at some national clearing house on the basis of a system similar to the excellent index devices now employed by the police department of almost every large city. These local systems, however, are useful only in identifying property which is recovered in the same city in which the report of loss has been made. A central bureau would make possible the identification of property reported stolen in one city and recovered in another. Indeed a central bureau can do much more. The establishment of a national *modus operandi* system which would record and classify information regarding the distinguishing characteristics in the commission of major crimes, would lead to the identification of criminals who cover a wide area in the course of their operations.[1]

In addition to maintaining and developing these several branches of identification, a central bureau of this kind could also serve as a clearing house for information of every sort which would be useful to the police departments of all cities. Such a combined identification and information bureau could aid in bringing about standardized practices in the keeping of crime records, as well as in methods of transmitting descriptions of persons wanted

[1] Such a system is now employed by the California State Bureau of Criminal Identification and Investigation. For a detailed discussion of the *modus operandi* system see *European Police Systems,* Chap. IX.

352

or of property stolen. A national bureau too, would be in a position to devise and establish an efficient cipher code for use in transmitting messages between police departments. It is to purposes of this kind that Scotland Yard is lending its good offices, and while the size of America, as compared with Great Britain, complicates our task, with patience and ingenuity a solution can be found.

CHAPTER X

THE PREVENTION OF CRIME

Place of crime prevention in work of department.— Attack on the breeding places of crime.— Special conditions making for crime.— Educating the public.— The police and ex-convicts.— Juvenile delinquency.— Poverty.— Other crime prevention methods.— The development of the crime prevention bureau.

THE activities of the uniformed and detective forces represent our conventional methods of fighting crime. The policeman patrolling the city block, like his prototype, the rattle-watchman of 250 years ago, is there to prevent disorder, and to catch, if he can, any person who breaks the law. Conceivably, therefore, if he is alert and conscientious, no crimes will be committed in his vicinity. Highway robbers will not operate, burglars will not break in from the street, and pickpockets will be restrained from activity. If it were possible to maintain enough policemen continuously to cover all our city blocks, we could be guaranteed against the commission of crime *in our streets.*

Similarly the detective force, while engaged primarily in ferreting out the criminal who has already committed a crime, exercises a restraining influence upon those who would break the law. The pickpocket is far less apt to succumb to temptation if he feels that his actions may be watched by men in plain clothes who know the ways of the trade.

354

The Prevention of Crime

All police work has as its goal the prevention of crime. It is a matter for surprise, therefore, to learn that even were we to secure 100% efficiency in our patrol and detective work, most crimes would still go unhindered. Arthur Woods, formerly police commissioner in New York, put the case as follows: " Given perfect patrolling work, perfect (if there is such a thing) detective work, along the conventional lines, what proportion of crimes would still be committed? I discussed this at an Inspectors' meeting some time ago. One Inspector said it was ' fifty-fifty,' meaning that one-half the crimes that were then being committed in his district could not be prevented, even if the regular patrol and detective work were as good as they could be. This Inspector had a district thickly populated with foreigners. An old experienced Inspector, whose district is largely residential, on the west side of Manhattan, said he believed only one per cent of the crime in his district could be prevented by perfect police work. The other estimates varied between these two. If these men were right in their estimates — and they were the highest officers on the New York Force — if from fifty to ninety-nine per cent of crime would be committed in spite of perfect police work along the conventional lines — you can see why it is that we are cudgelling our brains to try to devise new methods, even if unconventional, with which to fight the outlaw." [1]

One cannot review the activities of the police in many cities without realizing that this point of view is the exception rather than the rule. Too many police administrators are content to develop the conventional methods of

[1] *Crime Prevention,* Princeton University Press, 1918.

policing and are inclined to disclaim responsibility for any crimes committed in a way that these methods cannot be expected to meet. If a burglar enters from the rear while the policeman is patrolling the front, if a theft is an " inside job," committed by a servant, if goods are stolen from a truck left carelessly in a yard, it is assumed that from the standpoint of prevention these are cases with which the police have nothing to do. Indeed so visionless are some police executives that the more this type of case increases the more do they stress the enlargement of the very conventional methods which have proved useless in thwarting it. Every crime-wave, therefore, is apt to be met with a request for more policemen, whereas a smaller number of men, working with resourcefulness and imagination might perhaps better handle the new condition.

The average police department is still too much merely an agency of *law enforcement,* divorced from responsibility for the *causes* of crime. Its energies are consumed in defensive measures, in efforts to correct the manifestations of crime rather than attack its roots. So long as this is the case, the policeman will continue to represent, as he does in so many places at present, the city's bewildered and futile attempt to beat back the spasmodic outcroppings of disorder which are continually in process of manufacture in the inner currents of city life. There is as much room for crime prevention in our communities as for fire prevention or the prevention of disease, and in this endeavor to limit the opportunities of crime and keep it from claiming its victims the police department must take the leading part.

The Prevention of Crime

The Breeding Places of Crime.

Just as yellow fever was successfully attacked by draining the swamps and morasses where it bred, so the attack on crime is, in part, at least, a matter of eliminating its breeding places. Crime develops from contact and bad environment. Every city has its vicious spots — its points of contagion — distributing their contamination over smaller or larger areas. Often these spots are unknown to the police; sometimes when known they are not treated. The old " red-light " districts which disgraced our cities for so many years, but which have now gradually given way before an aroused public opinion, were flagrant examples of breeding places of crime unmolested by the police. Quite apart from the conditions of immorality which they fostered, they let loose upon the community an army of pick-pockets, shop-lifters, and petty robbers, of both sexes, who found retreat and stimulation in the protected district. " I never knew where that brood of small-fry crooks was coming from," the chief in a southern city told me, in explaining the decrease of crime complaints which followed the closing of the district in his town.

Similarly, gambling and pool-selling places, and the various rendezvous where narcotics are illegally obtained, are breeding grounds of crime to which the conscientious police executive will give careful attention. Particularly is this true of the sale of habit-forming drugs. There is scarcely a city in the country where this insidious practice has not gained a foothold, and the methods employed to evade the law are numerous. It has recently been esti-

357

mated that there are 300,000 persons addicted to the use of narcotic drugs in the city of New York alone.[1] The Inspector of Pharmacy of the police department of Washington, D. C., says: " It is alarming to note the terrible evils of the drug habit and almost impossible to estimate its enormous proportions, as it is fostered in secrecy and is responsible for a large portion of the crimes against the community." [2] Chief of Police Long of Newark in speaking of the relation between the use of drugs and the commission of crime said: " Men and women who ordinarily commit no crime, when under the influence of their favorite ' dope ' will hesitate at none. When the craving is long unsatisfied it becomes a strong and merciless driver, forcing its victims to take chances of securing the necessary means by methods from which they would shrink when in normal condition." [3]

The same remark is true of the existence of gambling rendezvous, which in most cases are nothing but clearing houses for criminals. Commissioner Enright of New York speaks of them as follows: " Such places are invariably the headquarters of the most dangerous criminals, as the vast majority of society's enemies appear to have a passion for games of hazard, a reflection of their precarious existences, perhaps. Besides, many of the keepers of such resorts are ex-convicts and if not, then

[1] From a statement in the *Journal of the American Institute of Criminal Law and Criminology*, Nov., 1919, by Albert J. Weber, Foreman of Grand Jurors, Southern District of New York. This estimate is concurred in by other writers.

[2] Annual Report of the Metropolitan Police of the District of Columbia, 1918.

[3] From an address before the annual convention of the International Association of Chiefs of Police, 1915.

they are apt to be surrounded by such men and women
and are not at all averse to financing the criminal projects
of their hangers-on and the vicious parasites who flock to
every gambling house to which access can be had. . . .
The suppression of these establishments, no matter what
their disguise, is preventive police work of the highest
quality." [1]

The modern police head will not only attack the swamps
and morasses whose existence and location are more or
less patent, but he will be zealous to seek out and discover
secret sources of infection which lie hidden in the dark
places of city life. For example, here is a locality in a
city credited with a larger number of crime complaints
than circumstances would seem to justify. It may be a
matter of poor policing along conventional lines; it may
be the work of local or of travelling criminals. However, the question on which the conscientious executive
will want to be assured is whether in this particular locality specific conditions exist which encourage the commission of crime. These conditions may take the shape of
disorderly gangs, unregulated dance-halls and other places
of amusement, policy-shops, vicious " back-rooms," or
rendezvous for idlers and loafers. They may be traceable to unnecessary temptations to theft or to any one of
a dozen other factors. As important as the arrest of the
offenders, in the mind of the zealous police chief, will be
the discovery and the elimination, if possible, of the conditions which hatched the present crimes, and which, if
not treated, will send out a swarm of new offenders.

It was this conception that prompted Commissioner

[1] Annual Report, New York Police Department, 1918, p. 29.

Woods in New York to inaugurate his system of " crime prevention patrolmen." Carefully chosen officers were assigned to the more busy precincts of the city to ferret out conditions which seemed to be having a tendency to lead people astray, particularly boys and girls. Many temptations to petty stealing were discovered which could be eliminated, and other situations were traced through the influence of which thoughtless, growing boys were turned into law-breakers. Commissioner Woods' experiment did not have time to prove itself before he left office, but it illustrates the new technique in police work for diminishing the supply of crime.[1]

Special Conditions Making for Crime.

The prevalence of crime is often traceable to certain special conditions which are controllable by the police. The existence of disorderly gangs, for example, has frequently led, particularly in our larger cities, to open defiance of the law and a reign of terror among peaceful citizens. In the districts infested by these gangs the merchant and the shopkeeper are especially made the prey. The New York police in 1914 reported that it was a common experience for a small storekeeper to have a member of one of these gangs walk into his place of business, produce a number of tickets for a dance, and demand that they be purchased for fifty dollars. The entertainment perhaps was never to be given, but the purchase was quickly made and no questions asked. Ordinary prudence dictated prompt compliance. In addition to black-

[1] See Annual Report of New York Police Department, 1917, p. 78, issued just before Mr. Woods' retirement from office.

mailing shopkeepers, gangsters soon became bold in robbing and stealing, holding up citizens on the street and invading restaurants and cafes with drawn pistols. Keepers of disorderly houses have frequently paid them tribute, each gang having its domain and granting protection from other gangs within that sphere of influence. Gunmen of this type have not hesitated to assault or murder citizens for hire. Commissioner Woods in reporting upon the situation existing when he took office in New York in 1914, made the following statement:

" Strikers would approach gang leaders and hire them to assault men who continued to work in spite of warnings from the strikers to desist. Employers hired men of like character, attached to so-called ' detective agencies,' who used ' strong arm ' methods against the strikers. In various strikes occurring in this city during the period mentioned, almost every conceivable crime was committed by ' guerillas ' hired by one side or the other, including robbery, extortion, assault, arson, riot, and murder." [1]

It was only by a systematic and concentrated attack upon these gangs that certain congested sections of New York City were freed from the terrorizing experiences which had occurred spasmodically for years. Many of the bands were composed of highly trained and highly paid specialists. Some used weapons such as black-jacks, gas-pipes, or bottles containing fluids, but the majority carried pistols. Most of them took their names from their leaders, and the gangs were known by such titles as

[1] Annual Report of New York Police Department, 1917, p. 38.

"Dopey Benny," "Joe the Greaser," "Hudson Dusters," "Sirocco," "Ownie Madden," "Skush Thomas," "Slaughter House," "Pearl Button," "Little Doggie," "Pansy," "Frog Hollows," and "Jew Murphy."

The police concentrated their attention on these gangs one by one, and special squads were formed to familiarize themselves with individual thugs and guerillas, as well as with their habits and places of rendezvous. The so-called "ball rooms" where the criminals congregated were closed, the law forbidding the possession of pistols without permits was strictly enforced, and gradually by careful study and surveillance, the ring was tightened and the bands were broken up.[1] Every city of any size has its heroes of the underworld about whom are gathered weak-willed imitators and hangers-on, who will follow their leaders in vice and crime to almost any extreme. But the customary method of proceeding against these lawless gangs has been to await the commission of some major crime that may offer an opportunity to give these leaders or their associates prison sentences.

In this connection the law against the carrying of weapons is worthy of special note. The so-called Sullivan Law in New York has effectively served to reduce the number of homicides. Unfortunately, however, this law is not applicable to neighboring states, with the result that weapons can readily be purchased within easy distance of New York City. In spite of this disadvantage,

[1] In this campaign, a card catalogue was compiled at police headquarters of the names and aliases of 1,352 known gangsters. Previous to this time many a gunman had escaped the deterrent effect of a severe sentence by reason of the fact that he had never been finger-printed, and his previous record appeared under some other name. (Annual Report 1917, p. 39.)

squads of detectives in New York are constantly employed in rounding up vicious characters and relieving them of revolvers and other dangerous weapons which they have no right to possess, and the result has undoubtedly been of great value in preventing the commission of contemplated crime. During 1918, the members of the detective force of New York took 336 revolvers from persons not authorized to carry them.[1] Major Pullman, late head of the force of Washington, D. C., in urging a somewhat similar law for the District of Columbia, expressed himself as follows: " At the present time a person may purchase a firearm by going into any store or second-hand shop and putting down the money for the weapon, then going out and perhaps killing a person in the next half hour. Many crimes result from persons buying revolvers in this manner and shooting while in a fit of passion." [2]

Educating the Public.

One of the principal measures which an enterprising police force can adopt in reducing the volume of crime is a systematic education of the public in regard to criminal methods and practices. In a few cities, notably New York, Detroit and Washington, D. C., a very extensive propaganda has been carried on under the direction of the police to educate the citizens for self-protection. Moving picture films, lectures and literature have been used to illustrate the fatal consequences of leaving doors unlocked, handbags easy to open, or notices on the door-bell

[1] Annual Report for 1918, p. 41.
[2] Report, Metropolitan Police, District of Columbia, for 1918, p. 13.

that nobody was home.   Campaigns have been conducted against particular forms of carelessness which result in thefts from vans, drays and storage lofts.   Because a substantial percentage of crimes in our large cities nowadays is the work of dishonest employees, special emphasis has been laid upon the advisability of requiring careful references.   The police cannot directly prevent an " inside job," but they can indirectly discourage it by emphasizing in vivid and appealing form the necessity of scrupulous care in hiring servants.   Similarly, the police have advised with business houses as to the best methods of protecting them, and have sent experts to inspect and suggest; they have emphasized the urgency of safety devices on automobiles to prevent their being stolen, and have consulted with insurance people as to more effective measures for avoiding the things they were insuring against.

A circular issued by the police of Washington, D. C., and widely distributed to the citizens, contains such pertinent advice as follows:

Do not admit to your home telephone inspectors, water inspectors, gas inspectors, health office inspectors, or any other kind, unless they give proper credentials and show authority.

When you leave your home, do not advertise the fact by pulling down the shades or leaving a note in the letterbox saying you will be back at such and such an hour.   Sneak thieves profit by such advice, and it is an invitation for them to enter.

Do not make your home a safe deposit vault for silverware and jewelry while you are away.

The Prevention of Crime

Women, do not when shopping lay your handbag on counters while looking at goods. This is an opportunity thieves are always waiting for.

Neither strangers nor any one else, for that matter, should expose their money in public unnecessarily; nor should men carry their wallets in the hip pocket. Pickpockets would have to go out of business if men became careful in handling their money. Four-fifths of all pickpocket jobs are made easy because so many carry their money in their hip pockets and have it lifted while getting on a car or while in a crowd. Keep your coat buttoned up and an eye on your pockets.

A large percentage of crime committed in Washington, and all other cities for that matter, may be prevented if the citizens are careful and do not make it easy for the criminal to do his work.

Always keep your eyes open and your wits about you. Regard the policeman as your best friend. He is paid to serve you by keeping the streets safe and orderly. He is entitled to your help.

Such advice as this, if vividly and dramatically set forth, and constantly brought home to the citizens in ways which modern advertising methods suggest, can help materially in reducing crime complaints. Without the co-operation of the public, the police themselves cannot successfully attack the problem of crime. Education and propaganda are indispensable aids in every modern police department.

Men Out of Prison.

The bulk of crime, certainly of crime against property, is committed by those who have previously been in the hands of the police. The chief problem of any police organization is furnished by the professional or habitual criminal, by the man upon whom the possibility of another prison sentence exercises no restraint. Too often the attitude of society and the police has made any other career than crime impossible for an ex-convict. The handicap of his previous record, his inability to secure employment, and the constant " hounding " by the police, make it difficult for him to rehabilitate himself and easy to continue in a life of crime. Some time after Commissioner Woods took office in New York, he spoke to the inmates of Sing Sing prison, and promised them that as long as he was head of the New York police force there was going to be no " hounding " of convicts. He told them that if they came to New York and wanted to earn an honest living and lead an honest life, the police would not merely give them a chance, but would try to assist them to find positions. In response to this invitation, 176 ex-convicts got in touch with police headquarters in New York when their terms at Sing Sing had expired. They had been sentenced for such crimes as homicide, burglary, grand larceny, robbery, forgery, etc., and many had served two and three terms. For these 176 men, 203 positions were obtained.[1] A careful record was kept of every case and at the close of Mr. Woods' term, of the 176 men, 120 were working, nine had been re-sentenced to prison, twenty were lost track of, and 27 cases were pending.[2]

[1] Only those positions which were actually worked at for a week or more are included in the calculation.
[2] For a full discussion of these cases, see Leroy Peterson, loc. cit., p. 18 ff. In placing these men in positions, every effort was made to find work that was really suitable to them and from which they could earn enough money to support themselves and their families. Employers were always told the full facts, and each case was han-

The Prevention of Crime

There was nothing emotional in the approach of the New York police to this problem. Primarily, they were interested in preventing crime, and the method which they pursued was adapted directly to this end.

Juvenile Delinquency.

In November, 1916, of the seven people in the death house in Sing Sing, awaiting execution, five were boys under 21 years of age.[1] The following arrests were made in Washington, D. C., in 1919, of children under seventeen years of age. [2]

Crime charged	Number of arrests
Murder	4
Robbery	36
Assault with dangerous weapon	7
Forgery	12
Grand larceny	71
House breaking	189

Statistics such as these furnish indisputable evidence that criminals are recruited from the ranks of childhood. The rollicking, mischievous boy of today, uncontrolled and out of hand, is the hardened offender of tomorrow. In their efforts to prevent crime, therefore, the police have no more fruitful field of work than is presented by the boys and girls of our cities.

died on its own merits. If a man had been sentenced for grand larceny, he was not given a position where he would be continually tempted. If he seemed to be a weak individual without stamina or backbone, he was placed in a job where he could do real work without being subject to easy chances for continued thieving.

[1] From an unpublished report by Leroy Peterson on the social activities of the New York Police Department from 1914 to 1917.

[2] Annual Report of the Metropolitan Police of the District of Columbia for 1919.

American Police Systems

In this connection it must be admitted at the outset that the path of the police is beset with difficulty. The policeman seems to be the natural and inveterate enemy of the growing boy. He is the represser of everything that a red-blooded boy instinctively wants to do, such as build bonfires, play ball in the streets, climb trees in the park, and throw snowballs at teams and pedestrians. It must be admitted, too, that the police are often stupid in handling the boy problem. Too often the policeman is a sort of glorified town bully, and boys are arrested as criminals and haled to court for mischief that should have been overlooked or at the most reprimanded. It is discouraging to examine in the police stations of some cities the records of juvenile arrests. Boys are locked up for stealing a bottle of milk, for calling a policeman " copper," for loafing on street corners, for calling the iceman " Dago," for boating in the park after hours, or for pulling an old man's beard. True, the boys are generally discharged by the court, but the mischief has been done; the boy has been branded as a criminal and the memory of the brief prison experience remains.

The modern police executive realizes that growing boys must be continuously active — that if because of the cramped conditions of city life, bonfires and snowballing have to be forbidden, something else must be substituted in their places. He realizes, too, that in this search for positive opportunities for recreation and the employment of leisure time the police must take a leading part.

It was with this idea in mind, therefore, that Commissioner Woods in New York established his system of

Junior Police. Before he left office there were 6,000 members between the ages of eleven and sixteen, organized in 32 different precincts of the city under the regular police captains. The boys were uniformed and drilled; they were given lessons in first-aid, safety-first, the rules of the road, and law and order; they had their games and athletic meets — all under the direct control and management of the police. "We feel that the results have been good," said Mr. Woods in 1917. "The boy comes to feel that the policeman whom he has considered his natural enemy is really a man whom he can look to for help in doing the things that he most likes to do. We notice a marked falling off in juvenile delinquencies in precincts where there are Junior Police Forces."[1]

Similarly Commissioner Woods threw the influence of his department into the development of city playgrounds. In the more congested districts whole blocks were laid out as "play streets," and traffic was excluded between three o'clock and six o'clock every afternoon. Through the help of private agencies "backyard" playgrounds were opened up in those districts where the figures of juvenile delinquency were especially high. Sixteen such play spaces in all were developed with results that proved conclusively the relationship between delinquency and the lack of a rational opportunity to play.

Another method which progressive departments have adopted in establishing a better relationship between the policeman and the children has been to assign policemen in uniform to talk to the children in the public schools.

[1] Annual Report of New York Police Department, 1917, p. 81.

American Police Systems

In Washington, D. C., a series of addresses by police officers on "Why is a Policeman" has been especially successful.

The plan of Christmas parties in the precinct station houses for the children of the neighborhood was adopted in New York in 1915 and was followed in other cities, notably in Detroit. Lists of children were made up by precinct commanding officers through information furnished them by patrolmen on post. As far as possible these lists were composed of children who would not otherwise be provided for on Christmas day. Each child received one or more useful articles of clothing, a toy, a box of candy and some fruit. The station houses were decorated and each had a large Christmas tree. Instead of prisoners, the cells contained holly and toys and fruit. On Christmas day the stations were filled with happy mothers and laughing children instead of the usual procession of deserted mothers and crying children. The police captain in each precinct acted as Santa Claus and the program of entertainment frequently was run in shifts to take care of all the children in the neighborhood. Over 40,000 children were entertained in this fashion in New York during the Christmas of 1916. It is scarcely too much to say that the event marked almost a revolution in the relation of the policeman to the neighborhood. As one beaming, perspiring patrolman said to Commissioner Woods: "Well, Commissioner, I believe those kids will believe now, when we tell 'em to cut out hitching on wagons, that it's a friend that's talking!"[1]

One further method of socializing the relations of the

[1] *Crime Prevention*, p. 120.

police department with the children was developed by Commissioner Woods in the institution of so-called " welfare-officers." In January, 1917, ten precincts were selected for this experiment, a carefully chosen patrolman being assigned in each precinct with the single duty of looking after the boys and girls who seemed to be going wrong. " Think of the gain to the city," said Commissioner Woods, " if we can take a boy who would otherwise become a burglar, who has started to master that profession, and turn him into a self-respecting, self-supporting citizen. That is what these welfare officers are working for." [1]   Gradually the system was extended until forty-seven precincts were thus covered. By the end of 1917, 9,300 cases had been investigated and some action had been taken in each instance. These cases often involved truancy and were frequently the result of destitute home conditions which could be corrected by enlisting the aid of some private welfare association. Special forms of delinquency among the boys also included petty larceny, crap playing, stone throwing and carrying cans of beer. The girls were mostly charged with loitering around parks and armories. In only two per cent of all these cases was it found necessary to make arrests. The solution of the difficulty was obtained sometimes by the mere friendship of a big brother policeman, sometimes by connecting the child with the home through the authoritative but kindly influence of a man in uniform. [2]

In Chicago during the year 1918 there were 19,019 investigations of cases of delinquency and complaints in-

[1] *Ibid.*, p. 112.
[2] For discussion, see Report of New York Police, 1914–1917, pp. 76–78.

volving children made by 39 patrolmen assigned to juvenile work at various precinct station houses.[1] Of these cases, 16,320, or 85.8%, were adjusted out of court and delinquency petitions were filed in the remainder.   In the nine month period from April to December, 1918, a single officer working in the sixth and seventh precincts investigated 1,141 cases, only 82 of these cases going to court.

A juvenile delinquency division was established in Detroit in 1882.   Although its personnel is made up of regular policemen, the division operates as an independent bureau and even has headquarters in a building separate from any other police division.   A captain is in command of the division and there are ten juvenile officers none of whom are uniformed.   Other divisions of the police department refer matters affecting children to the juvenile division which assumes full responsibility for investigation and action.   In Los Angeles a juvenile bureau constitutes a separate division of the department.   It is commanded by a chief juvenile officer and includes both patrolmen and policewomen.   The chief juvenile officer described the work of the bureau as follows:

" In general this Bureau has to deal with minor children who are placed under arrest by any officer of the department, or against whom reports are received from parents or other citizens.   This Bureau also deals with reports and charges made against adults where children are the victims.   Officers of this Bureau are required to inspect dance halls, skating rinks, cafes, penny ar-

[1] Following the closing of seven precinct stations during 1918, the number of patrolmen assigned as juvenile officers was reduced from 39 to 24.

372

cades, public parks and other places frequented by juveniles." [1]

In many cities such as Indianapolis, Newark and Seattle, it is the practice to detail policemen to assist probation officers attached to juvenile courts.

Obviously this work involves the constant association of the welfare or juvenile officers with representatives of other organizations and government departments such as the truant officers, the Children's Society, the probation officers, the Charity Organization Society, the settlements, the Big Brothers, the churches, etc. This is a point of great importance. Police work cannot be isolated from other welfare agencies of the community concerned with social problems. It cannot be divorced from all the organized influences that are working for better conditions in city life. Indeed unless the police are in a position to invoke the cooperation of schools, clinics, churches and other public and private institutions to supplement repression and if possible to supplant it with education and diversion, they cannot effectively handle the task which society has given them. The new policing demands a type of officer interested and trained in social service. With representatives of this character the police department should presently be able to stimulate every other community agency in dealing aggressively with untoward community conditions. [2]

[1] Annual Report of the Los Angeles Police Department, 1918–19.
[2] In this connection, see an interesting paper by August Vollmer, chief of police in Berkeley, California, in the June, 1919, number of *The Policemen's News,* entitled *The Policeman as a Social Worker.* Chief Vollmer's views on this whole question are progressive and stimulating.

American Police Systems

Destitution.

Poverty as a cause of crime is common knowledge to every policeman who patrols the streets in the congested portions of our cities. He sees it on every corner; he deals with it constantly in the jails and police stations. He knows that even when dereliction is not the direct result of want, crime and poverty are often associated. "I have seen many a prisoner," said Commissioner Woods, "who had been inexorably, it almost seemed with deliberate purpose, driven step by step straight into an eddy of fate where there seemed nothing else to do but steal. And one could not help wondering whether the rest of us, caught in the same swirling current, would have done any better." [1]

It cannot be expected, of course, that the police either as individuals or as organizations can grapple with the whole complex social and economic question of poverty. Nevertheless, as social agents dealing with the causes of crime they cannot leave it out of their calculations.

Not a few departments in the United States have made a beginning in placing upon the policeman responsibility for reporting conditions of individual distress. Policemen on beat probably come more intimately into contact with the life of the people than any other class of men, and their wide opportunities for observation can be harnessed to various forms of constructive social work. Commissioner Woods, in the winter of 1914–15, when conditions of industrial disorganization threw thousands of people out of employment, developed a comprehensive system of contact. A small fund was raised among the

[1] *Crime Prevention,* p. 37.

374

police themselves, and a plan was worked out which provided the captain of every precinct with a book of tickets, each marked " ten cents." [1]   The captains made arrangements with a grocer, a fuel dealer and a restaurant keeper in their neighborhoods to honor these tickets, sending their accounts to headquarters every week.   In any part of the city, therefore, when a policeman came across a case of distress, he took the sufferer to the station house, where the captain or lieutenant in charge would provide at once for his immediate needs and would then put him in touch with some private association or church where help would be continued as long as necessary.   " We believed it was the duty of the police," said Commissioner Woods, " to protect society by preventing as much as possible of the crime that might be committed by these unfortunate people in their distress." [2]   During the three years in which this plan was in operation in New York, 3,262 families and individuals were thus assisted. [3]

In addition, the police constituted themselves an employment agency for people out of work.   Frequently it was necessary to create jobs where none existed before. Thus, the people living in a city block would be induced by the police to employ a man to keep the street and sidewalks clean around the block, pick up waste paper and other litter, and generally to supplement the work of the Street Cleaning Department.   By this plan alone some scores of families were kept together that otherwise would have been reduced to privation and hopelessness.   During the three year period from 1914–17 in which this employ-

[1] Supplemented by private funds.   The total amount was $2,800.
[2] *Crime Prevention,* p. 39.
[3] Leroy Peterson, *loc. cit.,* p. 4.

ment agency plan was in operation, 3,040 men, women and children were placed in positions through the efforts of the police.

In this field, as in the field of juvenile delinquency, the work of the police brings them into intimate team-work with all the private agencies that are seeking in various ways to better community conditions. Every officer on the street becomes a representative of a coordinated social service.[1] In New York in the period just noted, it meant that the community had at its disposal 11,000 trained men enlisted in constructive social work.

Other Crime Prevention Methods.

It is impossible in a short chapter even to outline all the steps that can be taken by an alert and progressive police force in dealing with the problem of crime. The development of women police, for example, although still in a vague and uncertain stage, is a factor of supreme significance. The possibilities of their work with women and girls along preventive lines, as well as with the conditions which affect women and girls, are almost immeasurable.[2] Similarly, the whole new field of psychiatry

---

[1] During the three years in which this plan was in operation in New York the Police Department cooperated and worked with a total number of 82 relief, charitable and social organizations. In every case, existing machinery was utilized and no attempt was made in any way to duplicate facilities already in operation.

[2] In too many departments women police have been installed with no clear idea as to what functions they were to perform. Thus, in some cities they have been used merely as police matrons; in others they have been uniformed and assigned to ordinary patrol duty. In one large city at the time of my visit, the women police who had recently been appointed had been taught to shoot and were then given pistols and blackjacks and assigned to precinct stations! Gradually, however, the peculiar value of women police officers as preventive agents in working with women and girls has come to be

lies open for development, and the various questions of handling the mentally defective, so that he may not add his substantial contribution to the total volume of crime, are pressing for solution and action. Again, the use of police as parole officers, and the intimate sympathetic relationship between the police machinery and parole and probation systems, are problems that are coming rapidly to the fore in society's attack on crime.[1] In all these matters the police have an important part to play. As the police chief of Berkeley, California, expressed it: " The police must fight for everything that promises a reduction of crime. Society's greatest task with reference to criminals is to protect itself." [2]

Ultimately the attention of all police departments and of all police officials will be centered on the prevention of crime. The conventional phases of their work will not be neglected — for they are essential [3] — but no longer

recognized. In some cities the women police have proved particularly successful as detectives in certain types of cases.

[1] In New York, under Commissioner Woods, 84 police sergeants were detailed to act as parole officers in looking after men released from the work-house, the penitentiary and the reformatory. In all, 1,483 men and boys were assigned to the care of these officers, who were under instructions to help them get work and keep in touch with them at least once a week for one year. " Show your paroled prisoner at your first conference that you want to be his friend," ran the instructions to the police sergeants, "that you, as well as the department, stand ready to assist him to do what is right and keep out of jail. He naturally will be suspicious of you and your motives. Put it up to him good and strong that the big thing the department is trying to do is to prevent crime, and that everything that you can do along that line will be good police duty." (Leroy Peterson, *loc. cit.,* p. 32.) The St. Louis department maintains a parole bureau consisting of three officers as part of the organization of the force. In Los Angeles two probation bureaus are attached to the department, one for men and one for women.

[2] Personally communicated.

[3] " Whatever new methods are tried," said Commissioner Woods, " we must not neglect the old, for the essential basis of all good

will the departments be contented to spend their energies in sweeping back the continuous overflow of disorder without regard to its causes or sources. It is possible, indeed, that as this new technique develops, it will be made to constitute a separate branch of the department: a bureau of crime prevention — as distinct and important a division of activity as the detective bureau or the uniformed force — heading up under its direction all the conscious agencies of the department that are working to diminish the supply of criminals. Up to the present, whatever work the departments have done in this direction has been scattered through a series of squads or bureaus, maintaining no conscious or organic relationship with each other. Sometimes these squads are attached to the detective bureau with resulting confusion and inadequate direction. More often the department has not progressed as far as the formation of any squads, and crime prevention work is handed over as a detail to a few scattered patrolmen.

Whatever form of organization this new method takes, its basic idea gives shape to the police work of the future: not a conventional system of patrol or a systematized procedure for making arrests — valuable as these activities may be — but an unceasing fight, in cooperation with all the active forces of society, to keep criminals from committing crime and people from becoming criminals.

police work is the character and physical power of the individual men. They must be strong of body, stout of soul — sturdy, two-fisted specimens, knowing how to hold themselves in restraint even under severe provocation, yet prompt and powerful to act with force and uncompromising vigor when only that will maintain order and protect the law-abiding." (*Crime Prevention,* p. 3.)

CHAPTER XI

CONCLUSION

Contrast between American and European police departments.—Europe far in advance.— American progress seen by comparison of present with past.— Irregular character of improvement.— Our achievement sordid and unworthy.— Importance of the police problem.

To an American who has intimately studied the operation of European police systems, nothing can be more discouraging than a similar survey of the police of the United States. As he travels from east to west across the continent he is oppressed with the contrasts that meet him on every side. He remembers the conscious pride of European cities in their police, and the atmosphere of public confidence in which they carry on their work. He recalls the unbroken record of rectitude which many of their forces maintain and their endeavor to create, with the aid of expert leadership, a maturing profession. He remembers the infinite pains with which the police administrators are trained and chosen, and the care with which the forces are shielded from political influence. Vivid in his mind is the recollection of the manner in which science and modern business methods are being applied to the detection of crime, so that on the whole the battle with the criminal is being fought with steadily increasing effectiveness.

In America, on the other hand, the student of police

travels from one political squabble to another, too often from one scandal to another. He finds a shifting leadership of mediocre calibre — varied now and then by flashes of real ability which are snuffed out when the political wheel turns. There is little conception of policing as a profession or a science to be matured and developed. It is a *job*, held, perhaps, by the grace of some mysterious political influence, and conducted in an atmosphere sordid and unhealthy. It is a treadmill, worked without imagination or aim, and with little incentive except the desire to keep out of trouble. Instead of confidence and trust, the attitude of the public toward the police is far more often than not one of cynicism and suspicion, expressing itself, occasionally, in violent attacks which are as unjust as they are ineffective. In the interim between these spasms of publicity the average police force sinks in its rut, while crime and violence flourish.

This is not a happy picture, and the contrast between the situation on the two sides of the Atlantic is frankly disillusioning. It is only when we approach the facts from another angle that any ray of encouragement can be seen. A basis of comparison, perhaps fairer than the juxtaposition of European police and our own, is the contrast between what our system is today and what it was ten, twenty and forty years ago. Assuming that our present measurement by European standards is below our hopes, what has our own growth been?

It is this perspective which furnishes a substantial basis for encouragement. London's police department had thirty-five years of established tradition and achievement behind it when the draft riots broke out in New York in

Conclusion

1863.   And what was New York's police force then?   It was an undisciplined, half-uniformed mob, armed with clubs.   Between that day and this a revolution has been wrought in our police administration.   In the early seventies the police of San Francisco were little more than a sheriff's posse, and the hue and cry was the method of apprehending criminals.   San Francisco's police force today, with all its imperfections, represents a new era in, public service.   As late as the eighties our police everywhere were regarded by the citizens with a resignation bordering on complacence, as the private armies of the political parties in power.   Today the open and avowed connection of the police with politics arouses widespread though often futile protest.   It was in 1895 that the Lexow Commission in New York unearthed scandals in the police department of a kind and to a degree that would be almost inconceivable today.   Such flagrant conditions, in open defiance of public right and decency, may exist here and there even now, but unlike 1895, they represent the exception and not the rule.   Birmingham, Alabama, has none too compelling a reason to be proud of her police force, but even she can stand amazed at the recollection of the rival chiefs of police, who, under the political system existing only a dozen years ago, stumped the city for election and sought for votes by open promises of leniency in office.

There is hardly a police department in the United States where similar evidences of improvement cannot be found.   Only a blind man could fail to see that with all our shuffling incompetence in municipal affairs — and it is ominous enough — the cumulative effort of forty years for a decent standard of local government in the United States is bearing fruit, not so evident as yet, perhaps, in constructive results — although even here it has registered substantial gains — as in the general toning up of our political life, and in a public opinion far more sensitive to betrayal and abuse, and increasingly intolerant of laxity and ineptitude. From the influence of these silent but potent forces in American life our police departments have not escaped. Measured against the background of the past they show a real advance.

But the advance has been discouragingly irregular — a step forward, a slip back, with a net achievement slight and inadequate. Improvement is not permanent; we do not hold our gains. The constructive efforts of a progressive administration are likely to be wiped out by a reactionary successor, and carefully laid plans whose installation and development bear promise of good results are abandoned over night. Every police department is a graveyard of projects and improvements which, had they been developed to maturity, would have reconstituted the police work of the city. They have died because the particular administration sponsoring them has met the fate of all municipal administrations, and the succeeding regime, to justify its existence, has had to discredit the work and aims of its predecessor. In this mean play of politics, this recurring advance and reaction, our gains are often illusory.

We have, indeed, little to be proud of. It cannot be denied that our achievement in respect to policing is sordid and unworthy. Contrasted with other countries in this regard we stand ashamed. With all allowances for the

Conclusion

peculiar conditions which make our task so difficult, we have made a poor job of it. Our progress has fallen far behind our needs. Successful in the organization of business and commerce, pre-eminent in many lines of activity, we must confess failure in the elemental responsibility laid on all peoples who call themselves civilized, of preserving order in their communities. Surely in the new era upon which we are entering, with its challenge to forms of government and political faiths, the vision of America will not be blind to the grave importance of the problem and the resourcefulness of America will not be baffled in attempting the solution.

ORGANIZATION OF THE CHICAGO POLICE DEPARTMENT

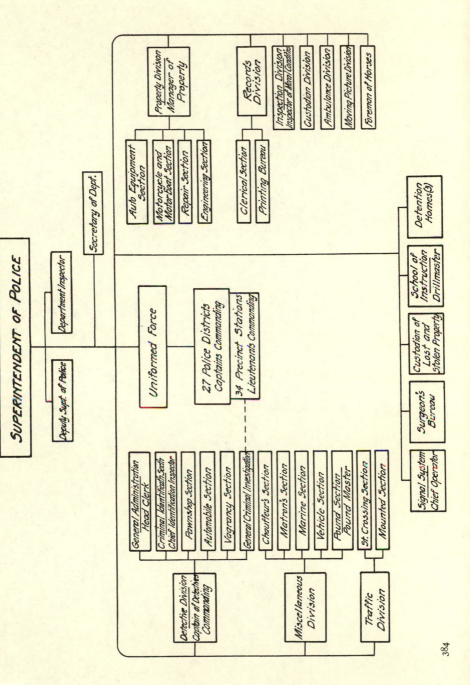

SUPERINTENDENT OF POLICE

Deputy Supt. of Police

Department Inspector

Secretary of Dept.

Uniformed Force

27 Police Districts
Captains Commanding

34 Precinct Stations
Lieutenants Commanding

General Criminal Investigation

Detective Division
Captain of Detectives Commanding

General Administration
Head Clerk

Criminal Identification Sect'n
Chief Identification Inspector

Pawnshop Section

Automobile Section

Vagrancy Section

Miscellaneous Division

Chauffeur's Section

Matron's Section

Marine Section

Vehicle Section

Pound Section
Pound Master

Traffic Division

St. Crossing Section

Mounted Section

Signal System
Chief Operator

Surgeon's Bureau

Custodian of Lost and Stolen Property

School of Instruction
Drillmaster

Detention Homes (3)

Property Division
Manager of Property

Auto Equipment Section

Motorcycle and Motorboat Section

Repair Section

Engineering Section

Records Division

Clerical Section

Printing Bureau

Inspection Division
Inspector of Mea. Conditns.

Custodian Division

Ambulance Division

Moving Picture Division

Foreman of Horses

384

ORGANIZATION OF THE DETROIT POLICE DEPARTMENT

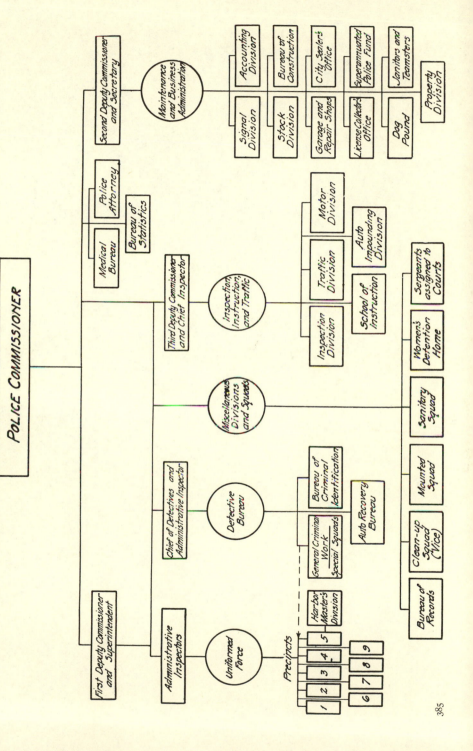

385

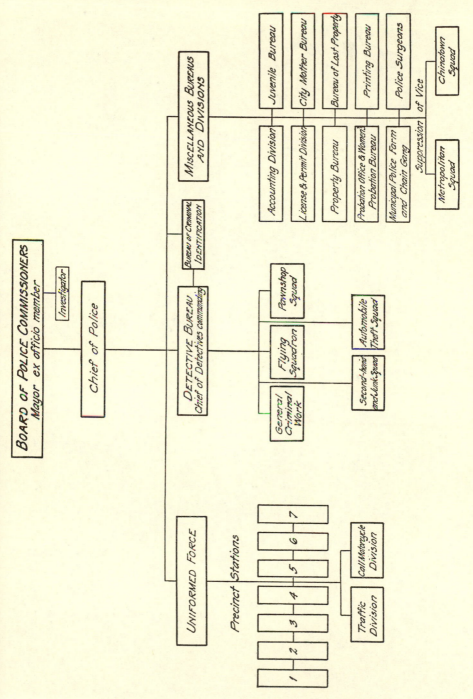

ORGANIZATION OF THE LOS ANGELES POLICE DEPARTMENT

BOARD OF POLICE COMMISSIONERS
Mayor ex officio member

Investigator

Chief of Police

UNIFORMED FORCE

Precinct Stations

1 2 3 4 5 6 7

Traffic Division

Call/Motorcycle Division

DETECTIVE BUREAU
Chief of Detectives commanding

BUREAU OF CRIMINAL IDENTIFICATION

General Criminal Work

Flying Squadron

Pawnshop Squad

Second-hand and Junk Squad

Automobile Theft Squad

MISCELLANEOUS BUREAUS AND DIVISIONS

Accounting Division

Juvenile Bureau

License & Permit Division

City Mother Bureau

Property Bureau

Bureau of Lost Property

Probation Office & Women's Probation Bureau

Printing Bureau

Municipal Police Farm and Chain Gang

Police Surgeons

Suppression of Vice

Metropolitan Squad

Chinatown Squad

ORGANIZATION OF THE NEW YORK POLICE DEPARTMENT

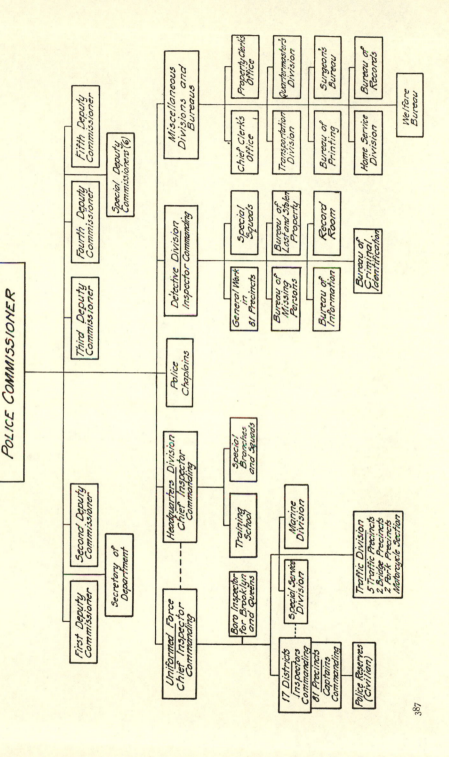

387

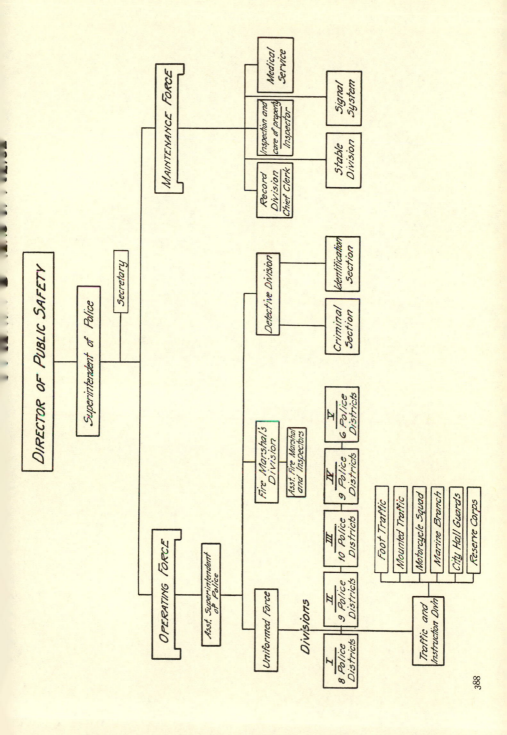

DIRECTOR OF PUBLIC SAFETY

Superintendent of Police

Secretary

OPERATING FORCE

Asst. Superintendent of Police

Uniformed Force

Divisions

I
8 Police Districts

II
9 Police Districts

III
10 Police Districts

IV
9 Police Districts

V
6 Police Districts

Traffic and Instruction Divn

Foot Traffic

Mounted Traffic

Motorcycle Squad

Marine Branch

City Hall Guards

Reserve Corps

Fire Marshal's Division

Asst. Fire Marshal and Inspectors

Detective Division

Criminal Section

Identification Section

MAINTENANCE FORCE

Record Division
Chief Clerk

Inspection and care of property
Inspector

Medical Service

Stable Division

Signal System

388

Organization of the St. Louis Police Department

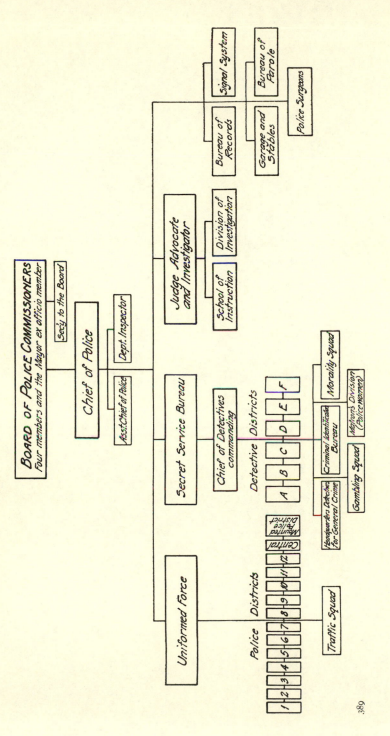

ORGANIZATION OF THE WASHINGTON, D.C., POLICE DEPARTMENT

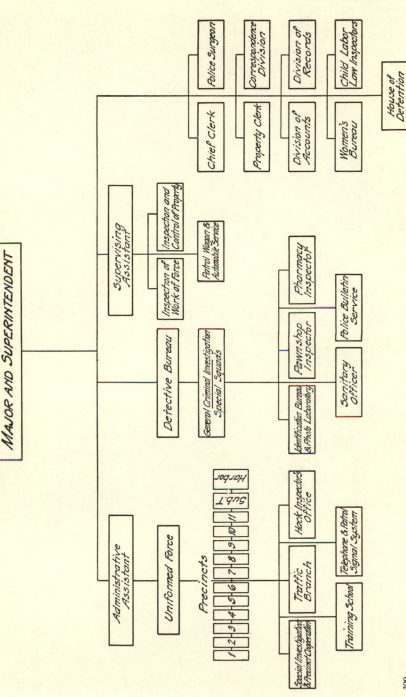

INDEX

Index

Banks, General, 90, note
Bay City, Mich., 174, note
Bayonne, N. J., population of, 167
Bedini riots, Cincinnati, 72
Berkeley, Cal., chief of police, 265; police training school system, 298; patrol system, 309–311; detective instruction at, 332; 348, note; in relation to crime prevention, 377
Berlin, foreign element in, 5; average of murders, 14; 111; jurisdiction of police president, 170; 237
Bertillon, Alphonse, system of identification, 207; decline of system, 348 et seq.
Bicycle squads, 189
Bingham, General, reorganization of New York detective bureau, 337
Birmingham, Ala., negroes in, 7; 52, 109, 137, note; commissioner's salary, 175, note; commissioner, 181; 182; police organization, 184; proportion of police to population, 201; chief of police, 258; police system, 270; chief of police quoted on police system, 274; detective bureau, 328, 334; police and politics, 381
Birmingham, Eng., 112; police administration, 233, 236, 244
Blankenburg administration, 193
Board, rise of the police, 76 et seq.; the bi-partisan, 103 et seq.; passing of the police, 107 et seq.; of state commissioners, 129 et seq.; 133; control vs. single-headed control, 137 et seq.; appointment, size and functions of police commis-

sioners, 138; weakness of police control, 140; administration a part-time task, 141–143; meetings of, 143; lack of unity in administration, 145 et seq.; politics in administration, 149–151; the elective, 151–154; supposed neutrality of bi-partisan, 154 et seq. See also Commissioners
Booth system, operation of, 309, 310
"Boss," the, 184; relation of, to police preferment, 271
Boston, foreign element of population, 5; genesis of police force, 59; 60, 62, 66, 96, 105, 107, 108, 109; in relation to state-controlled police, 119–123; 129, 130, 131, 136, 149, 159, 162, 164; suburban development, 166, 167; 169; police commissioner, 170; 200; proportion of police to population, 201; legislation in relation to police, 209, 210; irrelevant functions of police, 212; 239; police methods, 277; 280, 281, 283, 292; plan of police promotion, 293 et seq.; Commissioner O'Meara quoted on system of promotion, 294, note; police strike, 318, 320; detective bureau, 328, 331; organization of detective bureau, 333; 338
Boulogne, 5
Bradford, Ernest S., *Commission Government in American Cities*, cited, 174, note
Breeding-places of crime, 358 et seq.
Bremen, 5
Brigade de Sureté, Paris, 4
Bridgeport, 137, note; 155, note;

392

Index

police arrangements, 202; police system, 271, note

Bribery, 287 et seq.

Bristol, Eng., 112

Brooklyn, 75, 82, 168

Bruere, Henry, *The New City Government,* cited, 174, note

Brussels, Belgian national board of identification, 351

Budapest, 5

Buffalo, 79, 107, 109, 137, 162, 172, 174, note; 175; commissioner's salary, 175, note; 182; director of public safety, 193, 194; 208; police methods, 277; 281; organization of detective bureau, 333; method of detective supervision, 343

Bureau of Municipal Research, New York, cited, 32, note; 278, 279; 344, note; 345, note

Burglary, comparative statistics, 15 et seq., table, 16

Cahalane, Inspector Cornelius, quoted, 269

Calhoun, Patrick, trial of, 37, note

California State Bureau of Criminal Identification and Investigation, 352, note

Cambridge, 138, note; 162, 164, 165

Camden, police system in, 271, note

Canada bureau of identification, 351

Canterbury, Eng., 245

Carabinieri, 3; Italian patrol system, 201

Carmack, Senator, 37, note

Carter, James Coolidge, quoted on unnecessary laws, 47

Centennial History of Cincinnati,

Charles Theodore Greve, cited, 63

Centralization *vs.* decentralization in detective bureau organization, 333 et seq.

Chap, Thomas, case of, 40

Charleston, S. C.: negroes in, 7; 95

Charleston, W. Va., 174, note

Charlottenburg, 170

Charts, of police department organization, Chicago, 384; Detroit, 385; Los Angeles, 386; New York, 387; Philadelphia, 388; St. Louis, 389; Washington, 390

Charters, city, 203–216, *passim*

Chicago, 4; character of population, 5; 6, 10; comparative table of murder in, 11; homicide, 13; murder record, 24; *Tribune,* quoted, 27; Taft's speech at, 1909, quoted, 28; homicide calculation of *Tribune* quoted, 33; law's delay in, 35, 36; 37, 41, notes; 67; 75, 114, 115, 137, 162, 164, 192; police department, 196; patrol system, 199; irrelevant functions of police, 212; police commission, 217 et seq.; cost of police department, 218; 220; police system, 222; police administrative experiments, 228; police methods, 271, 279, 280, 281–285; civil service entanglements in, 291, 292; police training school system, 298 et seq.; detective bureau, 327–329; organization of detective bureau, 333, 341; method of detective supervision, 343; inadequacy of police records, 345, 346, 350; chart of police department organization, 384

Index

Index

Index

Index

Index

Index

Index

Lucas, George, the case of, 36
Lynn, Mass., 174; personnel of commission, 176
Lynchburg, Va., 174, note

Machine, the police forec as a, 313
Macon, Ga., 283
Manchester, Eng., 112; police administration, 233; 236; 245
Manchester, N. H., term of chief of police, 256
Marseilles, 223; police administration, 233
Massachusetts, state control, 123; 240
Matsell, Chief of Police, New York, 72, note
Mayne, Sir Richard, first chief of Metropolitan Police Force, 83, 84; term of service, 236
Mayor-commissioner, salary of, 175, note
Memphis, negroes in, 7; murder record, 25; 52, 137, note; 162, 174, note; mayor-commissioner's salary, 175, note; commissioner of fire and police, 179, 181; term of chief of police, 254; 282; detective bureau, 328
Metropolitan Police Force, London, 3, 4, 111, 201, 233
Meudon, 170
Michigan, police legislation, 203
Milwaukee, 105; 107; size of police board, 138; powers of police board, 139; 155, note; other functions combined with police, 188, note; proportion of police to population, 201; irrelevant functions of police, 212; police methods, 279; 280, 281, 283
Minneapolis, 102, 107, 137, 162; term of chief of police, 254,

255; police system, 271; 280, 281
Missouri, police control, 119; state-controlled police expenditure, 135; police legislation, 207
Mobile, board of public safety, 188, note
Mobilization, types of police, explained, 215 et seq.
Montgomery, Ala., police control in, 119
Morgan, Governor, New York, 84; quoted, 88
Moscow, 6
Motor vehicles, part played in patrol work, 309 et seq.
Munich, 244, 245
Municipal Freedom, Oswald Ryan, cited, 174, note
Municipal *vs* state control, 118–159, *passim*
Munro, William Bennett, *Principles and Methods of Municipal Administration*, cited, 120, note
Murder, comparative statistics, 10 et seq.; trials, 33–37

Naples, 245
Napoleon, establishment of Paris police organization by, 111
Nashville, 52; negroes in, 138, note; 162, 174, note; 175; commissioner of fire and police, 179
National Bureau of Criminal Identification, 351
National Municipal Review, cited, 186, note
National Police Journal, cited, 350, note
Negro, relative population, table, 7; criminal record in Washington, D. C., tables, 22, 23; riots in East St. Louis, 41, note; 65

Index

Index

402

Index

Index

Index

Index

Index

Index

and result of his efforts, 366; establishes Junior Police, 369; quoted, 369; and city playgrounds, 369; 370; quoted on poverty, 374; 377, 378, note

Worcester, Mass., 137, 162, 164

Wright, William, case of, 36

Young, Matthew, 62

Youngstown, 138, note

Zurich, 3

PATTERSON SMITH REPRINT SERIES IN
CRIMINOLOGY, LAW ENFORCEMENT, AND SOCIAL PROBLEMS

1. Lewis: *The Development of American Prisons and Prison Customs, 1776-1845*
2. Carpenter: *Reformatory Prison Discipline*
3. Brace: *The Dangerous Classes of New York*
4. Dix: *Remarks on Prisons and Prison Discipline in the United States*
5. Bruce *et al: The Workings of the Indeterminate-Sentence Law and the Parole System in Illinois*
6. Wickersham Commission: *Complete Reports, Including the Mooney-Billings Report.* 14 Vols.
7. Livingston: *Complete Works on Criminal Jurisprudence.* 2 Vols.
8. Cleveland Foundation: *Criminal Justice in Cleveland*
9. Illinois Association for Criminal Justice: *The Illinois Crime Survey*
10. Missouri Association for Criminal Justice: *The Missouri Crime Survey*
11. Aschaffenburg: *Crime and Its Repression*
12. Garofalo: *Criminology*
13. Gross: *Criminal Psychology*
14. Lombroso: *Crime, Its Causes and Remedies*
15. Saleilles: *The Individualization of Punishment*
16. Tarde: *Penal Philosophy*
17. McKelvey: *American Prisons*
18. Sanders: *Negro Child Welfare in North Carolina*
19. Pike: *A History of Crime in England.* 2 Vols.
20. Herring: *Welfare Work in Mill Villages*
21. Barnes: *The Evolution of Penology in Pennsylvania*
22. Puckett: *Folk Beliefs of the Southern Negro*
23. Fernald *et al: A Study of Women Delinquents in New York State*
24. Wines: *The State of the Prisons and of Child-Saving Institutions*
25. Raper: *The Tragedy of Lynching*
26. Thomas: *The Unadjusted Girl*
27. Jorns: *The Quakers as Pioneers in Social Work*
28. Owings: *Women Police*
29. Woolston: *Prostitution in the United States*
30. Flexner: *Prostitution in Europe*
31. Kelso: *The History of Public Poor Relief in Massachusetts: 1820-1920*
32. Spivak: *Georgia Nigger*
33. Earle: *Curious Punishments of Bygone Days*
34. Bonger: *Race and Crime*
35. Fishman: *Crucibles of Crime*
36. Brearley: *Homicide in the United States*
37. Graper: *American Police Administration*
38. Hichborn: *"The System"*
39. Steiner & Brown: *The North Carolina Chain Gang*
40. Cherrington: *The Evolution of Prohibition in the United States of America*
41. Colquhoun: *A Treatise on the Commerce and Police of the River Thames*
42. Colquhoun: *A Treatise on the Police of the Metropolis*
43. Abrahamsen: *Crime and the Human Mind*
44. Schneider: *The History of Public Welfare in New York State: 1609-1866*
45. Schneider & Deutsch: *The History of Public Welfare in New York State: 1867-1940*
46. Crapsey: *The Nether Side of New York*
47. Young: *Social Treatment in Probation and Delinquency*
48. Quinn: *Gambling and Gambling Devices*
49. McCord & McCord: *Origins of Crime*
50. Worthington & Topping: *Specialized Courts Dealing with Sex Delinquency*

PATTERSON SMITH REPRINT SERIES IN
CRIMINOLOGY, LAW ENFORCEMENT, AND SOCIAL PROBLEMS